Personal Finance For Overseas Americans

Personal Finance For Overseas Americans

Barbara Frew

GIL Financial Press

Sterling, Virginia

PERSONAL FINANCE FOR OVERSEAS AMERICANS
By Barbara Frew

Published by:

GIL Financial Press
A Unit of GIL Incorporated
21055 Hawthorne Court
Sterling, VA 20164
USA
info-gil@GILFinancialPress.com

This publication is designed to provide information in regard to the subject matter covered. Every effort has been made to make this publication as accurate and as complete as possible. However, there may be mistakes both typographical and in content. It is sold with the understanding that the author and publisher are not engaged in rendering legal, accounting, and other professional services. If legal or accounting advice, or other expert assistance is required, the services of a professional should be sought. The author and GIL Financial Press shall have neither liability nor responsibility to any person or entity with respect to any loss or damage caused, or alleged to be caused, directly or indirectly by the information presented in this publication.

Printed and bound in the United States of America

ISBN: 0-9700651-1-6

Library of Congress Catalog Card Number: 00-103363

To Don, my life's choice.

CONTENTS

PART 1
FINANCIAL PLANNING 11

1. CHOICES 13

2. SETTING YOUR GOALS 15

3. WHERE DOES YOUR MONEY GO? 19
Net Financial Worth Statement 21
Understanding Your Net Financial Worth Statement 23
Monthly Net Income Statement 25
Understanding Your Monthly Net Income Statement 30

4. SPENDING BY CHOICE 35
Plan Your Spending 36
Identify Harmful Spending Patterns 38
Changing Your Harmful Spending Habits 39

5. TARGETING YOUR GOALS 43
Short-Term Financial Goal—Less Than Six Years 46
Short-Term Financial Goal Worksheet 49
Medium-Term Financial Goal—Six to Ten Years 50
Medium-Term Financial Goal Worksheet 56
Long-Term Financial Goal—Over Ten Years 57
Long-Term Financial Goal Worksheet 64

6. TARGETING RETIREMENT 67
Time Horizon 68
Amount Needed to Retire 68
What to Set Aside Each Month 86
Net Income Concerns 87
Net Worth Concerns 87
Combining Taxable and Tax-Deferred Accounts 87
Saving for Retirement Worksheet 90

PART 2
MONEY MANAGEMENT 93

7. CASH MANAGEMENT 95
Bank Accounts 95
Brokerage Accounts 101

8. DEBT MANAGEMENT 107
Mortgage Loans 107
Consumer Loans 117
Credit Cards 119
Your Credit Rating 122

9. FINANCIAL RISK MANAGEMENT– INSURANCE 125
Insurance 127
Buying Insurance 128
Property and Casualty Insurance 133
Health and Disability Insurance 143
Life Insurance 160
Life Insurance Benefit Worksheet 172

10. FINANCIAL RISK MANAGEMENT–
SOCIAL SECURITY 175
Eligibility and Benefits 176
Social Security Benefits Under Totalization Agreements 183
Annual Exemption Amounts 186
Receiving U.S. Social Security Benefits While Overseas 188

11. INVESTMENT MANAGEMENT 191
Basic Investment Principles 191
The Investment Process 202

12. TAX MANANGEMENT 217
Taxes and Investing 217
Income Taxes 220
Tax Treaties 225
Social Security Taxes 228
Taxation of U.S. Social Security Benefits 230

AFTERWORD 233

APPENDIX A
FINANCIAL STATEMENTS 235
    Net Financial Worth Statement 236
    Monthly Net Income Statement 238

APPENDIX B
FINANCIAL PLANNING WORKSHEETS 243
    Short-Term Financial Goal Worksheet 244
    Medium-Term Financial Goal Worksheet 245
    Long-Term Financial Goal Worksheet 246
    Saving for Retirement Worksheet 248
    Life Insurance Benefit Worksheet 251

APPENDIX C
FINANCIAL TABLES 253

GLOSSARY 269

INDEX 281

PART 1
FINANCIAL
PLANNING

1. CHOICES

Chances are that during your life you will have more desires than you have money and time to pursue. In that case, you have some choices to make. What activities do you most enjoy? What could you do without? Which pursuits will give you the most gratification in your life? In short, you need to decide what you will and will not pursue and when. To do that you need to set goals and a time frame for achieving those goals. Part 1, Financial Planning, helps you understand the tradeoffs involved in setting and achieving your goals, near term and long term.

Goals need to be financed. To increase your chances of achieving your goals you need to make informed choices about money management. Part 2, Money Management, gives you detailed information on managing cash, debt, financial risk, investments, and taxes. Not all of this information will be pertinent to your situation. Skim the chapters in this part, stopping to carefully read those sections of interest to you now. As your situation changes, refer back to this material, it is meant to serve as a reference.

This book is not a panacea—there is no panacea in personal finance. This book is designed to give you the tools and information you need to make the choices that are best for you. It provides detailed information, but not country specific information—with the exception of the United States. As overseas Americans live and work all over the world, one book could not hope to cover the financial nuances of every country. In addition, some complex financial issues, such as estate planning, deserve a book of their own and are not covered in this text.

The goal of this book is to give you the information you need to assess the financial tradeoffs you will face. With this knowledge you will make better decisions on how to spend your limited time and money, making sure more of each is spent achieving those goals you find most important in your life.

2. SETTING YOUR GOALS

It is important to remember that the financial aspects of your life are just that—aspects of your life. Your finances are not walled off from other parts of your life any more than your health or professional life is separate from the rest of your life. As such, your financial goals must be driven by your broader life goals. In working through this chapter bear in mind that you want to list and then prioritize your life goals—not just those goals commonly thought of as "financial goals". Most of your life goals have financial ramifications. This book helps you understand what you need to do financially, to make your most important goals a reality.

Goals reflect your values and circumstances. Your circumstances change over time. For example, the most important goal for many graduating college students is landing a good job. This goal reflects the value of striking out on your own and gaining financial independence from your parents. As new people play an important role in your life, your goals change to accommodate their interests. For example, when couples become parents, funding their child's college education often takes precedence over many other goals. Your individual interests and circumstances will dictate the nature and relative importance of your goals.

It is important to consider the timing of your goals. When you hope to achieve each goal depends on many factors. Chances are, you are striving to achieve several goals at any one time. Therefore, you have to know what priority to give each goal. Establishing priorities allows you to evaluate the tradeoffs you make in day-to-day spending that affect your ability to achieve the goals that are truly important to you.

As a first step, be sure to pay off your credit cards. When you regularly carry a balance on your credit card you greatly increase the price of the things you buy with that card leaving you with less money to put toward your goals. Once your credit cards are paid off, build a self-insurance fund equal to three to six months of your aftertax income. Your self-insurance fund allows you to cover unexpected expenses, including possible periods of unemployment, without disturbing your long-term investments and possibly forfeiting important goals. It also allows you to save money on insurance by buying policies with larger deductibles.

First, prepare a preliminary list of goals. When setting your goals go beyond the obvious, such as providing for your retirement or, if you have children, providing for their college education. Take a look at your interests and what you enjoy doing. How do you spend your free time? How would you like to spend your free time? This is helpful in thinking about what you want to do when you retire, choose to work less, or have more free time because the children are grown. Choose realistic goals. Remember, you want to achieve these goals, not to be disappointed. List your goals and briefly describe why you value each of them. Group your goals into categories based on their relative importance: One for the most important, two for the middle tier, and three for the less important. Assign a relative importance to each goal within these three categories. Each member of the family should do this separately and privately.

Once you have this preliminary list of goals, it is time to fine tune the list in terms of priority. For families, remember each person's values and goals are valid. Be willing to give and take as the family decides on the prioritized list of family goals. Try to include your children in the process as much as possible. The more people have a say in the decision making process the more they will be willing to do to achieve the family's goals. Prioritizing can mean selecting the goals to pursue now versus later. More often than not, you will need to pursue several goals simultaneously—for example saving for retirement and for a new car or a child's college education. Prioritize the goals that will get more or less of your financial resources. Mark any goals that can be postponed. Jot down when you hope to achieve each goal: in less than six years; in six to ten years; or in more than ten years.

Remember that you can adjust your goals. If you want a new car it does not have to be a BMW or a Mercedes if paying that much would keep you from achieving other goals. Look at the underlying value you associate with each goal. If, for example, you would like to enhance your status by owning a Mercedes, but that interferes with reaching other goals, consider volunteer work or running for a leadership position in an organization you admire as an alternative means of achieving your goal of enhancing your status in the community. Be willing to explore innovative ways of pursuing each goal to make financial resources available to achieve other goals.

Changing circumstances may cause you to adjust your goals. For example, a couple may decide to have a child. This will impact the family's goals and simultaneously the family's resources. It costs $125,000 to $300,000 to raise a child, excluding college costs. The couple may also choose to have one parent stay home with the child and forego a second income until the child enters school. A less dramatic impact occurs when you accept a new assignment and move to another country. The cost of living abroad and your income level may leave you better or worse off than you were before the move. You will also have out-of-pocket expenses associated with the move.

Remain flexible as you monitor your progress. Your goals are not carved in granite; you can adjust them, add new ones, or drop old ones at any time.

Now that you have prioritized your goals, you need to see what financial resources you have available to put toward achieving those goals.

3. WHERE DOES YOUR MONEY GO?

The first step in evaluating your current financial situation is a little like doing your income taxes. The difference is that you, not a tax authority, benefit from your effort. You do not have to evaluate your financial situation every year: Reviewing your financial situation after a move or other major change or once every few years should be sufficient. Start by looking at the net financial worth, and the monthly net income statements provided in this chapter. These two financial statements tell you what financial resources you have and how those resources are currently being used.

Gather together your financial records: last year's income tax return, credit card statements, pay stubs, check book register and bank statements, and any other financial information you think you might need to complete the net financial worth and the monthly net income statements.

Many of the line items in the monthly net income statement may not apply to you. The monthly net income statement is very detailed to give you an idea of all the different services and products you purchase in the course of a month. This exercise can help you decide exactly how much you value each purchase you make relative to the goals you hope to achieve in the future. If you use a computer program such as Quicken®, Microsoft Money®, or a spreadsheet of your own design, you may already have a good idea of where your money goes and what your net worth is at the moment. You may want to modify how your accounts are organized or your reports are designed if they do not give you the information you need to answer the questions posed at the end of each financial statement.

Appendix A of this book contains extra copies of these financial statements. Feel free to make additional copies for yourself as your circumstances change and you need a fresh evaluation of your financial condition.

NET FINANCIAL WORTH STATEMENT[1, 2]

DATE _____

Assets

CASH ASSETS[3]

Checking Accounts _____

Savings Accounts _____

Money Market Accounts _____

Brokerage Accounts[4] _____

Life Insurance Cash Value _____

TOTAL _____

INVESTMENTS

Stocks _____

Mutual Funds _____

Bonds and T-Bills _____

CDs _____

IRAs _____

401(k) Pension Plans _____

Other _____

TOTAL _____

REAL ESTATE[5]

Land _____

Primary Home _____

Second/Vacation Home _____

TOTAL _____

---

[1] This statement reflects the value of your possessions minus what you owe as of the date you enter. This differs from your net income statement, which reflects your average monthly income and expenses over the course of a year.

[2] Convert all local currency figures into dollar amounts based on the current exchange rate.

[3] These are assets you can access via check or can easily convert to cash. Your self-insurance fund may be held in any of these accounts, except life insurance.

[4] Include cash holdings only; investments are covered separately.

[5] Use market value. If that is not available use what you paid for the property.

PERSONAL PROPERTY

Automobiles (resale value)   _____

Recreational Vehicles (resale)   _____

Household Items[6]   _____

Collections (antiques, etc.)[7]   _____

Original Art[8]   _____

Luxury Items[9]   _____

Other   _____

TOTAL   _____

Total Assets   _____

(Total Cash Assets, Investments,
Real Estate and Personal Property)

Liabilities[10]

Mortgage Balance   _____

Bank Loans   _____

Educational Loans   _____

Auto Loans   _____

Recreational Vehicle Loans   _____

Life Insurance Policy Loans   _____

401(k) Pension Plan Loans   _____

Balance on Credit Cards   _____

Other Loans   _____

Total Liabilities   _____

Net Worth   _____

(Total Asset - Total Liabilities)

---

[6] Include only the more expensive items; use your best estimate of their resale value.

[7] Items such as stamp or coin collections should be professionally appraised. If that is not practical use what you paid for these items as an estimate. Include only the more expensive items.

[8] See footnote 7 for details.

[9] Items may include fur or jewelry. See footnote 7 for details.

[10] At least once a year you should receive a statement showing the amount of principal remaining on each of your loans, use that figure minus any payments of principal made after each statement's date.

UNDERSTANDING YOUR NET FINANCIAL WORTH STATEMENT

The net financial worth statement gives you long-term strategic information. By examining your net financial worth statement you can tell, for example, how your assets are allocated. Do you have enough cash assets to cover your current (short-term) liabilities plus a self-insurance fund to take care of financial emergencies—such as becoming unemployed or disabled for a short period of time? Are you happy with the balance between the value of your real estate and the money you have in financial investments? If you want to change the balance between your assets and liabilities you can do so by paying down your debts (as described in the section, Understanding Your Monthly Net Income Statement later in this chapter), or by increasing your assets by adjusting your saving and spending patterns (as described in the next chapter, Spending By Choice).

What can you learn from your net financial worth statement? If your net worth (total assets minus total liabilities) is positive you have financial resources that can be applied to achieving your goals. If it is not, are you just launching your career? Many people have a negative net worth at some point, particularly when they are just starting their careers. They have little or no assets and may be saddled with student loans. If your net worth is negative it means you are technically insolvent and that if you (or your heirs) liquidated all your assets today, the cash value of your assets would not cover your debts. A negative net financial worth means you need to pay serious attention to your finances before you face major financial hurdles like buying a home, putting your children through college, and retirement. Getting out of debt and building up your assets should be your top priority. You are not in a financial position to pursue your life goals until your net financial worth is positive.

Examine the asset side our your net financial worth statement. If your personal property assets are larger than the other categories you need to dedicate some serious attention to your finances. It takes time to sell personal property, particularly cars, art and jewelry. In an emergency, you may not be able to sell these items for needed cash. Many personal property items (vehicles, furniture, and electronics) drop in value over the years and you may have to sell them at a large discount to the price you paid for these items should you face a major crisis. In addition, personal property value is the most uncertain of your assets. If you have had jewelry or art appraised at a certain value that does not guarantee you could actually realize that amount, if you decided to sell them. In general, you cannot count on using these items to meet your goals.

Real estate, like personal property, usually cannot be sold quickly to raise cash. However, you can usually borrow against the equity in your home to meet other goals. For most real estate owners, the market value of their property will exceed that of their investments and other assets. Over time, however, financial investments should become your largest asset class. It is far easier to sell mutual fund shares than a share in your house to meet living expenses during retirement. You will increase your financial flexibility and ability to meet your goals if your investments are larger than your other assets.

Compare your cash assets to your total investments. Are you just starting to accumulate the wealth you will need to meet your financial goals? Are you selling long-term investments to have the cash needed to realize a goal? If you answered no to both of these questions and you have most of your investments in cash you are much too conservative for your own good. The only time you should have large sums of cash and short-term investments is when you are within a couple years of achieving one or more of your goals. During other times, your investment holdings should exceed your cash holdings.

What is the minimum you should have in cash and short-term holdings? You need at least three to six months of your monthly expenses—which is your self-insurance fund. To determine your monthly expenses you need to complete the next financial statement, your monthly net income statement.

MONTHLY NET INCOME STATEMENT[1]

Income

EARNINGS
Salary and Wages _____
Self-employment Income _____
Housing Allowance[2] _____
Other Overseas Allowances[3] _____
Bonuses _____
TOTAL _____

INVESTMENTS
Capital Gains[4] _____
Interest Income _____
Dividend Income _____
Mutual Fund Distributions[5] _____
TOTAL _____

OTHER INCOME
Rental Income _____
Social Security Benefits _____
Alimony/Child Support _____
Other _____
TOTAL _____

Total Income _____

---

[1] Enter monthly figures. In many cases it will be necessary to estimate the monthly amount using yearly figures and dividing by 12. Convert all foreign currency figures into dollars using the current exchange rate.

[2] If your employer pays you a housing allowance, include the amount here. Housing paid directly by your employer should not be included.

[3] Include only those allowances paid directly to you by your employer.

[4] Only include capital gains net of capital losses on investments you sold during the year and divide by 12.

[5] As an estimate, you can use last year's figures from your federal tax return, Schedule D, and divide by 12.

TAXES[6]
U.S. Federal Income Taxes   _____
U.S. State & Local Income Taxes   _____
Other U.S. Taxes[7]   _____
Host Country Income Taxes   _____
Other Host Country Taxes   _____
TOTAL   _____

Total Net Income   _____
(Total Income - Total Taxes)

Expenses

HOUSING
Mortgage/Rent (overseas home)[8]   _____
Mortgage for U.S. Home[9]   _____
Home Repairs, Improvements   _____
Management Fees (U.S. home)   _____
Home Owners Assoc. Fees   _____
Real Estate Taxes   _____
Other[10]   _____
TOTAL   _____

FOOD
Groceries   _____
Dining Out   _____
TOTAL   _____

---

[6] Not all taxes apply. Some taxes may be due in both your host country and the United States. Use last year's tax returns as an estimate and divide by 12.
[7] For example, personal property taxes. Exclude real estate taxes. They are listed separately under housing expenses.
[8] If you pay your rent or a mortgage directly—even if your employer pays you a housing allowance—include that amount here. If your employer pays your rent or mortgage directly, do not include that amount here.
[9] Enter your mortgage payment (principal and interest only) here. Real estate taxes and homeowners insurance are listed separately under property taxes and homeowners/renters insurance respectively.
[10] This might include housing costs for a second home.

UTILITIES[11]
Phone (local) _____
Phone (international) _____
Electricity _____
Gas _____
Water/Sewage _____
Garbage Removal _____
Cable/Satellite TV _____
On-line Computer Services _____
Other _____
TOTAL _____

TRANSPORTATION
Car Loan Payment _____
Auto Repairs _____
Gasoline _____
Public Transportation _____
Other [12] _____
TOTAL _____

INSURANCE
Auto _____
Homeowners/Renters _____
Disability _____
Health _____
Life _____
Long-term Care _____
Other _____
TOTAL _____

CLOTHING _____

---

[11] If covered by your employer, enter zero.
[12] Exclude travel for vacations and other recreational travel; recreation is covered separately. Include any other travel not covered by your employer.

HOUSEHOLD FURNISHINGS

Furniture and Appliances   _____

Other Household Items   _____

TOTAL   _____

MISCELLANEOUS DEBTS

Educational Loans   _____

Personal Loans   _____

Credit Card Debt Payments   _____

Other Loan Payments   _____

TOTAL   _____

HEALTH CARE[13]

Doctor Visits   _____

Dentist Visits   _____

Prescriptions   _____

Hospital and Other Expenses   _____

TOTAL   _____

PERSONAL CARE

Dry Cleaning   _____

Barber/Hair Dresser   _____

Other   _____

TOTAL   _____

RECREATION

Vacation   _____

Weekend Trips   _____

Other Weekend Activities   _____

Books, Music CDs   _____

Movies/Theater/Concerts   _____

Other   _____

TOTAL   _____

---

[13] Only include expenses not covered by your insurance policies.

OTHER

Daycare _____

Alimony/Child Support _____

Tuition _____

Pet Care _____

Magazines _____

Gifts _____

Other _____

TOTAL _____

Total Expenses _____
(Total all expenses except taxes)

Savings _____
(Total Net Income
- Total Expenses)

Savings Ratio _____
(Savings ÷ Total Net Income,
see text for discussion)

Total Debt Payments _____
(Mortgage Payments
+ Car Loan Payments
+ Total Miscellaneous Debts)

Debt Service Ratio _____
(Total Debt Payments
÷ Total Income,
see text for discussion)

UNDERSTANDING YOUR MONTHLY NET INCOME STATEMENT

How confident are you in your figures? Have you recently moved? It usually takes more than six months for your spending habits to get back to normal after a move. It is a good idea to track your spending for the first full year after a move to get a clear reading of your expenses in your new location. In addition, if you do this you will have an idea of how much you typically spend on household furnishings and other items as part of a move. Prior to your next move you can plan to have that much money available for similar moving expenses.

Even if you have been settled for some time, you may not have kept all your receipts for groceries, meals eaten out and other incidentals. And of course, you pay cash for many items, particularly when living in countries that are more cash based than the United States. To get a better idea of how much you are really spending on these items keep your receipts and jot down what you spend in cash each day on a calendar or a notepad. After a month, you will have a clearer idea of how much you actually spend on these items. You can track this spending for several months to get an idea of how much you spend, on average, for these items.

Once you are confident that you have a good idea where your money is going, what should you make of the results on your net income statement?

How much money are you saving per month? Remember to include in savings any money you contribute automatically to a retirement savings plan. To calculate your savings ratio divide your savings amount by your total net income. For most Americans that number varies from 0.05 to 0.10 otherwise expressed as 5%–10%. You should aim for a minimum of 10%. If practical in your current circumstances, 10%–25% is a good goal.

To calculate whether you have enough of a self-insurance fund, take your total cash assets from your net worth statement and divide that number by your total expenses number from the monthly net income statement. The result gives you the number of months you could maintain your current lifestyle if you lost your source of income. Ideally, your self-insurance fund should cover three to six months of your net income.

Is too much of your income spent making debt payments? To calculate your debt service ratio, first calculate your total debt payments by adding your mortgage payment from the housing section of expenses to your automobile loan payment under transportation along with your total miscellaneous loan payments to find your total debt payments. Divide that number by your total income (before taxes) and you will have your debt service ratio. If this number is greater than 0.35 (35%) you have too much debt and need to make reducing your debt a top priority. Note that a debt service ratio of 35% does not mean you are carrying an ideal debt load, it means that you are carrying the largest debt load that your current income can maintain. Carrying that much debt may rob you of the financial flexibility you need to achieve your goals. You should try to keep your debt service ratio below 25%.

There are many reasons for wanting to reduce your debt load. As discussed above, you may need to lower your debt service ratio, or you may not be happy with the balance between your assets and liabilities from your net financial worth statement. Under some circumstances paying down your debts may be the best investment you can make. Paying off a debt is a risk-free investment that pays you and not the lender the interest you would otherwise owe on that debt.

Consider your credit card loans first. Do you carry a balance on your credit cards? If so how much money do you have outstanding on your credit cards? What interest rate are you paying on that balance? The interest you pay is money that could be invested elsewhere to earn a return for you rather than a return for the company that issued the card. Credit card debt is listed in this statement under short-term debt because you should pay your credit card balances off every month—that way you never pay any interest. Used in this way credit cards work to your advantage. Between the time you make a purchase with a credit card and the time you pay the total balance due on that card, you can earn interest on your money while it sits in your interest bearing checking account. Even if your checking account does not pay interest, you still get an interest free loan from the card issuer between the time you make a purchase with a credit card and the time you pay the total balance due. If you carry a balance on your credit cards the card issuers benefit, since they get the money you pay to them in interest—usually at a higher interest rate than for other loans. If you are carrying debt on your credit cards that you cannot afford to pay off this minute from extra money you have categorized as cash in your net financial worth statement you need to use a longer term, lower interest rate loan to pay off your credit cards. You need to do that today, do not wait. Look for the lowest interest rate you can get on a loan to replace your credit card debt. Ideally, the loan you use to pay off your credit cards will have no prepayment penalty. Where possible, plan to make extra payments on the principal of this loan to pay it off early. Once free of credit card debt, stay free of it. Do not carry a balance on your credit cards from one billing cycle to the next; that only enriches the credit card companies at your expense.

Once you are free of credit card debt pay down the loan with the highest interest rate first, with the exception of your home mortgage or home equity loan. You probably do not want to pay off these loans early. In addition to the tax deduction, which lowers the effective rate of interest you pay on these loans, the deductible interest from these loans may allow you to itemize other deductions such as real estate taxes, which together with the interest paid and other qualified deductions, can easily exceed the standard deduction. If the interest on your mortgage and home equity loan, plus any other itemized deductions does not exceed the standard deduction, then there is no tax advantage to these loans and the effective aftertax interest rate equals the stated interest rate on the loan.

To calculate the effective aftertax interest rate on a tax-deductible loan use the steps illustrated in the following example. If you are in the 28% tax bracket your U.S. tax liability will be reduced by 28% of the interest you pay on tax-deductible loans. This means a 10% interest rate is effectively a 7.2% interest rate after receiving a tax break on that interest (10% × (100% - 28%) ÷ 100% = 7.2%).

Use the aftertax interest rates of your tax-deductible loans when comparing interest rates of your various loans. If the aftertax interest rate is higher than that of your non-deductible interest loans and paying down the tax-deductible loan will not effect your ability to take other deductions then you want to pay down the tax-deductible loan before the non-deductible loan.

Rather than paying down your mortgage, you may be able to save money by refinancing your home if mortgage rates have dropped significantly below the rate of your current mortgage. To determine if you are further ahead refinancing your home divide the closing costs you would have to pay by the amount you will save on your mortgage payment. This gives you the number of months it will take to recoup your closing costs. If you will remain in your home beyond that point then you may benefit from refinancing your home. Shop around.

Once you bring your debt service ratio down, you need to decide whether you would be further ahead to pay down your remaining debts (excluding your mortgage) before you begin investing money for long-term goals. To do this you need to compare the interest rates you pay on your remaining loans to the aftertax rate of return you might earn in other investments. Historically, investments in stocks have provided about an 11% pre-tax annual rate of return. A pre-tax rate of return of 11% would equal an aftertax rate of return of 7.9% for a person in the 28% tax bracket (11% × (100% - 28%) ÷ 100% = 7.9%). Compare this aftertax rate of return to the interest rates you are paying on your remaining loans to determine if you should pay off additional loans before beginning to invest money for your long-term goals.

When you pay down a loan, you are doing more than reducing the amount of debt you owe; you are also saving the interest you would have had to pay on that debt. By paying down your loan, you are investing in debt reduction at a rate of return equivalent to the interest rate on your loan. In addition, after you pay off the loan, the money that was spent on loan payments can then be put toward achieving your other goals.

You now have a good grasp of ways to reduce your debt burden. Effective use of loans is discussed in detail in Chapter 8, Debt Management.

According to information from the U.S. Department of Labor Statistics the average American in the United States spends about 13% of aftertax income on food. To calculate your percentage, divide your total under the food category in the net monthly income statement by your total net income and multiply by 100. The average American spends roughly 8% of aftertax income on food eaten at home, and about 5% on food eaten away from home. The amount spent on groceries does not include the cost of household items such as cleaning products that people frequently purchase when they buy food. Housing costs are about 31% of aftertax income for Americans, while utilities total about 6.5%. Household furnishings consume about 4% of aftertax income, clothing and shoes about 5%, health care 5%, recreation 5%, and insurance almost 7%. Total transportation costs for the average American consume almost 18% of aftertax income, composed of vehicle purchase expense (8%), oil and gasoline (3%), and miscellaneous expenses that include repairs, license fees, vehicle insurance, and any use of public transportation (7%). These average figures may or may not apply to your particular case, since living overseas often skews your expenses in different ways than when you live in the United States. They do give you a rough idea of where the average person's money goes. Your priorities may be different from the average and you may want to keep things that way, but you need to know where your money goes.

There are many different ways to spend money. The monthly net income statement details many types of expenses, so you can gain as good a picture as possible of how you spend your money. If you are not happy with how you are currently spending your money or you need to allocate more money toward your future goals, you need to change your spending habits to make sure your money goes where you want it to go. That is the topic of the next chapter, Spending by Choice.

4. SPENDING BY CHOICE

Having worked through the previous chapter you now know where your money goes. This chapter helps you prioritize your spending, making sure you spend your money the way you want to and as effectively as possible.

The total income you will earn over the course of your life is limited. Chances are that you will not work your entire life, but will retire at some point. In total, how many years can you expect to work in your life? If you started your career when you graduated from college, in your early twenties, and plan to retire in your early sixties, you will earn an income for roughly 40 years.

How long can you expect to be retired? Currently, people who are 65 years of age have a life expectancy of 90. Over the past century advances in medicine and improved living standards have doubled life expectancies and the trend toward longer life expectancies continues. Chances are your retirement will last for at least 35 years.

Where is the money going to come from when you no longer earn a living? Government provided social security and employer provided defined benefit pensions currently account for only 20%–40% of the average retiree's income. Future retirees can expect social security and employer provided pension payments to provide even less of their income. Your income in retirement will come primarily from money you do not spend during your working years. If you spend all of your income as you earn it you will not be able to maintain your standard of living when you retire. You may have to work in retirement to survive in your later years. Retirees whose retirement years are truly golden are financially disciplined, debt-free and have set money aside for their retirement throughout their working careers.

How much of your current income should you set aside for later use? Between 10%–25% depending on your situation and future goals. If you are not setting aside at least 10% toward retirement—or if you are not satisfied with the amount you are saving to reach your other goals—you need to read the rest of this chapter carefully before moving on to the rest of the book.

PLAN YOUR SPENDING

While much of our spending is fixed (mortgage payments, student loans, insurance premiums), much is not (food, clothes, entertainment). Are you spending money on these variable expenses the way you want to? Do you know how much you spend on these variable expenses? When recording expenses on your income statement, did you base your answers on actual receipts and account statements or on your best guess? If your entries are mostly guesses you need to keep track of your actual spending for a while by collecting receipts or keeping a log of your purchases. Take a notepad with you whenever you go out and keep a record of purchases you make by phone or mail. You can tally your purchases later either by using a computer program like Quicken®, Microsoft Money®, or a spreadsheet, or with paper and pencil. The first step in planning your spending is to look at how you spend your money now; the more accurate that information is the better.

Even if there is some question about the accuracy of your current spending, you can still plan your future spending. You only have so much money coming in. You earn each dollar only once and you can spend each dollar only once. Once spent, that money is not available for something you may want even more than the item you just bought. All spending decisions involve tradeoffs. What criteria should you use to decide which tradeoff to make? That depends on your needs and wants and how important they are to you. Refer back to your list of goals. Which of them are the most important to you? What values do you associate with them?

Keep these values in mind as you answer the next set of questions. Which do you value more, your current spending habits or your future goals? Which areas of current spending are you willing to reduce so that you have more money available for your future goals? Are some of your goals less desirable than your current spending? For families, each family member should identify areas where they can either reduce spending or eliminate future goals to help the family attain their most desirable goals. Be specific about the amount of money to spend on each variable expense and the amount you are trying to save for your future goals. (Determining the specific amounts you need to save for your goals is covered in chapters 5 and 6. For now, you can set a savings ratio target of 10%–25%.) You will not spend exactly the amount you plan to spend each and every month but, on average, you want to spend money according to your plan. Let's look at some specific areas where spending can be reduced so more money is available for your future goals.

What spending can you easily curtail? Can you reduce restaurant dinners and instead eat at home one more night per month? Perhaps that will free up $40 per month. Can you take your lunch to work rather than buy it? If you typically spend $8 a day to buy lunch and it costs you $3 a day to take a lunch from home, you will have an additional $110 per month to put toward your goals by brown bagging your lunch.

Try to find ways to spend your money more efficiently. For example, make sure you are not overpaying for things. Compare prices. Wait for items to go on sale before purchasing them. Return defective merchandise. What things can you make rather than buy? What can be repaired rather than replaced? Do you shop for groceries from a list or do you buy what strikes you at the moment? Do you forget items you need and have to make extra trips to the store?

Eliminate wasteful spending. For example: Do you pay off your credit cards each billing period? If not, the price of items you purchase with those cards is increased by the interest you pay. For example, a $7,000 outstanding balance (the national average) on a credit card with an annual interest rate of 15% costs you $1,050 in interest each year. That's $1,050 you could be putting toward future goals. Stop supporting the bank and start paying yourself instead. Make paying off your credit cards a top priority. Chances are that the interest you pay on your credit card balance is the highest interest rate of all your loans. Once your credit cards are paid off, do not allow a balance to build up again.

Americans living overseas often end up paying finance charges and late fees because they do not receive their U.S. bills in time to meet payment deadlines. In this case, you cannot rely on the statement to remind you to pay the bill. You need to create a system that guarantees you will pay the bills in time. For credit cards this means keeping track of your charges so that you know how much you owe without having to wait for your statement. You pay that amount by mailing your payment in time to beat the due date and then reconcile the difference when the statement arrives. For more details on setting up such a system, see the section on Credit Cards in Chapter 8, Debt Management.

IDENTIFY HARMFUL SPENDING PATTERNS

Poor spending habits can waste large amounts of your hard-earned money. Besides finance charges and late fees, there are many ways to waste money, but the most harmful is impulsive spending. How often do you buy something on the spur of the moment? Unless your answer is, "almost never", read the rest of this chapter and identify the triggers that lead to your unplanned purchases. Remember, you are going to spend money. The trick is to spend it to your best advantage rather than to the advantage of the merchandiser.

To get a sense of the circumstances that encourage you to spend impulsively, you need to keep a log of your spending. Whenever you make an unplanned purchase record what prompted you to go shopping, why you made the purchase, how you felt when making the purchase, and how you felt after making the purchase. You are looking for what triggered your spending and how you decided to make the purchase. The log entries should be made as soon after the purchase as possible; remember to include purchases you make online or by catalog.

Review your log entries about once a week. Do you go shopping only when you need something or is shopping a way to pass the time? When you go window-shopping, do you always end up buying something? Do you tend to compare prices, or do you just enjoy the outing? Do you go shopping to cheer yourself up? Do you go shopping alone or with someone? Do you always make more unplanned purchases when you go shopping with a friend? How did you decide whether or not to make each purchase? What criteria did you use? Rate how good you felt about the purchase at the time. As you review each purchase, rate how you feel about the purchase after the fact.

CHANGING YOUR HARMFUL SPENDING HABITS

In the process of reviewing your spending log, you may identify spending patterns you want to change. Let's look at the various spending habits people can have and ways to change them.

The first step is to avoid situations that lead to unplanned purchases. If you go shopping to pass the time, cheer yourself up, or to be with a friend, find another activity to take its place. Go for a walk in the park, exercise, read, spend more time socializing away from shopping areas, or become involved with an organization you admire. Start thinking about what else you enjoy doing. Come up with a list of three to six activities you would like to be doing. Whenever the urge to go shopping strikes you, choose one of these alternative activities instead.

We cannot avoid the impulse to buy altogether. Examine how you decided to give in to the impulsive to buy. When you thought about whether or not to make a purchase what criteria did you use? Did you base your decision on how much you valued having that item when weighed against your future goals or did you buy it for the thrill of the moment? How long did that thrill last? Are you still satisfied with the purchase? When you were debating whether to buy or not, did you give in because it was on sale? Even buying something at 50% off, you still spent a dollar for every dollar you saved. You didn't actually receive the money you "saved" you just didn't spend additional money to make the purchase. If it was something you had planned to purchase before spotting it on sale it may have been a good deal. If the purchase was whimsical it almost certainly was not a good deal. The money you spent is now gone. When making the purchase did you tell yourself you would spend less somewhere else to make up for that impulse purchase? Are you doing that?

What is the best way to combat the impulse to buy? The choice to buy or not to buy needs to be based on what you value, not on a momentary desire. Look at your goals. Your goals are based on what you value. When you achieve those goals you will enjoy the lasting satisfaction of having what you most want. The question to ask yourself is: What am I giving up when I buy on impulse? The answer: What you most want—your goals. Keep your most important goals in mind when you shop. Your goals are easy to forget since it may be years before you realize them, but that is what you are trading away when you make unplanned purchases. When the impulse to buy strikes you, weigh the instant gratification of that purchase against the long-lasting gratification of reaching your goals. You will gain more control over how you spend your money if you practice this procedure. Keep a copy of your goals with you, and when you are about to make an unplanned purchase, ask yourself whether this purchase is worth more to you than the goals on your list. If you decide it is not, don't buy it.

As you try to change your spending patterns, remember it takes three weeks to break a habit. Only after the old habit is broken does the new habit begin to establish itself. Do not deviate from your new habit until it is entrenched. Be specific about the behavior you wish to change. For example, make a decision that you will not shop when your are feeling blue, or that you will take a lunch to work at least two days a week. Try to change only one habit at a time. Look at changes that will give you the most benefit. Paying off your credit card and breaking the habit of carrying a credit card balance between billing periods should be your top priority. Once you have reached that goal look at the various other ways money slips through your fingers. Prioritize the spending habits that cause waste or ineffective use of money. Once you have replaced an ineffective spending habit with an effective one, move on to the next ineffective habit. Make the changes with the greatest positive impact first. The idea is to get the most for your money. That way, more money goes toward achieving your goals- —getting what you most want.

5. TARGETING YOUR GOALS

It is not necessary to strike the bull's eye when targeting your goals: So long as your estimate is reasonable you will acheive your goals. Various factors influence how close to the bull's eye you will be. The single most important factor is your time horizon: That is, the time you have available to achieve each goal. The worksheets in this chapter are geared toward the three time horizons you assigned to your goals: Short-term—less than six years, medium-term—six to ten years, and long-term—over ten years. (For an explanation of why these time horizons where chosen, please see Chapter 11, Investment Management.) You should use the worksheet that fits the time horizon of your goal. Each worksheet has an example goal: Buying a new car, putting a down payment on a house, and providing a college education are covered in the short-, medium-, and long-term goal sections respectively. (Retirement is a special case long-term goal and is covered in the next chapter.) College costs are complicated to estimate, which is why saving for a college education is one of the example goals. If your goal is one of the example goals, but with a different time horizon, use the worksheet that matches your time horizon. When calculating how much money you will need, refer to the Amount Needed section of the worksheet with the example goal that matches your goal. Once you have determined the amount needed, return to the worksheet that matches your time horizon.

For each goal, you want to estimate the amount needed to achieve your goal and how much money you need to set aside each month to accumulate that amount. Your time horizon affects both of these. Inflation tends to push prices up over time. In most cases, the amount needed to achieve your goal will be based on that goal's current cost adjusted upward to account for the effect of inflation over your time horizon. However, the cost of some items will increase faster than inflation. For example, for the last few decades college costs have been increasing at more than twice the rate of inflation and home prices have risen by the rate of inflation plus 1%–2%. Because college costs and home prices increase at a rate that differs from the historical inflation rate of 3%, they are among the examples given in this chapter. In these cases (and others) you will have to determine how costs for your goal have risen in the past to get a more realistic idea of how costs for your goal are expected increase in the future. The amount needed will then be based on the goal's current cost adjusted upward by the goal's historic rate of cost increases over your time horizon.

The longer your time horizon, the longer your savings can remain invested, compounding your earnings and reducing the amount of money you need to set aside each month to achieve your goal. Your time horizon affects the types of investments you use. Initially, you will want to accumulate savings in a money market account with your discount broker or bank. If you have only a short time horizon, you will want to restrict your investments to these money market accounts, possibly supplementing them with CDs or U.S. Treasury bills. If your time horizon is medium- or long-term, you can invest in equity mutual funds that offer a higher rate of return once you have accumulated enough money to meet a fund's minimum purchase requirement. Even with a medium- or long- term horizon, you should stop putting new savings into stock mutual funds as you near the end of your time horizon. Savings during the last two to three years of your time horizon should be invested in CDs, U.S. Treasury bills, or money market accounts. During the last two to three years of your time horizon, you should start to move older long-term investments out of mutual funds and into CDs or U.S. Treasury bills that mature near the end of your time horizon. By the end of your time horizon all of your investments should be in your money market account where they will be liquid and available to spend on your goal. If you are unfamiliar with many of the terms used here, please see the glossary and Chapter 11, Investment Management, for a discussion of these concepts and several others related to investing.

Taxation of your investments is another factor. Unless your investments are in an educational, Roth or standard IRA account or some other tax-deferred account, you will have to pay, at a minimum, U.S. federal taxes on your investment earnings. If your host country also taxes your investment earnings you should be able to take a foreign tax credit for the amount of that tax on your U.S. federal tax return. (For more details, refer to Chapter 12, Tax Management.)

Other factors in your estimate include the assumptions you choose to make when using these worksheets. There are many. How much does your goal cost now? (Do you use an average price or an actual price?) How quickly are costs for that goal increasing? (At the rate of inflation or some other rate?) What rate of return will you earn on your investments? (The historical average or some other rate?) These worksheets provide you with a reasonable way to estimate how much a given goal will cost you based on a particular set of assumptions. In some cases it will not be clear which assumptions are more realistic. When this occurs it is best to recalculate the cost of your goal using an alternate set of assumptions. This will give you a "price range" for your goal. We encourage you to do this "sensitivity analysis", so you will see the impact these assumptions have on the amount of money you will need to set aside to achieve a given goal. These worksheets will not give you the exact cost of any given goal. They will give you a reasonable idea of how much your goals will cost and how much you need to save and invest to achieve them.

Additional blank worksheets and the tables you will need to estimate what your goals will cost you are provided separately in Appendices B and C. The impact working toward and then achieving your goal will have on your overall financial condition is discussed in the last two sections of each worksheet under the headings: Net Income Concerns and Net Worth Concerns. The rest of this chapter presents and explains how to use each worksheet.

SHORT-TERM FINANCIAL GOAL—LESS THAN SIX YEARS

Example Goal

Buying a new car.

Time Horizon

A short-term financial goal should have a time horizon of less than six years. In this example Elly and Elliot Ellicott want to buy a new car in four years. Use the time horizon appropriate for your own goal and circumstances.

Amount Needed

The amount needed depends on your goal. The Ellicotts' goal is to buy a second car. They will keep their current car, so its trade-in or resale value will not affect the amount needed. The amount the Ellicotts need depends solely on the type of car they plan to buy. The car they want to purchase costs $17,760 today. The cost of cars will increase over the next four years, generally at the rate of inflation, which historically has been 3% a year. The Ellicotts use an inflation rate of 3% for their estimate, as should you unless you know that the price for your goal will increase at a different rate. From Table 1, Growth Factors, in Appendix C, the growth factor for four years at 3% per year is 1.126. The estimated amount the Ellicotts will need four years from now is the current price times the growth factor. The total amount they estimate they will need is $20,000 ($17,760 × 1.126, rounded up).

Types of Investments

For short-term financial goals, avoid using stock mutual funds. Instead, invest the money you save in money market accounts or CDs. Once you have accumulated $1000, you can also invest in U.S. Treasury bills that mature in time to meet your goal.

Rate of Return

The rate of return on the above investments may vary over the course of your time horizon. It is difficult to predict interest rates—even professional economists shy away from predicting interest rates more than a year in advance—so it is best to assume current rates of return for your chosen investments. If interest rates change significantly you can re-estimate how much you will need to save. The Ellicotts assume a rate of return of 5.0%. You will have to pay taxes on your investments while saving for this goal, so you need to determine your aftertax rate of return. With a short time horizon, nearly all of your investment returns will be in the form of interest, which is taxed at your marginal tax rate. The Ellicotts are in the 28% bracket for their U.S. income taxes. Their assumed aftertax rate of return is then 3.5% (5.0% × (100% - 28%) ÷ 100% rounded to the nearest 0.5%).

What to Set Aside Each Month

Use Table 2, Monthly Savings Factors, in Appendix C, to determine your monthly savings factor. The Ellicotts check Table 2, and find the monthly savings factor is 0.01944 for a time horizon of four years and an aftertax return of 3.5%. To determine the amount to save each month, they multiply the total amount needed by the savings factor. They should save $389 ($20,000 × 0.01944) each month to have approximately $20,000 in four years if their savings earn 3.5% aftertax.

Net Income Concerns

An alternative to saving for the car is to buy their second car, in four years, by taking out a loan for the $20,000. They find the rates on a 48-month new car loan are approximately 7.5%. Assuming that interest rates are the same in four years they use Table 3, Monthly Loan Payments, in Appendix C, to find that the monthly loan payment factor is 0.02418 for a four year loan at 7.5%. Multiplying this by $20,000 they find the monthly payment is $484 per month. By saving for the car rather than taking out a loan, they will save $95 a month that can be used elsewhere.

Net Worth Concerns

In general, a car's value deteriorates quickly and does not add substantively to your net worth. After four years the market value of most cars falls to roughly 50% of its value when new. If the new car is financed with a loan, the amount of the loan negates the value of the car. For example, a new $17,760 car would add perhaps $15,760 to your assets: A car loses value once you drive it off the lot. If that car is financed with a $17,760 loan, your liabilities would be $17,760 initially, leaving you with a net worth impact of negative $2,000 for a brand new car. Banks and other lending institutions closely examine a person's net worth and debt load when considering loan applications.

SHORT-TERM FINANCIAL GOAL WORKSHEET

1. TIME HORIZON
How many years before you need the money?   4

2. AMOUNT NEEDED
a. What does your goal cost now? $17,760
b. How quickly are costs increasing on a
   yearly basis? Use 3.0%–4% for most goals.   3%
c. Determine the growth factor for your
   time horizon. Use Table 1 for the time
   horizon in line 1 and the rate in 2.b above.   1.126
d. Calculate how much you will need to reach
   this goal. Multiply the growth factor in
   line 2.c by the amount in line 2.a above. $20,000

3. PRETAX RATE OF RETURN
What is the expected rate of return for the
investments you will use?   5%

4. YOUR MARGINAL TAX RATE   28%

5. AFTERTAX RATE OF RETURN
line 3 × (100% - line 4) ÷ 100%   3.5%

6. SAVINGS FACTOR
Using Table 2, find the monthly savings factor
based on your time horizon in line 1 and the
aftertax rate of return in line 5.   0.01944

7. MONTHLY SAVINGS NEEDED
line 2.d × line 6 $389

MEDIUM-TERM FINANCIAL GOAL—SIX TO TEN YEARS

Example Goal

Saving for a down payment and closing costs on a house.

Time Horizon

A medium-term goal has a time horizon between six and ten years. If you are saving specifically for a house, but have a different time horizon use the worksheet appropriate for your time horizon. When determining the amount you need to save to buy a house follow the Amount Needed section in this worksheet and then return to the worksheet that matches your time horizon. For a discussion of how owning your home impacts on your financial condition, refer to the Net Income Concerns and Net Worth Concerns sections in this worksheet. In this example, Elly and Elliott Ellicott plan to buy a house in six years. Use the time horizon and worksheet appropriate for your goal.

Amount Needed

The amount needed is based on the current cost of your goal. When your goal is buying a home the amount needed depends primarily on the area where you are considering buying your home and how large of a mortgage you can afford. The national average home price is $150,000. However, prices vary widely depending on location. To get more accurate housing prices, contact realtors in the locations you are considering, or search online. In the area where the Ellicotts want to buy, a home like they want to own costs approximately $150,000. Use the amount appropriate for your chosen location and home.

To reduce the amount of your mortgage payment, increase the size of your down payment. If you put less than 20% down on a house the lending institution will charge you for private mortgage insurance (PMI), which protects the lender, not you. Should you choose to make a down payment of only 10%, charges for PMI will add $55–$75 to your monthly payment for a mortgage of this size. For a $150,000 house, 10% is $15,000, leaving $135,000 that must be financed. To determine whether you can afford a mortgage of this amount, refer to Table 3, Monthly Loan Payments, in Appendix C. From Table 3, the monthly loan payment factor on a 30-year loan at 8% is 0.00734. (Use the interest rate and time period appropriate for your situation.) The monthly payment for such a mortgage is $991 ($135,000 × 0.00734). Add PMI of $64 and your monthly mortgage payment would be $1,055. Property taxes and homeowners insurance can easily bring the monthly payment to $1200 or more. Utility costs are also a factor; on average these are 6.5% of net income. From your Monthly Net Income Statement (in Chapter 3), see if you can comfortably afford these mortgage and utility payments. If not, you may want to consider making a larger down payment. For a $150,000 house, 20% is $30,000, leaving $120,000 that must be mortgaged. Using the assumptions above, the monthly payment for this mortgage would be $881 ($120,000 × 0.00734). With a 20% or higher down payment you will not be charged PMI, so you will shave a total of $174 ($991 + $64 - $881) from your monthly mortgage costs; this may make the same house affordable. If not, you may need to consider a less expensive house.

In this example, the Ellicotts decide to make a down payment of 20%, or $30,000. The amount they need to save is $30,000 plus closing costs.

Closing costs depend on the terms of the purchase contract, but in general they can vary from 2%–5% of the value of the house. The Ellicotts assume they will need 4% or $6,000 ($150,000 × 4% ÷ 100%) for closing costs. In total they expect to need $36,000 ($30,000 + $6,000) to cover the down payment of 20% and associated closing costs for a $150,000 house. You should use the amount appropriate for your goal.

Historically, inflation has been 3% and for most goals you should adjust the amount needed upward to account for the effect of inflation over your time horizon. If buying a home is your goal, you need to use a different rate. Residential property values, on a national average basis, have increased at the rate of inflation plus 1%–2%. However, home prices can increase or decrease at different rates depending on location. The Ellicotts assume home prices will increase 4.5% a year for the next six years. From Table 1,

Growth Factors, in Appendix C, they find the growth factor for six years at 4.5% per year is 1.302. The amount they will need six years from now is approximately the amount needed today to achieve this goal times the growth factor or $46,872 ($36,000 × 1.302). You should apply the historical rate of inflation—3%, to your goal, unless you know the cost of your goal is likely to increase at a different rate.

Types of Investments

For a medium-term time frame you can invest in stock mutual funds during the initial years of your time horizon. During the final two to three years of your time horizon, all new savings should be placed in a money market account with your discount broker or in CDs or U.S. Treasury bills. During the final two to three years of your time horizon you should also start to shift older investments out of stock mutual funds and put the aftertax proceeds in safe, liquid investments such as CDs, U.S. Treasury bills or your money market account.

Rate of Return

The rate of return on the above investments may vary over the course of your time horizon. As it is difficult to predict investment returns, it is best to assume historical rates of return for your chosen investments. If rates change significantly, you can reestimate how much you will need to save. The Ellicotts assume a rate of return of 11%, the historical rate of return for stocks.

You will have to pay taxes on your investments while saving for this goal, so you need to determine your aftertax rate of return. With a medium-term time horizon, a small portion of your investment returns will be long-term capital gains, which are taxed at 20% or less in the United States. A major portion of your returns will be short-term capital gains, interest, or dividends, which are taxed at your marginal tax rate. The Ellicotts have a U.S. marginal income tax rate of 28%, so they assume their aftertax rate of return will be 8% (11% × [100% - 28%] ÷ 100%, rounded to the nearest 0.5%).

In any investment plan, it will be necessary to move money out of stock mutual funds and into liquid and guaranteed investments some time before the money is needed. As a general rule, it is best to move your money into short-term investments such as a money market account, U.S. Treasury bills, or CDs when you are two to three years from the end of your time horizon. These short-term securities ensure you avoid losses if the market turns down just as you are preparing to use your money. New money saved during the last two to three years should also be placed in these types of investments. Your overall rate of return for the entire time horizon will be lower than estimated above because of this. For a medium-term financial goal, your expected aftertax rate of return should be lowered by at least 2% because of this. In this example, the time horizon is only six years, so the Ellicotts lower their expected rate of return by 3%. Their expected aftertax rate of return over the entire six-year period is 5% (8% - 3%). If your time horizon is eight to ten years you can reduce your expected rate of return by 2%.

What to Set Aside Each Month

From Table 2, Monthly Savings Factors, in Appendix C, the monthly savings factor for a time horizon of six years and an aftertax rate of return of 5% is 0.01194. Based on this, the Ellicotts estimate they will need to save $560 per month ($46,872 × 0.01194) to have $46,872 in six years.

Net Income Concerns

Normally, a mortgage or rent payment is a substantial portion of one's monthly income. Frequently, employers provide housing for their employees while they live overseas. If you live overseas with housing paid for by your employer, it will be easier to save for a down payment and closing costs. Take advantage of this opportunity.

Net Worth Concerns

While saving for the down payment and closing costs for your house, your net worth will increase. Initially, when you buy your home, your net worth will drop by the amount of the closing costs. Over time, however, there are two ways the equity in your house—and therefore your net worth—can increase. The most obvious increase comes from paying your mortgage. Initially, you will pay off the debt on your mortgage very slowly. On the $120,000, 30-year, 8% mortgage the Ellicotts considered in this example, the first payment of $881 consists of $800 of interest expense—only $81 goes toward paying off the $120,000 debt. It is not until the twenty-second year that half of the monthly mortgage payment goes to paying off the then remaining debt of $65,500. After 22 years, equity in this house will be the $30,000 down payment plus $54,500 ($120,000 - $65,500) or $84,500. People frequently move as their families and situations change. If you wished to buy a bigger home after seven years, your equity in the house would be the $30,000 down payment plus $9,000, or $39,000. At any point during the term of the loan, your mortgage lender can tell you the principal amount outstanding on your loan, which you can use to calculate the total equity in your house.

For a 15-year mortgage the interest rate is typically 0.25%–0.5% lower than for a 30-year mortgage. Wanting to consider this alternative, the Ellicotts find a 15-year mortgage at 7.5%. From Table 3, they find that the monthly loan payment factor on a 15-year, 7.5% mortgage is 0.00927. Their mortgage payments would be $1,112 a month (0.00927 × $120,000). In the first month, $750 would go toward interest and $362 would be used to reduce their mortgage debt. In the sixth year, half of the mortgage payment goes toward paying off the then remaining $88,300 of debt. After seven years, the debt outstanding on their mortgage would be $80,100. Their equity in the house with a 15-year mortgage would be their $30,000 down payment plus $39,900 ($120,000 - $80,100) or $69,900. This is considerably more than the $39,000 for the 30-year mortgage described above. You can borrow against the equity in your home, usually at low rates, to meet college or home improvement costs.

The second way your net worth will increase is if the value of your home increases. Unfortunately, home prices do not always go up. For a rough estimate of the magnitude and direction of the change in your home equity from changing home prices, watch the real estate pages of your local newspaper for sales of houses similar to yours in your neighborhood. Collecting a few such examples should give you an idea of what your house is now worth. Subtract the purchase price of the house from your estimate of your home's current value. Add this to the equity from the discussions above to determine your total equity in your home.

MEDIUM-TERM FINANCIAL GOAL WORKSHEET

1. TIME HORIZON
How many years before the money is needed?   6

2. AMOUNT NEEDED
a. What does your goal cost now?   36,000
b. How quickly are costs increasing on a
   yearly basis? Use 3.0%–4% for most goals.   4.5%
c. Determine the growth factor for your
   time horizon. Use Table 1 for the time
   horizon in line 1 and the rate in 2.b above.   1.302
d. Calculate how much you will need to reach
   this goal. Multiply the growth factor in line
   2.c by the amount in line 2.a above.   46,872

3. PRETAX RATE OF RETURN
What is the expected rate of return for the
investments you will use?   11%

4. YOUR MARGINAL TAX RATE   28%

5. AFTERTAX RATE OF RETURN
line 3 × (100% - line 4) ÷ 100%   8%

6. REDUCTION IN RETURN
for the time your money is in short-term
investments   3%

7. FINAL AFTERTAX RATE OF RETURN
line 5 - line 6   5%

8. SAVINGS FACTOR
Using Table 2, find the monthly savings factor
based on your time horizon in line 1 and the
aftertax rate of return in line 7.   0.01194

9. MONTHLY SAVINGS NEEDED
line 2.d × line 8 $560

LONG-TERM FINANCIAL GOAL—OVER TEN YEARS

Example Goal

Saving for a child's college education.

Time Horizon

A long-term financial goal should have a time horizon longer than ten years. If your time horizon is less than six years refer to the short-term worksheet; if your time horizon is from six to ten years refer to the medium-term worksheet.

If you are saving specifically for a child's college education but have a different time horizon, use the worksheet appropriate for your time horizon. When estimating the amount you will need, follow the Amount Needed section in this worksheet and then return to the worksheet that matches your time horizon. Various federal and state tax-deferred college savings plans are discussed in the Rate of Return section of this worksheet. For a discussion of how this goal impacts on your financial condition, refer to the Net Income Concerns and Net Worth Concerns sections in this worksheet.

Ideally, you should start saving for a child's college education before the child is born. In this example, Elly and Elliott Ellicott have a new baby who they hope will enter college 18 years from now. Use the time horizon appropriate for your goal and circumstances.

Amount Needed

The amount needed depends on the cost of your goal. If your goal is providing a college education there are several organizations you can consult to obtain recent college costs. Each year the U.S. Department of Education publishes figures on college tuition and related costs. According to their information for 1997–98, the average tuition for a 4-year public university was $3,110 per year. Add $4,518 for room, board, and expenses (books and related materials) and the total annual cost was $7,628 in 1998. The average tuition at a 4-year private college was $13,392 per year. Add $5,751 for room, board, and expenses and the total annual cost came to $19,143 in 1998. Most students attend public universities. Out-of-state tuition varies greatly but is often twice in-state tuition rates. As an American living outside of the United States you may not qualify for residency in a particular state, or if you do your child may not wish to attend a university in that state. The Ellicotts assume they will have to pay the higher out-of-state tuition rate. Using the figures above, they begin with the estimate that the cost of one year at a public university with out-of-state tuition is about $10,738 ([2 × $3,110] + $4,518). If your long-term goal is not providing a college education determine what your goal costs now and use that amount here.

For most long-term goals, it is appropriate to assume the price of your goal will increase at the historical rate of inflation—3%. However, college expenses have increased much faster than the rate of inflation. From 1980–1994, college tuition and expenses increased 8.5% annually. Recently, rates have increased 5% to 7% annually and many experts expect this will continue into the future. The Ellicotts assume college costs will increase 6% per year. To determine how much tuition will cost 18, 19, 20, and 21 years from now, (when their child will be in college) they refer to Table 1, Growth Factors, in Appendix C. From Table 1, the growth factor for 18 years at 6% a year is 2.854. For 19, 20, and 21 years at 6% the growth factors are 3.026, 3.207, and 3.400 respectively. Thus an estimate of the total amount they will need is:

Time Horizon	Current Cost		Growth Factor		Expected Cost
18	$10,738	×	2.854	=	$30,646
19	10,738	×	3.026	=	32,493
20	10,738	×	3.207	=	34,437
21	10,738	×	3.400	=	36,509
TOTAL					$134,085

They will need approximately $134,000 18 years from now to send their child to a public university for four years. Some financial planners argue that you can save while your child is in college. It may be difficult to save $36,500 in three years while your child is in college. During the first year you will also have other expenses as the child moves away from home. Throughout your child's college education you may have expenses such as air travel, phone bills, and miscellaneous living expenses for your college student. If you are living overseas when your child enters college some of these expenses may be substantial. You may also have more than one child in college at a time. If at all possible, have the entire amount needed for each child saved before that child enters college. If you cannot save the entire amount, save as much of it as you can. The figure used in this example is a rough estimate of the average cost. There are many good universities that have substantially lower tuition and room and board rates.

Types of Investments

The time frame for this goal is long-term; so stock mutual funds are appropriate investments to use in achieving this goal. During the final two to three years of your time horizon, all new savings should be placed in a money market account with your discount broker, or in CDs, or U.S. Treasury bills. During the final two to three years of your time horizon you should start to shift earlier investments out of stock mutual funds and put the aftertax proceeds in safe, liquid investments such as CDs, U.S. Treasury bills or your money market account.

Rate of Return

The actual rate of return on investments will probably vary over the course of your time horizon. As it is impossible to predict actual rates of return, it is best to assume historical rates of return as an estimate for your chosen investments. If returns on your investments change significantly you can re-estimate how much you will need to save. The Ellicotts assume a rate of return of 11.0%, the historical average for stocks. To meet this goal you will use taxable investments, so you need to determine your aftertax rate of return. Since this is a long-term goal, much of your return may be in the form of long-term capital gains, which are currently taxed at 20% in the United States. To get an idea of how much of your return may be subject to regular income taxes we examined the income and capital gains distributions over the past ten years for the mutual funds we track (roughly 200 funds). This examination also included the tax on the proceeds from selling these mutual funds after ten years. The results indicate that only 8% of distributions would have been taxable at your marginal income tax rate. The Ellicotts assume a U.S. long-term capital gains tax rate of 20% plus 1% to account for distributions that will be taxed at their marginal tax rate. If you are in a high tax bracket (greater than 35%) you should add two or three percent rather than one percent to your 20% effective tax rate. Using the one percent correction, an estimate of the aftertax annual rate of return from stock investments is 8.5% (11% × [100% - 21%] ÷ 100%, rounded to the nearest 0.5%).

In any investment plan, it will be necessary to move money out of mutual funds and into liquid and stable investments some time before the money is needed. As a general rule, it is best to move your money into short-term investments such as your money market fund with your discount broker, or U.S. Treasury bills, or CDs when you are two to three years from the end of your time horizon. These short-term securities ensure you avoid losses if the market turns down just as you are preparing to use your money. New money saved during the last two to three years should also be kept in these short-term investments. As a result, your overall rate of return for the entire time horizon will be lower than our estimate above. For a long-term financial goal, your expected aftertax rate of return should be lowered by about 1% because of the lower rate of return your money will earn during the final two to three years of your time horizon. The Ellicotts estimate their aftertax rate of return over the entire 18-year period will be about 7.5% (8.5% - 1%).

There are several tax-deferred options to help you save for college. You may want to consider educational IRAs, but only for a portion of your savings. Currently, you can only place $500 each year into an educational IRA. As you will see shortly, this is far short of the annual sum most people need to save for their child's college education. If your adjusted gross income is over $110,000 (or $160,000 for a married couple filling jointly) you are excluded from using educational IRAs. Finally, some colleges consider educational IRAs to be part of the student's assets, which will reduce the amount of financial aid your family can receive. If you qualify to use an educational IRA your total rate of return from using such an account may increase by only 0.25%–0.75% because the amount you can earn tax-free in such an account is so limited.

Other options include using either a state prepaid tuition plan or a state college savings plan. As of October 1999, 18 states offer prepaid tuition plans and 23 offer state savings plans. Only 17 plans are open to those who are not state residents and as an American overseas you may be restricted to these 17 plans.

If you qualify to participate in a state's prepaid tuition plan you may make contributions of $2,500–$10,000 each year (depending on the state). Federal income tax on these accounts is deferred; they are free of state taxes if you are a resident of the state. The prepaid tuition plans cover in-state tuition costs only. Other costs such as room and board are not covered. If the child attends a college in a different state the plan will pay tuition up to the average in-state tuition cost for colleges in the state where you have your prepaid tuition plan. If the child does not attend college you can designate another family member as the beneficiary. If that is not possible the state will refund your money to you plus a "reasonable" rate of return, which is frequently equivalent to money market rates.

If you can participate in a state's college savings plan you can make much larger contributions, totaling $100,000 or more in some cases. Federal income tax on these accounts is deferred; they are free of state taxes if you are a resident of the state. The child pays federal taxes (currently 15% of income above the standard deductions) on the money when it is withdrawn at the end of the plan's tenure. This money can be used to cover tuition, room and board, books and supplies and a computer. If the child does not attend college another family member can be designated as the new beneficiary for the account. If that is not possible you will have to pay all back taxes on the sum in the account at your marginal tax rate plus a penalty of 10% or more.

If you enroll in a state prepaid tuition plan or a state college savings plan, you have no say over how the money is invested. In many states, the state's pension fund managers take on this extra responsibility. Pension fund managers do not face the same competitive pressures or the same scrutiny of their performance that managers of mutual funds face. Increasingly, states are selecting independent, established investment firms to handle their college savings plans, which will increase competition and hopefully reduce the cost of managing these funds.

If you are dissatisfied with the rate of return you receive from your state tuition plan your options are limited. You can withdraw from the plan. For savings plans this means you will have to pay all federal and state back taxes (at your tax rate, not your child's) plus a 10% penalty. For prepaid tuition plans, you may not be able to withdraw your funds or if you can, you will receive your contributions plus a reasonable rate of return that may be the money market rate. Your only other option is to save additional money outside the plan, to make-up the shortfall.

The Ellicotts are assuming an aftertax rate of return of 7.5%. So any state tuition plan will have to return more than 7.5% to match this performance. Most state plans invest in bonds as well as stock mutual funds. Because bonds are used, the overall return in the long term will probably be less than that of stock mutual funds. In these plans, the bond component increases as the child reaches age 18, further reducing the overall return. Because of the many caveats associated with state tuition plans, you may wish to retain control over your money and invest it yourself. The Ellicotts decide not to use a state tuition plan.

What to Set Aside Each Month

From Table 2, Monthly Savings Factors, in Appendix C, the monthly savings factor for a time horizon of 18 years and an aftertax return of 7.5% is 0.0022. The Ellicotts estimate they will need to save roughly $295 per month ($134,000 × 0.0022) to have $134,000 in 18 years.

Net Income Concerns

An alternative to saving the entire amount is to plan to take out loans during the later years of your child's college education. In some cases this will be necessary. There are complications to taking this route since you may be approaching retirement at that point and may not be able to pay off the loan before you retire, or you may not be able to continue to save for your retirement while paying off the loans.

Net Worth Concerns

While saving for college your net worth will increase, but during the four years your child is in college, your net worth will decrease by the amount of the tuition and college expenses. If you own a home and have considerable equity in your home you may borrow against it, usually at a lower rate than is available with other educational loans. (See the Net Worth Concerns section of the Medium-Term Financial Goal Worksheet for a discussion of 15-year versus 30-year mortgages and their effect on your equity in your home.) Again, you need to consider the effect on your retirement before taking a home equity loan.

LONG-TERM FINANCIAL GOAL WORKSHEET

1. TIME HORIZON
How many years before you need the money?   18

2. AMOUNT NEEDED
a. What does your goal cost now? $10,738
b. How quickly are costs increasing on a
   yearly basis? (For college, the figures have
   been 5%–7% a year.) Use 3.0%–4% for
   most long-term goals.   6%
c. Determine the growth factor for your goal.
   Use Table 1 for the time horizon in line 1
   and the rate in 2.b above. Multiply this
   factor by the amount in line 2.a above.
   Repeat this process for each additional
   year your child will attend college.

Time Horizon	Current Cost		Growth Factor		Expected Cost
18	$10,738	×	2.854	=	$30,646
19	10,738	×	3.026	=	32,493
20	10,738	×	3.207	=	34,437
21	10,738	×	3.400	=	36,509

TOTAL $134,085

3. PRETAX RATE OF RETURN
What is the expected rate of return for the
investments you will use?   11%

4. YOUR EFFECTIVE TAX RATE   21%

5. AFTERTAX RATE OF RETURN
line 3 × (100% - line 4) ÷ 100%   8.5%

6. REDUCTION IN RETURN
for time money is in short-term investments   1%

7. FINAL AFTERTAX RATE OF RETURN
line 5 - line 6   7.5%

8. SAVINGS FACTOR
Using Table 2, find the monthly savings factor
based on your time horizon in line 1 and
the aftertax rate of return in line 7.   0.0022

9. MONTHLY SAVINGS NEEDED
line 2.c total × line 8 $295

6. TARGETING RETIREMENT

Targeting any goal involves making a number of assumptions. Targeting your retirement goal is a more complicated process because there are several more assumptions involved, including the impact of career moves. In particular, portions of your retirement income may or may not be provided by your employer(s) or by government(s). If your overseas career spans several employers and countries you may not work for any one employer or in any one country long enough to be eligible for an employer provided pension or social security benefits. If your overseas career spans only a few employers and countries, you could, in principle, qualify for multiple employer provided pensions and possibly more than one social security benefit.

While, retirement benefits are not the primary factor in deciding on a career move, they should be a considered. For example, if you wish to change employers before you are eligible to take your current employer's pension plan benefits with you, you can determine how much you would forfeit in retirement benefits and negotiate with your new employer for a signing bonus equal to the lost benefit. Generally, you will have many options as your career unfolds and each option will have an impact on your retirement. As with spending, any retirement decision involves making tradeoffs. This chapter helps you examine how those tradeoffs might affect your retirement.

In this chapter, we use the same general format as the long-term goal worksheet presented in Chapter 5, Targeting Your Goals. However, determining the amount of money needed to retire is quite complicated and involves the following steps:

1. Determine how much of your current income you will need in retirement
2. Determine what percentage of your retirement income will be provided by employer or government pensions; you will need to supply the remainder from your personal savings
3. Taking inflation into account, determine your retirement income needs in your first year of retirement
4. Determine how long you expect to be retired
5. Taking inflation into account, determine the lump sum you need to supply your retirement income for the duration of your retirement

This chapter also gives you an indication of how much money you need to set aside each month to maintain your life style during retirement.

TIME HORIZON

Ideally, you should start saving for your retirement as soon as you start working. Your time horizon for retirement is the number of years from now until you plan to retire. In this example, Elly and Elliott Ellicott are 40 and plan to retire 25 years from now at age 65.

AMOUNT NEEDED TO RETIRE

How much of your current income will you need to retire and maintain your life style? Many financial advisors take a simple approach and assume you will need some fixed percentage of your current income in retirement, typically 60%–80%. While this is a rough estimate, it assumes you will have paid off any large debts before you retire. It also assumes that your living expenses will drop once you retire because you will no longer need to commute to work, eat lunch out, and buy and maintain an expensive business wardrobe. These assumptions may not apply to you. In addition, people are living longer and healthier lives. Most retirees do not stay home and sit on the front porch: They take up new activities and pursue interests they never had time for when working. You will likely do the same. Money now spent on commuting, lunches, and business attire can be used to finance other interests in retirement.

If you can, try to have your house paid for by the time you retire. For many people, their mortgage payment is 20% or more of their pretax income. If you will have paid off your home mortgage before retiring enter the amount of your mortgage payment—principal and interest only (you will still have property taxes and homeowners insurance to pay)—on line 3 of the worksheet. If you plan to move to a more expensive home later in retirement or buy a second home you should not reduce your income needs by the full amount of your mortgage payment, even if your present home will be completely paid for before you retire.

Once you retire you no longer need to save for retirement, so your retirement income can be reduced by the amount you were saving for retirement. For example, if you are currently saving 10% of your pretax salary in a 401(k) plan, you can reduce your retirement income needs by 10% of your gross salary. The Ellicotts, who are doing just that, have a current annual income of $50,000, so in retirement they could reduce their required income by $5,000 ($50,000 × 10% ÷ 100%). If you have not yet started to save for retirement 10% of your gross income is a good first estimate of what you may need to save. If you expect to have additional expenses during retirement—for example, if you plan to travel extensively—you should not plan on reducing your retirement income by the full amount of any discontinued savings. Money going toward current savings can instead go to cover the costs of new activities.

The Ellicotts will still have to make mortgage payments and plan to travel extensively during retirement. For these reasons, they decide they will need all (100%) of their current income during retirement. If you can reduce your expenses in retirement your percentage will be lower.

Retirement Income From Defined Benefit Pensions

You may not have to supply all of your retirement income from your savings. From your employer, determine whether you have a defined benefit retirement plan, a defined contribution plan, both, or neither. A defined benefit plan is often paid entirely by your employer. There is usually a set time before you are *vested* in such a plan, meaning you must work for the employer for some number of years before you are entitled to this benefit. Defined benefits are often calculated on the basis of years of service with your employer and a benchmark salary you earned at some point in your career with that employer. For example, if your defined benefit plan stipulates you will receive 0.5% of your salary for each year of service with the company, then after 35 years of service your employer will pay you 17.5% (35 × 0.5%) of your benchmark salary for the rest of your life. If you participate in such a plan find how they calculate your benchmark salary and the percentage that applies to you and multiply it by the number of years you will have worked for your employer before you retire. Elly Ellicott has been with her employer for ten years already and plans to remain with the same employer for another 25 years before retiring. Her employer offers a defined benefit retirement plan that will pay her a benefit of 0.5% of her benchmark salary for each year she has worked with the employer. Thus she expects to receive a defined retirement benefit of 17.5% of her benchmark salary.

If you are married you probably want to stipulate that your spouse should continue to receive your pension benefit if you die first. Most defined benefit pension plans offer this survivor benefit option, but your benefit will be reduced, usually by about 15%. If Elly Ellicott wants to take this option her benefit will be reduced to 14.875% of her benchmark salary (17.5% × [100% - 15%] ÷ 100%). She plans to do this, and so estimates that her defined benefit will be 15% of her benchmark salary, rounding up. If you want to be conservative, round down.

Most defined benefit plans are indexed to inflation, so payments will increase each year. If your plan is not indexed to inflation, reduce the percentage of your income covered by this benefit according to how long you expect to be retired. (See the section,

Retirement Income: Year One and Beyond, later in this chapter.) For example, if you expect to be retired for 30 years and have no inflation protection in your pension plan cut the percentage of income provided by that benefit in half. If Elly's pension had no inflation protection she would assume that only 7.5% of her income—over the course of her retirement—might be covered by this benefit.

The above discussion assumes you work for only one employer during your career. This is an unlikely scenario. On average, people change employers four times during their careers. When deciding between potential new employers, favor those that offer a defined benefit pension plan. Of those employers that offer a defined benefit pension, favor those with higher percentages per year of service and those with shorter vesting periods.

The above issues are not your only considerations: Timing plays an important role with respect to your defined pension benefits. The vesting period for many defined benefit pension plans is five years. In the beginning of your career, you may choose employers with particular areas of expertise to gain the skills you need to position yourself for a particular line of work later in your career. You may not need to spend five years with each of these earlier employers to acquire the skills you want. How will changing employers early in your career affect your defined pension benefits? Not as badly as would be the case were you to change employers late in your career. When you leave an employer after becoming vested in that employer's defined benefit pension plan, your benefits will be based on your years of service, the percentage stipulated in the plan, and your benchmark (often final) salary with that employer. If you switch jobs your final salary with former employers will most likely not be your highest. Early in your career, your salary will be considerably lower than your salary just before retiring. The defined benefit from your initial years of employment will be a small fraction of your final salary. For example, if your salary at the end of your first five years of work is a quarter of your final salary just before retiring your defined pension benefit based on those first five years will cover only 0.5% of your final salary.

Some examples will show the effect of switching employers early in your career versus late in your career. We assume in each example that you will work for four employers over the course of a 35-year career. Each employer offers a defined benefit pension plan with a 0.5% per year of service benefit and a five year vesting period. We also assume that your salary will increase five percent annually, that the benchmark salary is your final salary, and that you are married and decide to accept a reduced benefit so your spouse can continue to receive your pension benefit should you die first.

Example one—If you work for three employers during the first nine years of your career, each for less than the 5-year vesting period, you will not be eligible for defined pension benefits for any of your work during that 9-year period. However, you will be with your fourth and last employer for a total of 26 years. When you finish your career, your benefits will be 11% of your final salary at retirement.

Example two—If you work for three employers during the first 15 years of your career, managing to work five years with each so that you are vested in each employer's defined benefit pension plan, your benefits when you finish your career will be 10% of your final salary at retirement. This is slightly worse than the previous example because you will work for your final employer for only 20 years rather than 26.

Example three—If instead you work for ten years for each of your first three employers and only five years with your last employer, your benefits will be only 8.5% of your final salary.

As a general rule, plan to stay with your last employer for as long as possible. Your total years of service will be longer and that number will be applied to a benchmark probably linked to your final salary at retirement, which generally will be your largest. If you decide to switch employers try to do so early in your career rather than late in your career.

Increasingly, employers do not offer defined benefit pension plans to new employees; they offer defined contribution plans instead. These will be covered in a later section.

Many employers are converting existing defined benefit pension plans to *cash balance* plans. Cash balance pension plans are a kind of defined benefit plan—the employer agrees to pay the employee a certain monthly benefit after retirement—but unlike traditional defined benefit pension plans they are portable. A traditional defined benefit plan promises the employee a monthly benefit that depends on the length of that employee's employment with that employer and the salary that employee earned during some benchmark period, often the employee's final years with that employer, when income is usually at its peak. Looking at this from the employer's perspective, there is some large amount of money that the employer needs to ensure is available when the employee retires that will provide the promised income to the employee for the rest of his or her life. (This calculation is similar to the one we will do later in this chapter to estimate how much you will need to save for your own retirement.) With a cash balance plan, the employer and employee contribute to the employee's cash balance account, and the employer guarantees the amount in that account will grow at some specified rate. If you leave your employer after you are vested in the plan, but before you retire, the sum in your retirement account can be transferred to your new employer's pension plan.

The upshot is that cash balance plans have the advantage of being portable, and they often result in more pension money being available for those who leave a company after a few years, but after the pension vesting period. The disadvantage is that for those who have been working for the same employer for a long time, the traditional defined benefit plan usually promises better retirement benefits. With a traditional defined benefit plan, employees may earn nearly half of their pension benefits during the final five to ten years of their employment. If your long term employer switches from a defined benefit pension plan to a cash balance plan during your final years of employment you can lose a substantial portion of your retirement benefit. For this reason there are political and legal questions (and suggestions of age discrimination) related to cash balance plans that are not yet resolved as of this writing. There is no guarantee your defined benefit plan will still be in place in its current form when you retire.

The Ellicotts are pleased with how Elly's career is progressing and they expect to remain with her current employer throughout her career. Being cautious, the Ellicotts think it likely that Elly's employer will convert its defined benefit pension plan to a cash balance plan and her overall benefit will be reduced by a third. For retirement planning purposes, the Ellicotts assume only 10% of Elly's retirement income will be provided through her employer's defined benefit pension plan. Make adjustments to this worksheet to reflect your own situation.

There is one other "defined benefit" type of pension—social security—that we will cover before moving on to defined contribution pension plans.

RETIREMENT INCOME FROM SOCIAL SECURITY BENEFITS

You may receive a social security check in retirement. To be eligible for U.S. social security benefits you must have 40 quarters (ten years) of earnings on which you paid U.S. social security taxes. The amount of your U.S. benefit is based on those earnings. You may have to pay social security taxes to another country rather than, or even in addition to, your U.S. social security taxes. (For full details on social security taxation refer to Chapter 12, Tax Management.) Any earnings that where free of U.S. social security taxes will not be considered in determining your U.S. social security benefit.

You may qualify for social security benefits in other countries where you work. Many countries have a two-tiered system where the potential beneficiary must meet certain residency requirements as well as have a work history, often of ten years or more. Obtain detailed information on eligibility requirements from each country where you plan to work.

If you work in several countries, each for only a few years, you may not be eligible for social security retirement benefits from any country where you have worked. The United States has established bilateral agreements, called totalization agreements with 17 countries that may help you qualify for retirement benefits in one of the treaty countries or in the United States. In this case your U.S. social security retirement benefits will be based solely on earnings on which you have paid U.S. social security taxes. (See Chapter 10, Financial Risk Management—Social Security, for more details on totalization agreements.)

In principle, you may be eligible for retirement benefits from more than one country. If you qualify for U.S. social security retirement benefits and similar benefits from one of the totalization agreement countries your benefits from both countries will be reduced. In a worst case scenario, your U.S. social security retirement benefits could be reduced to $202 per month. This could occur if you worked briefly in the United States at the start of your career and then worked outside the United States thereafter. Your social security benefits from a totalization agreement country will be reduced according to that country's regulations.

The tradeoffs between career opportunities in different countries and government sponsored retirement benefits are difficult to assess. The totalization agreement countries have appeal: While working in one of these countries you pay only one set of social security taxes. However, your ultimate benefits may or may not be increased. In addition, the totalization agreements stipulate that you can work for only five years in one of the agreement countries. In some cases, it is possible to work for more than five years in one of the totalization agreement countries, but you may have to leave the country for a full year and return to a substantially different job.

If you plan to retire abroad research the retirement and health care systems of the country where you expect to retire. If that country provides good retirement and health care benefits you may want to finish your career there and work in that country long enough to qualify for those benefits. If the country does not have a good retirement system be prepared to provide more of your retirement income from your personal savings.

If you plan to retire in the United States you will increase the amount of your U.S. social security retirement benefits if you work in the United States during the later part of your career.

How much should you expect to receive in social security benefits? In 1997, the minimum U.S. social security retirement benefit was $8,940 per year for a couple. The maximum was $23,868 and the average $15,000. It is unlikely the social security system will maintain this average benefit. Benefits are paid from current social security taxes. Because of demographics going forward, the population will become increasingly older. There will be fewer people of employment age working and paying the taxes needed to provide benefits to an increasing number of social security recipients. Benefits will need to be reduced or taxes will need to be increased or both. It is impossible to predict how social security benefits will be handled in the future. Despite this uncertainty, you still need to make an assumption about the social security benefits that you expect to receive. A good starting point is to assume benefits for all Americans will be reduced by a third by the time you retire. Based on the figures above, that translates to an average benefit of $10,000.

To improve your chances of receiving this full U.S. social security benefit you should plan to pay U.S. social security taxes on your salary during the last ten years of your career. To determine your U.S. social security retirement benefits refer to the latest copy of your Social Security Statement. If you do not have a copy request one from the social security administration at:

Social Security Administration
PO Box 20
Wilkes Barre, PA 18767-0020
Phone: 1-800-772-1213
Website: http://www.ssa.gov

The Social Security Statement replaces the Personal Earnings and Benefit Estimate Statement. As of October 1, 1999, Social Security Statements are mailed annually to each employee who pays U.S. social security taxes approximately three months before their birthday. If you already have the requisite 40 credits your statement will indicate the benefits you might expect in retirement. If not, you will have to calculate your potential benefits using the earnings given in the report and any other income on which you expect to pay U.S. social security taxes during your career.

To calculate your potential benefits yourself start by using the index factor and maximum earnings for historical years given in Social Security Publication No. 05-100700, *How Your Retirement Benefit is Figured*, to determine your indexed earnings for each year of reported U.S. earnings. Add these yearly indexed earnings together. To that sum, add any future earnings on which you will pay U.S. social security taxes. Divide the sum by the total number of years you will have paid U.S. social security taxes. The result is your yearly average earnings. Divide that figure by 12 to get your monthly average earnings. Your social security benefits are based on your average monthly earnings in the following way: Assume you will receive 40% of the first $505 of your average monthly earnings or $202 ($505 × 40% ÷ 100%). On the next $2,538 of your monthly average earnings, assume you will receive 32% or a maximum of $812 ($2,538 × 32% ÷ 100%). Finally, if your monthly average earnings exceeded $3,043 multiply the excess by 15%. Add up the three results and multiply the sum by 12 to get your expected annual retirement benefits from social security. To be conservative do not go over $10,000 for your estimated yearly benefit.

If you do not plan to work in the United States for ten years, but you have at least six quarters of earnings on which you have paid U.S. social security taxes, you may still qualify for U.S. social security benefits by working in totalization agreement countries throughout most of your career. Under this plan, you can estimate your monthly U.S. social security benefit from the earnings reported in your Social Security Statement. Based on this information, estimate your average monthly indexed earnings. (Add up your indexed earnings from your Social Security Statement and divide by the number of months you worked.) Your social security benefits are based on your average monthly earnings exactly as described in the previous paragraph.

The Ellicotts estimate in this way that they will receive about $5,000 per year in U.S. social security benefits. They are not eligible for social security retirement benefits from any other country. If you expect to qualify for social security retirement benefits from a country other than the United States contact the appropriate government agency to find out the average retirement benefit paid in that country. Add that amount to any U.S. social security benefits and enter the total in the worksheet on line 6b.

Since U.S. social security payments are indexed to inflation, these payments will continue to cover the same portion of your income throughout your retirement. Elly Ellicott is currently making $50,000 a year. Social security benefits of $5,000 per year will finance 10% ($5,000 ÷ $50,000 × 100%) of her income throughout their retirement. This example assumes she will qualify for U.S. social security retirement benefits only. Your situation may be different and you should use the percentage most appropriate for your situation.

The Ellicotts estimate that a total of 20% of their retirement income will be provided by a defined benefit pension plan (10%) plus social security (10%). In today's dollars their investments will need to provide the remaining 80%, or $40,000 ($50,000 × 80% ÷ 100%) of their current income in retirement.

There are several tax-deferred options for your retirement savings and we now examine those options before calculating the inflation adjusted dollar amount needed for the first year of your retirement.

Defined Contribution Retirement Plans

Many employers now offer a defined contribution retirement plan, such as a 401(k) plan, instead of—or in addition to—a defined benefit retirement plan. With defined contribution plans you invest part of your pay in one or more of the tax deferred investments available through your employer sponsored plan. You decide how much to contribute and where the money is invested. Defined contribution plans benefit you in three important ways. First, all the money you contribute, up to the current legal maximum of $10,500 per year, is tax-deferred at the federal level. Second, earnings in your 401(k) account are tax-deferred. Lastly, many employers will make contributions to your retirement account, often matching some portion of your contributions. This is a benefit you should take advantage of, especially since employer contributions and their earnings are also tax-deferred.

Once you participate in a 401(k) plan, any contributions you make and any earnings on your contributions are yours. Contributions made by your employer and earnings on your employer's contributions are not yours until you are vested. Vesting periods vary from employer to employer. When switching to a new employer, be aware of any employer contributions and earnings on those contributions that you may forfeit if you are not yet vested. (Your retirement plan statement should give you a full breakdown of contributions and earnings.) If possible, try to negotiate a signing bonus or some other form of compensation with your new employer to cover any loss.

Your previous employer may drop you from its 401(k) plan once you leave. Arrange to have your 401(k) transferred to your new employer's 401(k) plan if your new employer offers one. If not, transfer your 401(k) to an IRA account that you set up or already have with your broker. It is important that you transfer your 401(k) directly to an IRA or eligible 401(k) plan with a new employer. If the transfer is not direct, the IRS will treat the move of funds as a distribution and a mandatory tax of 20% will be withheld and penalties for early withdrawal may be imposed. While it may be possible to convince the IRS that this was not a distribution, it may take a year or more to recover the 20% that was withheld. In the meantime, you will forfeit any earnings you could have made on the 20% that was not invested in your IRA or in a new 401(k) plan.

The above discussion assumes both employers are located in the United States. If you participate in a defined contribution retirement plan with a foreign firm you may not be able to transfer your account to an IRA or to a 401(k) plan with a U.S. employer. You will have to check with your employer to see what options are available to you.

If you have already been making contributions to a defined contribution retirement plan you will periodically receive a statement that indicates how much you have contributed, how much your employer has contributed, and how much you have earned on these contributions. Keep that total handy for later reference. To date the Ellicotts have accumulated $30,000 in Elly's 401(k) plan with her employer.

Other Employer Sponsored Plans

As your career takes you to different countries, you may participate in a number of pension plans. Often a pension plan works well until you leave that country, at which point you may not be able to make additional contributions or even retain membership in the plan. Even when you can maintain your membership, your new host country may tax the earnings on assets in pension funds outside its borders. To eliminate these difficulties, a large corporation may establish a pension plan offshore for its mobile executives. Some pension schemes are merely a promise to pay benefits at some point in the future—these plans are not actually funded.

When offshore pension plans are funded, the funds are deposited offshore, which makes reporting to the tax authorities the responsibility of the employee. If the plan is set-up properly your earnings may grow free of taxation by most countries, but not the United States. As an American, your worldwide income is subject to U.S. taxation. In addition, because of the structure of some offshore pension plans, your investment may be classified as a Passive Foreign Investment Company and taxed at an unfavorable rate. Failure to report earnings on these funds is a criminal offense in the United States and you could face not only fines and penalties, but also jail time.

Tax evasion is only one of the activities law enforcement agencies are investigating as they scrutinize offshore funds. Criminals frequently use offshore funds to launder money. Investigations by law enforcement officials could seriously disrupt the management of a fund and may cause it to be shut down.

There are other reasons an offshore fund may be unsuitable. Regulation of many offshore funds is lax and you may have no recourse if a fund manager embezzles the fund's assets and disappears. In addition, offshore funds are required to disclose only management fees. There are many undisclosed fees that, when combined with the management fee, often double the expenses of these funds and consequentially reduce your investment return. Finally, the overall performance of offshore funds has not been exceptional. You may be better off placing your money in a taxable U.S. mutual fund indexed to the U.S. stock market. Any offshore funds you consider should have a long-term performance track record that, after expenses, exceeds the aftertax return in a broadly based U.S. stock mutual fund.

Should you decide to invest offshore on your own, remember most offshore mutual funds are off limits to U.S. citizens and investment returns are subject to U.S. taxation. A few offshore mutual funds have passed the necessary Security and Exchange Commission regulatory hurdles and are registered to sell shares to U.S. citizens. Thoroughly research potential candidates. Be sure to compare each offshore fund's long-term performance and its fees with those of a U.S. Standard and Poor's 500 index fund. Historically, the Standard and Poor's 500 index has returned 11% annually. Any offshore funds you consider should have a performance track record that exceeds a return in a U.S. stock index fund. Keep in mind that most offshore funds, unlike U.S. mutual funds, will only disclose management fees. You may want to double any expense figure given to gain a better idea of total expenses. When making comparisons, deduct total expenses from the fund's historical track record. The Ellicotts do not plan to invest any of their money in offshore funds.

Individual Retirement Accounts

In addition to your employer sponsored retirement plans, you can save up to $2,000 per year—$4,000 if you are married—in a Roth or a traditional IRA. Earnings grow tax-deferred in traditional IRAs: During retirement, withdrawals from a traditional IRA are taxed as ordinary income. Earnings grow tax-free in Roth IRAs and withdrawals from a Roth IRA are free from taxation in retirement.

Contributions to a traditional IRA are exempt from federal income taxes for people who are not covered by an employer sponsored retirement plan. If your spouse is covered by an employer sponsored plan (but you are not) your joint adjusted gross income must be below $150,000 per year for your IRA contributions to be exempt from federal taxation. Those covered by an employer-sponsored retirement plan may still make tax-exempt contributions to a traditional IRA, but only if their adjusted gross income is below $50,000, if married and filing jointly, or under $30,000 if single.

Contributions to Roth IRAs are not exempt from federal income tax, regardless of your income. Depending on your income, you may be prohibited from making any contributions to a Roth IRA. If your spouse is covered by an employer sponsored plan (but you are not) your joint adjusted gross income must be below $150,000 per year to make contributions to a Roth IRA. Those covered by an employer-sponsored retirement plan may still make contributions to a Roth IRA, but only if their adjusted gross income is below $50,000, if married and filing jointly, or under $30,000 if single.

If you are able to invest all or nearly all of your retirement savings in a Roth IRA, you will not have to pay taxes on withdrawals in retirement—barring changes to the tax code in the future. Because you do not have to pay tax on this income, you can reduce the gross income you will need in retirement by the amount of the tax you would have paid. The Ellicotts made $50,000 last year and paid $8,500 in federal income taxes, a 17% effective tax rate ($8,500 ÷ $50,000 × 100%). The amount of tax they would owe on their income in retirement at this tax rate, if it came from a traditional IRA, would be $6,800 ($40,000 × 17% ÷ 100%). If your retirement income will come from a Roth IRA subtract taxes from the income you need in retirement. The Ellicotts would need only $33,200 in retirement ($40,000 - $6,800) if they can use a Roth IRA for all of their retirement savings. As with all long-term government provided benefits there are no guarantees that the tax treatment of these investments will be the same when you are ready to withdraw your money in retirement.

Because your adjusted gross income may exceed IRS limits, you may not be eligible to contribute to a Roth IRA. It is important to note that adjusted gross income, as the IRS defines it for both traditional and Roth IRAs, adds back the foreign earned income exclusion that is sheltered from U. S. federal income tax under most circumstances. It also adds back any foreign housing exclusion or deduction that may have lowered your taxable income. If you think your adjusted gross income will remain below IRS limits throughout your career you may wish to keep your retirement savings in a Roth IRA. Many Americans working overseas cannot use Roth IRAs when investing for their retirement. That is the case for the Ellicotts. If you can use a Roth IRA for all of your retirement savings then fill out line 9, a through e, Reduction For Taxes If You Are Using A Roth IRA, of the worksheet. Otherwise, enter the figure in line 8 onto line 9.e.

Do not move IRAs to banks or brokers outside the United States as the IRS will treat such a move as a distribution and will tax the entire amount and, where applicable, charge penalties.

Some other countries offer similar retirement savings schemes. In the United Kingdom they are known as Personal Equity Plans (PEPs). If you are considering work abroad as a local hire determine whether or not your host country offers such a program and if so how it works. Be sure to inquire about taxation issues, particularly if you plan to move to another country later. In many cases, these schemes are tax deferred in the country of origin, but earnings may be taxable if you move to another country. Currently, it is not possible to convert these IRA like schemes to U.S. IRAs. If you plan to retire in the United States you may have to liquidate the account, losing the tax-deferred benefit on future earnings. Even if your account can remain intact you will have to pay foreign exchange and transfer fees on withdrawals you bring to the United States.

That covers the main tax-deferred and tax-free retirement savings options. Now on to determining how large of a nest egg you will need to maintain your current life style in retirement.

Retirement Income: Year One and Beyond

The $40,000 of annual retirement income the Ellicotts must provide from investments does not take into consideration the effect of inflation, which historically has been 3.0%. The Ellicotts, and you, should assume your income needs to grow at the rate of inflation to maintain purchasing power and standard of living. For the Ellicotts, retirement is 25 years away. From Table 1, Growth Factors, in Appendix C, the growth factor for 25 years and 3.0% is 2.094. Twenty-five years from now they will need approximately $83,760 ($40,000 × 2.094) to have the same buying power that $40,000 gives them today.

That only takes care of their first year of retirement. How many years will they need to fund their retirement? The life expectancy figures below give some indication.

Life Expectancy

Age	Men	Women
55	76	80
60	78	82
65	80	84
70	84	88
75	86	89

These figures are the median life expectancy of a person at a given age. That means half of the people live beyond the ages given above and half do not. When estimating the number of years you need to fund your retirement, add some years to your life expectancy. By definition, life expectancy means you have a 50% chance of living longer than the numbers above suggest and a 50% chance of not reaching the median age given. The above table, while still widely used, dates back to 1964. Life expectancies have increased since then. The Ellicotts plan to retire at age 65. Elliott's life expectancy at that point is 80 from the table above and Elly's is 84. They add a few years to those estimates to cover themselves to age 90, bringing their total time in retirement up to 25 years (90 - 65). Your situation will depend on your age at retirement, your gender, and how many additional years you add as a hedge against the money in your retirement savings running out before you do.

Your nest egg may run out of money early if you invest it too conservatively by favoring money market accounts and bond funds. Plan to remain invested in stock mutual funds throughout your retirement. As you will be retired for an extended period of time— well over ten years—your nest egg can be invested in stock mutual funds where your expected rate of return may be the historical rate of return of 11%. You may wish to favor large capitalization and value investment styles of stock mutual funds in retirement. You can read more on this topic in Chapter 11, Investment Management.

Unlike most financial goals, all of your monthly retirement savings can be invested in stock mutual funds. In addition, you will not want to move your retirement savings into CDs or a money market account before you retire. Instead of shifting a large portion of your lump sum into CDs or Treasuries two to three years before you need the money, you can withdraw funds from your retirement lump sum on a monthly basis to meet living expenses. Table 4, Lump Sum Factors, in Appendix C, takes this into consideration. You will not need to reduce your expected rate of return.

Since much of your retirement savings are likely to be in a tax-deferred retirement plan or an IRA account, the return on your investments will not be taxed until you make withdrawals. Since the amount needed to retire is based on your gross income and not your aftertax income, income taxes on withdrawals are already accounted for in the amount needed. Your rate of return should not be reduced to account for taxes. In this example, the expected rate of return is 11%. (See the section, Combining Taxable and Tax-Deferred Accounts, if your entire retirement savings cannot be invested in tax-deferred accounts.)

Looking in Table 4, Lump Sum Factors, in Appendix C, the Ellicotts find the lump sum factor for 25 years and an 11% return is 10.7289. The figures in Table 4 take into account the need to increase the amount of withdrawals from the lump sum by 3% each year due to inflation. The total lump sum they need to fund 25 years of retirement with an initial inflation adjusted income requirement of $83,760 is roughly $898,650 ($83,760 × 10.7289). This means they need a total of about $898,650 to finance 80% of their income needs during 25 years of retirement starting 25 years from now.

The Ellicotts already have $30,000 saved in their 401(k) plan with Elly's employer. This $30,000 will continue to earn money, tax-deferred for the next 25 years, so the pretax and aftertax rates of return are the same for this money. Since this is a long time horizon, this money can be invested in stock mutual funds. Historically, stocks have earned a rate of return of about 11% and they use that figure in their estimate. To estimate how large $30,000 will be in 25 years they refer to Table 1, Growth Factors, in Appendix C. The growth factor for 25 years and 11% is 13.585. In 25 years, this $30,000 may grow to roughly $407,550 ($30,000 × 13.585). Instead of saving for a nest egg of $898,650, the Ellicotts only need an additional $491,100 ($898,650 - $407,550). For your own situation, substitute the amount you have saved so far for the $30,000 and use your own time horizon to determine how much of your nest egg you still need to fund.

WHAT TO SET ASIDE EACH MONTH

From Table 2, Monthly Saving Factors, in Appendix C, the Ellicotts' monthly savings factor for a time horizon of 25 years and an aftertax rate of return of 11% is 0.00063. They will need to save roughly $310 ($491,100 × 0.00063) a month to have $491,100 in 25 years, a total of $3,720 a year. Since this is below the $10,500 limit on contributions to Elly's 401(k), their entire retirement savings can be invested in the 401(k) with her employer. If her employer matches a portion of her contributions she will not have to supply the entire $3,720 each year herself.

The above emphasizes the importance of investing in stock mutual funds and of taking advantage of a good employer sponsored retirement plan with matching contributions. It also demonstrates the need to start early. If instead of 25 years the Ellicotts had only 20 years until retirement, they would need to save $762 a month or a total of $9,144 a year for 20 years to have a lump sum large enough to provide the same retirement income.

NET INCOME CONCERNS

Depending on your situation you may need to save for several financial goals at the same time. If you will not have sufficient money before retiring consider delaying your retirement or working for another employer after retiring if you cannot continue with your current employer. You may also consider self-employment. If you plan to live and work overseas after retiring be sure to read the section, Receiving U.S. Social Security Benefits While Overseas, in Chapter 10, Financial Risk Management—Social Security, before you begin working overseas. You can also examine your monthly net income statement to see where you may be able to reduce your expenses.

NET WORTH CONCERNS

If you own a home you may consider selling it to move into a smaller house in retirement. Many people had large homes to raise a large family or have lived in expensive locations to be nearer their office. In retirement, many people want a smaller home or wish to live in a less expensive location.

COMBINING TAXABLE AND TAX-DEFERRED ACCOUNTS

In the example of the Ellicotts we have assumed that all of their retirement savings are in tax-deferred or tax-free accounts. What happens if you must invest a portion of your retirement savings in a taxable account? The portion of your retirement savings invested in a taxable account will earn less on an aftertax basis. It may be possible to lower the taxes on earnings in such an account. Currently, long-term capital gains are taxed at a lower rate than short-term capital gains, interest, or dividends. Favor investments that produce long-term capital gains. Be careful in selecting tax-free investments for these accounts. The tax-free rate of return from these investments must exceed your aftertax rate of return from alternative taxable investments. (See Chapter 12, Tax Management, for a full discussion on how to make these comparisons.)

The good news is that unlike a traditional IRA or 401(k) account, you will not have to pay income taxes on withdrawals from taxable accounts. This means you can reduce the amount of money you will need in retirement by the amount of income tax you will not have to pay on money withdrawn from taxable accounts.

Here is the process to use if your retirement savings must be split between tax-deferred and taxable accounts. Once you have calculated how much you need to set aside each month for retirement you will ideally invest the maximum allowable in a traditional IRA, which currently is $2,000 if you are single—$4,000 if you are married, roughly $167 and $333 per month respectively. We will now modify the Ellicotts' example to illustrate the process. Only three assumptions will change. We assume Elly is single instead of married and that her employer does not offer a 401(k) plan. The $30,000 she has already set aside for retirement is in a traditional IRA instead of a 401(k). Since her income disqualifies her from investing in a Roth IRA ($30,000 is the limit if you are single and have an employer provided pension) her only tax-deferred option is a traditional IRA. At most she can put $167 each month ($2,000 a year) into a traditional IRA. How much of her nest egg will be built-up over the years in this account? Since $167 will be invested each month at an estimated 11% annual rate, she divides $167 by the savings factor in line 22 of the worksheet. In this example, roughly $265,050 ($167 ÷ 0.00063) will accumulate in her traditional IRA by retirement.

Initially, Elly expected to need $491,100. Since her IRA will only cover $265,050, she still needs $226,050. Because she does not have to pay income tax on withdrawals from a taxable account, she can reduce the income she will need in retirement by the amount of the tax. In this example, where Elly made $50,000 last year and paid $8,500 in federal income taxes she paid a 17% effective tax rate ($8,500 ÷ $50,000 × 100%). The amount of tax she would owe on this portion of her retirement income at this rate (were it taxable) would be $38,425 ($226,050 × 17% ÷ 100%). Since this portion of Elly's retirement income will come from a taxable account rather than a tax deferred account, she subtracts taxes from the income she needs in retirement. In this example, Elly would need to accumulate only $187,625 ($226,050 - $38,425) in a taxable account.

Elly plans to invest this portion of her nest egg to earn about 11% in stock mutual funds. In this example, she assumes a U. S. long-term capital gains tax rate of 20% plus 1% to account for distributions that will be taxed at her marginal tax rate. If you are in a high tax bracket (greater than 35%) you should add 2% or 3% to your effective rate rather than 1%. Elly's estimated aftertax annual rate of return is 8.5% (11% × [100% - 21%] ÷ 100%, rounded to the nearest 0.5%).

From Table 2, Monthly Saving Factors, in Appendix C, the monthly savings factor for a time horizon of 25 years and an aftertax rate of return of 8.5% is 0.0097. Elly will need to save roughly $182 ($187,625 × 0.00097) per month to have $187,625 in 25 years, a total of $2,184 per year.

Combining Elly's taxable account with her traditional IRA, she will need to save $349 ($167 + $182) or $4,188 per year. This is only $39 more per month than the $310 she would need to set aside if all of her money was invested in tax-deferred accounts. She should still be able to reach her targeted goal of maintaining her current life style in retirement.

SAVING FOR RETIREMENT WORKSHEET

1. TIME HORIZON
How many years before you retire?   25

2. YOUR CURRENT INCOME
How much are you currently making a year? $50,000

3. DISCONTINUED EXPENSES
What expenses will be discontinued
in retirement? (Annual amount)   0

4. DISCONTINUED SAVINGS
How much of current savings will be
discontinued in retirement? (Annual amount)   0

5. INCOME REQUIREMENT
What percentage of your salary
do you need in retirement?
(line 2 - line 3 - line 4) ÷ line 2 × 100%   100%

6. INCOME FINANCED BY OTHERS IN RETIREMENT
a. How much of your income will be met through a
   defined benefit retirement plan with your employer?
   (no. of years of service × percentage
   - reduction for survivor benefit if appropriate)   10%
b. Social security retirement benefits
   (expected benefits ÷ line 2 × 100%)   10%
c. Total financed by others
   line 6.a + line 6.b   20%

7. PORTION OF YOUR INCOME YOU MUST PROVIDE
line 5 - line 6.c   80%

8. AMOUNT OF CURRENT INCOME YOU NEED TO FINANCE
line 7 × line 2 ÷ 100% $40,000

9. REDUCTION FOR TAXES IF YOU ARE USING A ROTH IRA
a. How much did you pay in federal taxes last year?
b. What was your total income last year?
c. What was your effective tax rate last year?
   line 9.a ÷ line 9.b × 100%
d. The amount of taxes you will not owe is:
   line 9.c × line 8 ÷ 100%
e. Adjusted current income you need to finance
   line 8 - line 9.d $40,000

10. INFLATION RATE   3%

11. GROWTH FACTOR
From Table 1, find the growth factor for
the number of years until you retire in
line 1 and the inflation rate in line 10.   2.094

12. RETIREMENT INCOME NEEDED IN THE FIRST YEAR
line 9.e × line 11 $83,760

13. YEARS IN RETIREMENT
Based on your life expectancy at retirement age
plus a buffer for good measure: How long must
your nest egg support you?   25

14. LUMP SUM RATE OF RETURN
The rate of return you expect your lump sum
to earn during retirement.   11%

15. LUMP SUM FACTOR
From Table 4, find the lump sum factor for
the years in retirement in line 13 and
expected rate of return in line 14.   10.7289

16. LUMP SUM NEEDED FOR RETIREMENT
line 12 × line 15 $898,650

17. AMOUNT YOU HAVE ALREADY SAVED $30,000

18. BEFORE AND AFTERTAX RATE OF RETURN
What is the expected rate of return for the
investments you will use?   11%

19. GROWTH FACTOR
From Table 1, find the growth factor for the
time horizon in line 1 and the
aftertax rate of return in line 18.   13.585

20. AMOUNT OF LUMP SUM COVERED BY CURRENT SAVINGS
line 17 × line 19 $407,550

21. AMOUNT OF LUMP SUM YOU STILL NEED TO SAVE
line 16 - line 20 $491,100

22. SAVINGS FACTOR
Using Table 2, find the monthly savings factor
based on your time horizon in line 1 and
the aftertax rate of return in line 14.   0.00063

23. MONTHLY SAVINGS NEEDED
line 21 × line 22 $310

PART 2
MONEY
MANAGEMENT

7. CASH MANAGEMENT

The way you handle your money on an everyday basis plays a large part in your long-term financial future. Disciplined spending habits lead to successful saving, but how you manage that cash can also help you reach your financial goals. Money you are accumulating for future investments should typically be kept in a cash management account at a discount brokerage firm. Money you receive when you cash out of previous investments should also be kept in that account. Typically, your money earns a higher rate of return when kept in a cash management account at a discount brokerage firm than it does in a checking account at a bank. However, it is often more convenient to have money needed to pay monthly expenses in a checking account. Ideally you want to manage all your "cash" as effectively as possible. This chapter describes how to use various tools to help you manage your cash more effectively, namely: a checking account, a cash management account at a discount brokerage firm, a money market deposit account, and certificates of deposit (CDs) at a savings institution.

BANK ACCOUNTS

Use your bank or credit union to handle your everyday cash flow. Have your dollar denominated pay direct deposited to your U.S. checking account. Because of delays in international mail, arrange to have as many U.S. bills as possible automatically paid from your checking account. The easiest and cheapest way to automatically pay your U.S. bills is to have the billing company directly debit the appropriate amount from your checking account. Examples of bills that can be directly debited from your U.S. checking account are insurance premiums, student and automobile loan payments, mortgage payments, rental property management fees, and utility payments.

For convenience when paying bills in local currency, you may want to open an account with a foreign bank in the country where you live. Use this account for bill paying convenience only. Do not allow a large sum, beyond what you anticipate needing in the next few months, to accumulate in your foreign bank account. The amount you hold in a foreign bank, and therefore in a foreign currency, is subject to exchange rate risk. If the dollar declines while you hold a large amount of foreign currency you may make a lot of money, but if it strengthens the reverse is true. This is an unsuitable way to handle any money it would bother you to lose. Watch out for high fees associated with foreign bank accounts as well. The U.S. banking sector is more competitive than most in the world. The result, on average, is that customers of foreign banks pay higher fees and receive lower interest, when adjusted for local currency strength and inflation. To reduce transaction costs, lost interest, and exchange rate risks, make two to four transfers a year between your foreign and U.S. bank accounts.

If you are eligible to join a credit union you should explore that institution first. Since credit unions are non-profit organizations and pay no taxes, they often offer higher interest on their accounts and charge lower interest on their loans than banks. Many credit unions now offer most of the services that were previously offered only by banks.

Whether your account is with a bank or a credit union, or if you decide to keep accounts with more than one institution, it pays to shop around. Especially when you live abroad, it is important that the U.S. bank you deal with is financially sound. Accounts at these institutions are federally insured up to $100,000 by the Federal Deposit Insurance Corporation (FDIC), or National Credit Union Administration (NCUA) for participating credit unions. As your savings grow it is important to note that the $100,000 insurance is not per account, but per depositor. If you have more than $100,000 on deposit in any savings institution, in any number of insured accounts, your deposits are insured up to only $100,000. The only exception to this is a married couple that can theoretically have $300,000 in insured accounts: one for each spouse in his/her name, and a joint account. Your joint accounts in one institution are only insured to $100,000; it does not matter if you have two different accounts in the institution, whose name is first, or which social security number you use. There are ways to insure more money in one institution by setting up trusts, but unless you are regularly moving large sums you should not keep more than $100,000 in any single bank anyway as the return bank accounts offer is simply not that good.

Although your deposit with a savings institution is federally insured, if the bank goes out of business your life will become complicated. This is particularly true if you are living abroad when the bank goes under, as your account may be frozen for an extended period of time. Most banks that become insolvent are eventually taken over by other banks, which honor the prior commitments of the acquired bank, but rather than take that chance you should make sure the bank you deal with is in good financial shape.

Before opening an account with a financial institution you want to first establish that the institution is financially sound and unlikely to become bankrupt. There are a number of ways to check the financial strength of a savings institution:

Bauer Financial Reports sells reports on the financial stability of banks and credit unions. You can check their summary star ratings of banks and credit unions for free at their web site, or purchase more detailed reports from them for a fee.

Veribanc also sells bank safety information. They sell Instant Ratings of banks by phone for $10 each, and more extensive written assessments, they call Short Form Reports, for $25 each. They also publish a book titled the Blue Ribbon Bank Report that lists well run banks in every region of the country for $35. They add $5 to shipping and handling charges to send their Blue Ribbon Bank Report to an overseas address.

Weiss Research sells reports on the financial safety of banks, brokerage firms, and insurance companies. As of the writing of this
book their Personal Safety Briefs on Banks and Thrifts costs $25.
They also sell a list of recommended banks, insurers and brokers
for $55.

Contact information for these companies follows:

> Bauer Financial Reports
> Penthouse One
> Gables International Plaza
> 2655 LeJeune Road
> Coral Gables, FL 33134
> Phone: +1-305-445-9500
> Fax: +1-305-445-6775
> Website: http://www.bauerfinancial.com
>
> Veribanc
> PO Box 461
> Wakefield, MA 01880
> Phone: +1-781-245-8370 or 800-837-4226
> Fax: +1-781-246-5291
> They have no presence on the Internet or e-mail
> as of this writing
>
> Weiss Research
> 4176 Burns Road
> Palm Beach Gardens, FL 33410
> Phone: +1-561-627-3300 or 800-289-9222
> Fax: +1-561-625-6685
> E-mail: wr@weissinc.com
> Website: http://www.weissratings.com

In addition to finding a safe bank or credit union you want to find
one that offers competitive interest rates on deposits and loans,
and has low fees. Increased competition in the banking sector has
lowered interest rates on loans and therefore, banks' profits. In

response, savings institutions have increased the amount and number of fees they charge in an effort to make up for profits they are losing to lower interest rates.

Checking Accounts

Because of communications difficulties that come with living abroad, you should keep a slightly higher balance in your checking account than would be optimal when living in the United States. In choosing a bank account, weigh the minimum balance requirement against the interest paid on the account and any fees charged. If you cannot meet the minimum balance requirement for an interest bearing checking account look for a non-interest-bearing checking account with the lowest fees. Some banks waive or lower the minimum balance requirement, or reduce fees, if your pay is direct deposited to an account at their bank.

Especially when living abroad, get overdraft protection for your checking account; this will keep you from accidentally bouncing a check if international mail delays slow the arrival of a deposit leaving you temporarily short of funds in your account.

When the balance in your checking account grows above the amount you need in the short-term, transfer your excess money to a money market or brokerage account.

Money Market Accounts

Your self-insurance fund (equal to three to six months of take home pay) should be kept in a money market account. This money market account can be kept in your bank, or with your discount broker. Generally, you will earn a higher return on your self-insurance fund if it is kept in a money market brokerage account. One possible advantage of keeping your self-insurance fund at your bank is money can quickly and easily be transferred to your bank checking account when needed. As the amount in your emergency fund at your bank grows beyond what you need, transfer the excess to your brokerage account for use in long-term investments.

Money market accounts pool money from many people and invest it in conservative financial instruments that have high minimum investment requirements (often $100,000 or more) putting them beyond the reach of most individuals. These securities pay higher rates of return than are commonly available with smaller investments. Money market accounts, unlike the financial investments they invest in, usually require a minimum initial investment of just a few thousand dollars. Money market accounts available from savings institutions are known as *money market deposit accounts*; they typically pay slightly lower rates of return than their counterparts, *money market mutual funds* available at brokerage firms. The advantage of a money market account at your bank is that you can transfer money between your money market account and your checking account at the same institution almost instantly. In addition to being able to transfer money—usually for free—between your accounts, most money market accounts offer limited check writing privileges, and all are federally insured along with your checking account up to the $100,000 limit. You may be allowed to write only three or five checks per month from your money market account, and each check may have to meet minimum size requirement. This should not cause a problem since you will use your checking account for most of your bill payments and cash withdrawals. Several discount brokerage firms offer accounts with check writing privileges as well.

Certificates of Deposit

Certificates of deposit, particularly those with maturities of six months or less, are a safe and convenient way to invest excess money you want to keep on deposit at your savings institution. In an emergency they can be redeemed early, although the penalties for early withdrawal will probably eliminate any interest you would have earned. Because the savings institution is assured of the use of your money for a longer period, CDs usually pay a higher rate of return than money market accounts. Longer-term CDs are subject to interest rate risk, just like bonds. The danger here is that you will lock in an interest rate in a long-term CD, and then interest rates will rise. CD rates vary from bank to bank, and CDs that pay higher returns are also available from brokerage firms. Because of the early withdrawal penalty, and the fact that CDs are not as liquid as money market accounts—you cannot write a check drawn on a CD—no more than half of your self-insurance fund should be kept in short-term CDs.

BROKERAGE ACCOUNTS

Commissions on brokerage transactions used to be fixed throughout the industry. In 1975 commissions were deregulated and the discount brokerage business was born. All brokerage firms buy and sell securities, maintain various types of accounts, and hold securities in street name for their customers. The only differences between full service brokers and discount brokers are that discount brokers do not offer investment advice to their customers, and they charge commissions on transactions that are roughly 30%–80% less than those charged by full service brokers.

The Securities Investor Protection Corporation (SIPC) insures all national brokerage firms in the United States. The SIPC is not a federal institution like the FDIC, but is a cooperative industry association that exists to insure the accounts that customers have with brokerage firms. If needed, and at the discretion of the Securities and Exchange Commission, the SIPC also has a one billion dollar line of credit available from the federal government. The SIPC guarantees individual brokerage accounts to $500,000, but only guarantees that money will be protected if the brokerage firm goes bankrupt. There is no insurance to protect clients from losing money if the securities they own—including mutual funds—decline in value, or even become worthless. This is true whether the securities are held in an account with a brokerage firm, or with an account at a bank. Many brokerage firms carry extra insurance with private companies to insure their customers' money against the brokerage firm's insolvency to well over a million dollars per account. SIPC will not protect you from a poorly run or dishonest brokerage firm that costs you money by failing to execute a trading instruction you have given them.

The large commission discount is only one of the reasons to work with a discount brokerage firm. Although full-service brokers offer their clients investment advice, many full-service brokerage firms do not allow their account representatives—also known as registered representatives, the people who deal face to face with customers—to make their own investment recommendations. The account representative must choose investments from the company's recommended list. While many account representatives have their customer's best interests at heart, these interests are often at odds with the incentives their employers offer to maximize their and the firm's income. Full-service brokerage employees are paid based on the number of shares bought and sold, not on how much profit those transactions make for the customer. When a brokerage company has a large inventory of stock it does not want, it often offers special compensation to those employees who help unload the excess. Brokerage firms are notorious for always having recommendations to buy but not advising customers when to sell. One reason for this is that brokerage firms serve corporate clients as well as individuals. Full-service brokerage firms may be reluctant to say something critical about a firm that is a corporate client, for fear of damaging the relationship. When there is a conflict of interest between a corporate client and individual clients the needs of the corporate client will usually be served over those of the individual client, because corporate clients provide much more of a full-service broker's revenues and profits. For this reason sell recommendations from research departments of brokerage firms are usually made by telephone rather than in writing. Since individuals do not speak with research departments of such firms directly, they do not get recommendations on when to sell an investment they hold. This may be one reason brokerage firms are traditionally reluctant to publish the track record of their investment recommendations.

Brokerage firms offer many different kinds of accounts. The most basic ones are cash accounts, which simply allow customers to buy securities and pay for them by the transaction settlement date. In margin accounts, the brokerage firm will loan the customer some of the money needed to make the securities purchase, holding the purchased securities as collateral on the loan.

The most useful type of brokerage account is known as a cash management account. A cash management account—known at many brokerage firms as an asset management account, or by other names—is a brokerage account that lets you buy and hold securities, but regularly sweeps any idle cash in the account into a money market mutual fund. Most cash management accounts let you write checks on the cash in your account, including the amount in the money market mutual fund. Some cash management accounts offer you a Visa or MasterCard debit card. These debit cards draw cash directly from your brokerage account when you make a purchase rather than extending you credit as a traditional credit card does. The amount of money needed to open a cash management account can be substantial ($5,000 to $25,000 minimums), but the minimum can be in the form of mutual fund holdings or other investments transferred from another brokerage firm rather than cash. You need to shop carefully to avoid accounts that charge you extra fees.

Cash management accounts offer tremendous advantages to Americans living outside the United States. The settlement date for securities transactions is three working days. With so little time available to make payment for a purchase, you should have the cash available in your account before you give the broker the order to buy if you live abroad. A cash management account offers you a safe account paying a good return in which to accumulate money between purchases of mutual funds or CDs. As you accumulate cash in your brokerage account, or when you have a large sum of cash available after selling a security, you earn money market returns on that money. If you have a substantial sum you want to keep as cash for more than a couple months you can buy a U.S. Treasury Bill (minimum $1,000) through your broker and keep the bill on deposit in your account with your other securities. For example, you might want to park money in Treasury Bills (T-bills) when you are liquidating investments as your time horizon shortens and you approach the day when you will realize a financial goal. T-bills usually pay a higher rate of return than most money market funds, and since they are a direct loan to the federal government they are as safe an investment as is available.

As you set money aside each month for your future goals, the best place to put it is in your cash management account with a discount broker since they usually offer a higher rate of return than banks. Ideally, you would do this every month by writing a check and mailing it to your brokerage firm. Several of the major discount brokerage firms now allow you to link your U.S. checking account to your cash management account. Through this link you can move a fixed sum of money out of your checking account each month and place it in your brokerage account for free and without the hassle of writing a check or addressing an envelope. The link works the other way as well, allowing you to move money from your brokerage account to your bank account when needed. Such a brokerage account can eliminate the need for a money market account with your bank, if you are comfortable with such an arrangement.

You should choose a discount broker that offers a large selection of mutual funds. You always have the option of buying mutual funds direct from the fund company, but the ease of buying and selling mutual funds via your discount broker, the convenience of having all of your cash savings and investments in one place, being able to access them quickly and directly, and receiving one consolidated statement every month are all advantages.

When buying mutual funds to be held in your brokerage account you should buy the mutual funds in street name. Street name means your broker buys the mutual fund shares for you and registers those shares with the mutual fund company in the name of the brokerage firm, rather than your name. The fact that you are the actual owner of those mutual fund shares is kept on brokerage company records and is reflected in your brokerage account statement.

If you choose to buy mutual funds direct from the mutual fund company, rather than using a brokerage account, you purchase the mutual fund by mailing a check to the mutual fund company with a request to buy shares in the mutual fund. You will then receive regular statements direct from the fund company informing you of the balance of your account and any distributions the fund has made to you. With mutual funds held either in a brokerage account or directly, you have the option of receiving distributions from the fund, or reinvesting those distributions. If you hold the funds yourself they will mail you a check for the distributions, if you hold the funds in a brokerage account they will deposit the cash to your brokerage account. In either case, if you reinvest the distributions, that money will be automatically used to buy additional shares in the mutual fund company—although you will still be required to pay income tax on the distributions as if you had received them in cash. If you sell a mutual fund that you hold in a brokerage account the money from the sale is deposited directly into your brokerage account. If you sell a mutual fund that you own directly you may have to do so in writing and the mutual fund company will mail you a check for the value of your fund shares. In some instances mutual fund companies require notarized or bank guaranteed signatures when you sell a mutual fund. The reason behind this is two-fold: first, to make sure only you are allowed to collect the money from selling your investments, and second, to discourage people from selling mutual funds. When living overseas it is sometimes a nuisance to find a means of having your signature on such a document notarized or guaranteed.

When deciding where to place your cash, the primary factors are what the money is going to be used for and when you will need the money. Once you have selected the option that satisfies those two criteria, you can make your final selection based on the option that gives you the best deal, either in terms of the rate of return or in lower fees and costs.

8. DEBT MANAGEMENT

The way you handle credit is at least as important as the way you handle cash. People who misuse credit find it much more difficult to save the money they need to build toward their goals. They also risk damaging their credit ratings, making it more difficult to get important loans in the future. In its most serious form, misuse of debt can lead to personal bankruptcy.

MORTGAGE LOANS

Mortgages are different from other loans principally for historical and cultural reasons. Loans to buy one's home are of necessity large and long-term, since homes are expensive, but are also typically available with lower rates of interest than most other loans. That is because the home purchased is used as collateral and because our society has put in place various mechanisms to help make home ownership more affordable. For example, mortgages have tax benefits that few other loans currently enjoy.

In the United States two government sponsored organizations (commonly called Freddie Mac and Fannie Mae) have been formed to help keep mortgages affordable. In it's simplest form financial institutions take in money from depositors, pay them one rate of interest on their deposits, then loan that money to borrowers at a higher rate of interest, making money from the spread in interest rates between loans and deposits. These days, however, most mortgage loans are bundled together with similar mortgages and sold as bonds on markets that trade in mortgage backed securities. To be able to bundle individual mortgages together into large mortgage bond issues those mortgages need to have certain criteria in common. Mortgages that can be securitized and sold in this way are called conforming mortgages, and usually offer slightly better terms and lower rates than non-conforming mortgages, which need to be handled individually by financial institutions.

The following discussion refers to owner occupied properties purchased as a person's primary residence. The risk to lenders is greater for rental and second homes, and so the interest rates and down payments they require are greater as well. For those living overseas and buying a home in the United States this is sometimes an issue. Your lender may require some form of proof, such as a statement from your employer that you are to be assigned to the city where the property is located, before they will agree to give you a mortgage on a property as your primary owner occupied residence. Check any lender's requirements on these issues very carefully early in the process of shopping for lenders if this is an issue in your case.

The most traditional mortgage in the USA is the 30-year fixed rate conforming mortgage. Conforming mortgages are available up to a current maximum size of $252,700; mortgages larger than that are non-conforming. Traditionally, mortgage loans require a 20% down payment, although loans with smaller down payments are typically available today. In the mortgage industry a loan with a 20% down payment is called an 80% loan-to-value (or LTV) mortgage. For example, with a home purchased for (and so presumably worth) $100,000 the purchaser pays $20,000 and the lender makes a loan of $80,000—80% of the value of the property. With $20,000 of his own money invested in the property the purchaser is less likely to default on the loan, since the lender could then foreclose and the purchaser would lose the $20,000 down payment as well as the house. After foreclosing, the lender has a $20,000 buffer between the original value of the house, $100,000 and the original amount of the loan, $80,000. Unless the value of the property falls by 20% or more the lender should avoid a loss when foreclosing on the property. Because of the lower risk to the lender, mortgages with large down payments (10%–20%) often offer better terms for the borrower than mortgages with low down payments.

As was mentioned briefly in the example of a medium-term financial goal in Chapter 5, Targeting Your Goals, mortgages are structured so that early in the loan the payments are mostly interest, with very little paid to bring down the loan principal. It is not until year 22 of a 30-year mortgage that half of each payment goes toward principal. Since most American mortgages last only seven to ten years, most of the money paid toward mortgages is interest paid to the lenders. After ten years of paying a 30-year mortgage only slightly more than 12% of the loan principal has been repaid.

While this loan structure is good for the lender, current tax laws make it less onerous for the homeowner as well. Interest paid on mortgage loans is deductible on your US federal income taxes. Property taxes are also deductible. At one time most loan interest was deductible, as were most local and state taxes. Today interest on most loans is not tax deductible and neither are some state and local taxes, but the cultural bias encouraging home ownership has kept both mortgage interest and property taxes deductible. Mortgage interest, at least early in a mortgage when most of the money paid is interest, combined with property tax usually exceeds the standard deduction, making it worthwhile to itemize and deduct any additional deductible expenses.

The tax deductibility of mortgage interest lowers the effective interest rate you pay on these loans. Nevertheless, there may be circumstances in which you would want to pay off your mortgage early. Some mortgages have prepayment penalties, others do not, and some states have laws that forbid prepayment penalties on mortgages. One method of paying off a mortgage early is making extra mortgage payments either regularly or on an occasional basis. Unlike required payments, these extra payments go entirely toward reducing the principal of the loan, shortening the duration of the loan (and the total amount of interest paid) as a result. One formalized version of this is the biweekly mortgage payment. With biweekly mortgage payments a person makes 26 payments in the course of a year, each equal to half of a normal monthly payment. In this way they effectively make 13 monthly mortgage payments per year, with the extra payment going to pay off principal. It is better to not be locked into such a formal arrangement, but to make extra payments on your own if you want to pay off your mortgage. Some companies even try to charge consumers for biweekly mortgage arrangements, when the consumers could get exactly the same result for free by making an extra mortgage payment every year.

Qualifying for a Mortgage

Despite the relative safety of mortgage debt for the lender, any prospective lender examines the financial situation of any potential homebuyer very carefully before deciding whether or not to underwrite the loan. Among the more important factors they use in deciding whether to make a loan—and the terms of the loan they are willing to make—are the borrower's *front ratio* and *back ratio*. One other important factor lenders consider in making loans is the purchaser's FICO score. FICO stands for Fair, Isaac & Co., a company that produces a well-known credit worthiness score based on a person's credit history and financial situation. FICO scores range from a low of 450 to a high of 850. Those with a FICO score under about 650 will find more lender scrutiny and less willingness to provide loans with the most favorable terms. A good credit history—built by good management of consumer loans and credit cards—means you will have a higher FICO score, which usually means a quick approval and more favorable terms.

One immutable payment homeowners with mortgages must make every month is called PITI in the mortgage and real estate industry. PITI stands for Principal, Interest, Taxes and Insurance. It refers to the principal and interest payments of a mortgage along with monthly installments toward property taxes and homeowner's insurance. To avoid legal liens against a property, lenders are very particular about making sure that property taxes are paid, and that the homeowner carries and regularly pays for sufficient homeowner's insurance.

The PITI divided by your monthly pretax income is your front ratio. Conservative lenders like to see a front ratio of 28% (0.28, usually written as simply 28) or lower. In addition to the loan principal, loan interest, property taxes and insurance, the lender will probably add any relevant private mortgage insurance, condominium fees or homeowner association fees to the PITI when deciding whether or not to make a particular loan to a particular customer to buy a particular property.

To calculate your back ratio add any monthly loan payments you are required to make—auto loan, student loans, consumer loans, minimum payments on credit cards—to PITI and divide that sum by your monthly pretax income. Lenders like to see a back ratio of 36% or less (0.36, usually referred to simply as 36). The combined front and back ratios for certain loan conditions, or for a particular customer and particular loan, are often written 28/36 for a front ratio of 28% and back ratio of 36%.

Let's take an example to make this a bit clearer. Assume that a person making $60,000 per year with a monthly automobile loan payment of $450 and a monthly student loan payment of $200 per month, with no outstanding balance on their credit card wants to buy a house costing $200,000. If they have a 20% down payment saved they will need a mortgage loan of $160,000. We assume the interest rate for such a 30-year conforming mortgage is 8% at the time. We can calculate the monthly mortgage payment by first looking up the factor for 8% and 30 years in Table 3, Monthly Loan Payments Factors, in Appendix C, 0.00734. Multiplying this factor by the loan amount gives us the monthly payment amount, $1,174.40 ($160,000 × 0.00734). To this we add estimated property taxes of $150 per month and a monthly homeowners insurance payment of $30 per month to develop a theoretical PITI of $1354.40 per month. A $60,000 annual salary equates to $5,000 per month pretax, so with this PITI the purchaser's front ratio would be a reasonable 27 ($1,354,40 ÷ $5,000 × 100). To calculate the back ratio we would add the $450 per month automobile loan payment and the $200 per month student loan payment to the PITI for a total of $2004.40 ($1354.40 + $450 + $200), dividing this sum by $5,000 yields a back ratio of 40 (2004.40 ÷ $5,000 × 100). A back ratio of 40 is too big for some banks, although it is likely that one could find a bank willing to make a mortgage loan in this situation. That mortgage loan would not have the best of terms and might charge more than 8% interest (possibly boosting the back ratio beyond the range at which even that bank is comfortable making the loan). This all illustrates the impact of one's spending and borrowing habits on later choices.

A little sensitivity analysis with this example will illustrate some other points. If this mortgage had been available at 7% rather than 8% the purchaser's front and back ratios would have been 25/38, possibly low enough to have secured a loan on better terms. If the purchaser had only enough money saved to make a 10% down payment, the mortgage loan would need to be $180,000 rather than $160,000. For such a loan at 8% the front and back ratios would have been 30/43, and it is doubtful the purchaser could find a loan with good terms to buy the house.

Another factor that can affect a person's ability to afford a house is the requirement for private mortgage insurance. Private mortgage insurance, or PMI, is insurance paid by the homeowner that insures that the lender will be paid the full outstanding principal on the mortgage if the purchaser defaults and the mortgage needs to be foreclosed. Lenders often require such insurance on high LTV loans (those with small down payments), and the premiums for this insurance add to the effective PITI and so reduce the amount of home a buyer can afford. In the past most lenders required PMI on loans with LTV higher than 80%—those with down payments of less than 20%. Today several lenders offer 90% LTV loans without PMI that are structured into two separate loans. The first loan covers 80% of the value of the house and is offered at competitive rates. The second loan covers 10% of the value of the house and is offered at a substantially higher rate than the first loan. The lender can use the extra interest income to pay PMI premiums itself. However, you will usually pay the lender more than is needed to cover the PMI premiums allowing the lender to pocket the rest.

In addition to interest rates, mortgages charge points at the time the loan is originated. A point is one percent of the loan amount paid to the lender at the time the loan is made. Officially, points are considered a form of pre-paid interest, and so are deductible on federal income taxes. By increasing the points paid at origination the loan interest rate decreases. For a 30-year fixed rate mortgage one point is equal to slightly more than a tenth and less than an eighth of a percent of interest. When comparing different loans you need to compare mortgage interest rates and points. Watch for hidden charges; many lenders charge one point automatically at closing as an origination fee, but some banks waive this requirement.

Whether to pay additional points at origination in return for a lower interest rate is a complex decision and will depend on the length of time you expect to own the home. For example, if a $100,000 mortgage were available at 8% with no points or 7.5% with four points which would be a better bargain—assuming you have the extra $4,000 available to pay the four points at closing? Using Table 3, we see that the monthly principal and interest payments for the 8% mortgage would be $734 ($100,000 × 0.00734), while for the 7.5% mortgage they would be $699 ($100,000 × 0.00699). Paying $35 less per month ($734 - $699) it would take you over 114 months ($4,000 ÷ $35), or over nine and a half years to save in mortgage payments the $4,000 you paid in points at closing. If you were planning on selling this house within ten years the 8% mortgage with no points would be the better deal. If you planned to pay the full 30 years on the mortgage you would save money in the long run by choosing the mortgage with higher points and lower interest.

When shopping for a house you want to use every advantage possible. Sellers and their representatives (the real estate agents) naturally want to be assured that they are dealing with a person who is capable of getting a mortgage to actually buy the property, and so they frequently ask the potential buyer for detailed financial information. One down-side of this for the buyer is that this sharing of information gives the seller a good understanding of how much the buyer can really afford to pay, putting the buyer at a disadvantage in negotiating the price of the property. Two potential solutions to this dilemma are pre-qualifying for a mortgage and being pre-approved for a mortgage. To pre-qualify all a buyer must do is provide some fairly detailed financial information to a potential lender. The lender will then issue a pre-qualification letter stating that the lender has good reason to believe that they would be willing to make a mortgage loan to this buyer. The pre-qualification letter in effect tells any seller that there is a good chance this buyer can actually purchase a property up to some maximum price, and so can be used by the potential buyer in place of actually giving detailed financial data to the seller. Pre-qualifying is quick and almost always free, but it is no guarantee that the lender will actually make the loan to the purchaser.

Pre-approval of a mortgage, on the other hand, requires actually making a full loan application to the lender and paying a loan application fee. The potential purchaser must provide the lender with proof of certain financial details as well. In return the lender writes a pre-approval letter that obligates the lender to make the mortgage loan to this potential purchaser, as long as certain conditions are met. Pre-approval can give a potential purchaser extra bargaining leverage with a seller, particularly a seller who wants to sell a property quickly, since it means that the buyer has already been through the sometimes lengthy process of getting a mortgage approved, so the purchase can go to closing quickly.

One disadvantage of pre-approval is that it tends to tie the buyer with one particular lender, limiting the buyer's bargaining power in negotiating loan conditions with the lender. This disadvantage can be overcome by seeking pre-approved status from more than one lender. Your cost is the additional application fee.

Negotiating

Everybody is aware that in buying a home the buyer is expected to negotiate the price and conditions of the sale with the seller, but few people focus on the fact that details of the mortgage loan are also negotiable. Lenders naturally do not encourage buyers to negotiate the terms of their loans. The buyer is pretty much on his or her own to negotiate with the lender, which is often a large and imposing bureaucracy ready to imply, if not openly lecture individual buyers that negotiating mortgage loan terms is simply not good manners. In fact, there is a fair amount of leeway in negotiating the terms of the mortgage. A buyer who is a good credit risk, is making a sizable down payment, has negotiated a good price with the seller, and has other lenders willing to provide the mortgage loan has a fair amount of leverage to drive a good deal on a mortgage loan. After you have been approved for a loan by a lender, and while discussing the details of the loan, ask the lender for your FICO score. This will tell the lender that he or she is not dealing with somebody who is ignorant of how the mortgage industry works, and—assuming your FICO score is close to 800—puts you instantly in a stronger negotiating position.

In addition to negotiating the combination of interest rates and points with the lender, terms of the escrow account are also negotiable. Usually when making a mortgage payment a person pays the lender the entire PITI every month. The principal and interest go toward the loan, while the tax and insurance payments go into an escrow account that the lender holds to pay taxes and insurance for the homeowner. By paying these from an escrow account the lender ensures that the taxes and insurance are actually paid, and that the lender's investment in the property is protected. Of course property taxes and insurance are typically paid only once or twice per year, and the monthly amount paid into the escrow account is usually slightly larger than the amount actually needed to pay the taxes and insurance. The lender earns investment returns free of charge on the homeowner's money until that money is needed to pay taxes and insurance. If you would rather pay your taxes and insurance directly and earn the investment returns on that money yourself you can negotiate with the lender to eliminate all or part of the escrow requirement. Sometimes the lender will charge a fee of one eighth to one quarter percent of the mortgage to eliminate the escrow account. The exchange will work to your benefit if you plan to keep the house for several years.

Non-Traditional Mortgages

Lenders today offer many alternatives to fixed rate 30-year mortgages; the most common alternative is the 15-year fixed rate mortgage. The example of the medium-term goal in Chapter 5, Targeting your Goals, describes the advantages of lower total interest paid with a 15-year mortgage versus a 30-year mortgage. The disadvantage of a shorter duration mortgage is that the homeowner must make a larger monthly payment to buy the same property.

Adjustable rate mortgages, or ARMs became popular in the high-interest-rate era of the 1980s. An ARM is just what it sounds like, a mortgage loan with an interest rate that adjusts with prevailing interest rates. One advantage of ARMs is that they are available at starting interest rates significantly below the rates charged for 30-year fixed rate mortgages. One disadvantage is that the homeowner is never quite sure how much they will be paying per month years in the future.

A 1-year ARM is the most common. This kind of mortgage has one interest and payment adjustment per year. Rather than leaving the homeowner entirely at the mercy of prevailing interest rates, most ARMs have limits on the maximum rise in interest rates from one adjustment period to the next. Often they also have interest rate caps that limit the maximum interest rate the mortgage lender can charge.

In addition to interest rate limits, some ARMs also offer payment limits, which limit the amount a mortgage payment can rise in any period. If you consider an ARM with payment limits examine the possibility of negative amortization carefully. Under negative amortization the interest and principal not paid by the homeowner because of the payment cap gets added to the amount of the loan, extending the term of the loan until that additional money is ultimately paid to the lender.

The interest rates at which ARMs are initially available are not the interest rates at which they will remain. Initial rates are called teaser rates in the industry and are priced to attract new borrowers to these products. These interest rates are almost guaranteed to rise at the first opportunity. In fact when qualifying potential buyers for ARMs most banks do not use the first year rate, but rather assume that the borrower will be paying an interest rate one or two steps higher than the initial teaser rate.

In addition to various ARMs and fixed rate mortgages, many lenders offer convertible mortgages that start out as fixed-rate mortgages for some period—often seven years—then convert automatically to ARMs for the remainder of the mortgage. Such convertible loans safeguard the lenders from long term interest rate risk, while guaranteeing fixed interest rates and payments for homeowners who stay in their home the national average of about seven years.

One other alternative is the two-step mortgage which starts with one fixed rate for the first five or seven years of the mortgage, then adjusts to another fixed rate for the duration of the mortgage. This limits the fluctuation in mortgage payments the homeowner will experience while providing a measure of long-term interest rate protection to the lender.

In addition to loans that are paid off slowly during the life of the loan, some non-conforming mortgages are structured as balloon loans. In a balloon loan the homeowner is obligated to pay the entire principal of the loan at once at the end of some period, often 7–10 years. During the 7–10 years the borrower pays interest only. In taking a balloon loan the homeowner is betting that they will either move and sell the home at some point before the balloon payment is due, or that they will be able to secure another mortgage to pay the balloon payment at the end of the first mortgage. The homeowner does not build any equity in their home unless the value of their property increases.

CONSUMER LOANS

Most people use debt to make major purchases, such as automobiles, that are within their means, but for which they do not yet have the cash they need. A person's debt service ratio, which you calculated in Chapter 3, Where Does Your Money Go, should not exceed 35%. The 35% guideline is not an optimal debt load, it is the maximum amount of debt that you can service, and is sometimes used by mortgage companies and other lenders in deciding whether to extend credit to a potential customer. You will find it easier to save money, and have more control over your financial life, if you can keep your debt service ratio below 35%, below 25% is even better.

When borrowing money for a consumer loan, such as an automobile, shop around before deciding where to borrow the money. Car dealers often have relationships with lenders so that people can buy and finance a car conveniently all in one place. Before you go shopping for a car, go shopping for a car loan. The first place to check is your credit union, if you have one. Write down the interest rate, terms, loan origination fees and any pre-payment penalty, and compare them with other deals available from competing banks. Only when you have this information written down in your pocket should you walk into your first car dealership. When buying a car always negotiate the price of the car before you are willing to discuss whether you will finance the car or write a check for the purchase. Avoid giving the salesperson any financial information about yourself until you have a firm acceptable offer in writing. By looking at your financial situation before you have agreed on a price, the salesperson will get a good idea of how large a car loan you can afford and change his negotiating position accordingly to sell the car for as much as possible. After you have agreed on a price, and have it in writing, ask about the details of financing available at the car dealer. Recently, some car manufactures have offered exceptionally good deals in automobile loans as a tool to sell more cars. If the car manufacturer is offering to finance the car you may get an excellent deal by financing the car at the dealership. If the loan offered by the dealer would come from a commercial lending company you will probably get a better deal borrowing the money from a bank or credit union. Since you already have the information in your pocket about auto loans from other sources, you can quickly determine if the deal offered by the dealer is your best option.

If you use a loan to buy something remember that the thing you buy with the loan should always last longer than the loan. When 60-month (5-year) automobile loans first became available many people opted for the lower monthly payments these longer loans offered. Unfortunately, when many of these people decided to buy new cars three or four years later they found that the value of their old car had fallen by 40%–50% and was worth less than the balance they still owed on their automobile loans. All commercial loans are structured so that most of the interest owed over the life of the loan is paid first. This means that if the borrower repays the loan early the lender still makes a good profit on the loan. The fraction of a loan payment that goes to reducing principal does not get large until shortly before the loan is paid off.

Once you have taken a consumer loan you need to make timely regular payments. One way to make sure international mail delays do not cause your loan payments to arrive late is to arrange to have the loan payments electronically withdrawn directly from your checking account every month. Just make sure that you remember to subtract these regular payments from your checkbook ledger every month so that you know the correct balance of your checking account.

CREDIT CARDS

It is important to have a major credit card, especially if you live abroad or travel frequently. Major credit cards from American card issuers are convenient, can be used to buy goods in most currencies, put substantial emergency purchasing power at your disposal 24 hours a day, and expose you to only $50 of risk if they are stolen. Their very convenience also makes them a danger to people who have difficulty saving money. Properly used, as a cash float, credit cards can cost you nothing, and in fact can save you money. Improperly used, they can lead you down the road to bankruptcy.

The credit card you choose should be widely accepted around the world—some are almost unknown outside the United States—should have a low or no annual fee, and should offer you a grace period of 25 to 30 days. If the card is properly used the interest rate charged by a credit card is irrelevant.

When using a credit card as a cash float, you pay in full for all the purchases you make with the card during each billing period. When credit cards are used in this way the credit card company effectively loans you money, interest free, to make your purchases. As long as you pay the bill in full every month you never pay the credit card company any interest. You use their money for the grace period—up to 30 days—for free. Of course, if you do not pay your bill in time you begin paying interest to the credit card company at a rate far higher than you would pay for other consumer loans. If, during an emergency, you use a credit card to make large purchases pay off the credit card from your self-insurance fund. When the emergency has passed and your spending patterns return to normal, you can replenish your self-insurance fund. Only use your credit card for a cash advance in an emergency. There is no grace period for a cash advance: You begin paying high rates of interest immediately on the sum advanced.

It is much easier to use credit cards as a cash float when living in the United States than when living abroad. The delays in international mail sometimes cause you to receive your credit card bill after it is due. The solution to this is to keep a running tally of your credit card purchases yourself. Just as you record every check you write in your checkbook ledger, record credit card purchases in a ledger each time you make a purchase. Your credit card ledger need not be anything fancy, a list of the purchase cost, and date kept on a sheet of paper will do. To start, send a check to the credit card company along with a letter before your next bill arrives. The letter should tell the credit card company that the enclosed check is to be credited toward your credit card bill and include your name, billing address, and credit card number. The check should be for the sum of all purchases outstanding on your credit card. When the bill arrives, keep the billing stub to use when making your next payment. When you are ready to make your next payment, cross out the old due date and the amount printed on the stub and write in the correct due date and the amount outstanding based on a reconciliation of your previous statement and your ledger. Send the stub along with a check for that amount to the credit card company.

Many of your purchases will be in your local currency and you can never tell exactly what the exchange rate will be for the transaction. Therefore, you should keep your credit card account slightly overpaid, so that you have a credit balance with the credit card company of $50–$100 at all times to meet any fluctuations in the exchange rates. When the credit card bill arrives use the information on the bill to balance your credit card ledger, the same way you balance your checkbook every month. If your credit buffer drops too low because of exchange rate fluctuations include a little extra money in the next payment to cover future foreign exchange uncertainty.

In addition to being convenient, making local purchases with your credit card often gets you a better rate of exchange than you can find as an individual at local banks. This is because the credit card company lumps all of its monthly foreign exchange transactions together into a large transaction that is executed at a better exchange rate than is available to individuals.

You may want to explore local credit cards in the country where you live, but be careful about the terms of these cards. Be particularly careful about your potential liability if the card is lost or stolen. Before the Consumer Credit Protection Act was passed in the United States, credit card holders were liable for any charges made with a stolen card until that theft was reported in writing to the company issuing the card. This law now limits your liability on purchases made on a stolen card to a maximum of $50. Many countries do not have such legislation, so if your card is stolen your liability could be virtually unlimited.

For your protection, record on a separate piece of paper all of your credit card numbers, as well as the phone numbers to call to report the cards stolen, and your passport number and date of issue; keep this paper in a safe place. If you are traveling, carry this paper somewhere on your person where it is secure and will not be lost if your wallet or purse is stolen.

YOUR CREDIT RATING

It is important that you build and maintain a good credit history, reflected by your credit rating. You should check and correct your credit history with one or more of the major credit bureaus every three years or so. Credit reports, which potential lenders request and receive from credit bureaus when deciding whether to make a new loan, sometimes contain factual errors. It is in your best interest to make sure these errors are corrected: The major credit bureaus often seem not to care if the information they have about you is accurate; it is up to you to explain their mistake to them and ensure they rectify it. In addition to factual mistakes, it is important for married couples to make sure that all accounts for which either partner is individually or jointly liable are included in the credit report. Frequently, one partner is viewed as the principal income provider and credit for paying loans on time helps that person's credit rating, but is not reflected in the credit rating of the other partner. It is important that both married partners keep their individual credit ratings strong by both getting credit for prompt repayment of loans taken jointly.

Thanks to the Fair Credit Reporting Act you have the legal right to review any credit file held on you by a credit bureau in the United States. You also have the right to correct any inaccurate information. This law requires that credit bureau reports contain accurate, relevant and recent personal and financial information about the people they report on, so if you detect an inaccuracy in your credit report be tenacious in forcing the credit bureau to correct it.

If you have been denied a loan, the lending institution must tell you the reason your application was denied, and the name and address of the credit bureau whose report was used in making its decision. If you are denied credit on the basis of a credit report you are entitled to a free credit report from the credit bureau. Under normal circumstances you must purchase a copy of your credit report, which usually costs $10–$20.

The Equal Credit Opportunity Act makes it illegal for any lender in the United States to discriminate on the basis of sex, marital status, age, religion, race, or national origin. This act also makes it illegal for a lender to ask about an applicant's gender, marital status, or childbearing plans as part of a loan application. Prior to this law women, particularly women of childbearing age, were frequently targets of lending discrimination.

You can order a copy of your credit report in writing, by phone, and sometimes online from one of the major credit bureaus listed below. To purchase a copy of your credit report you will need to supply your name, address, date of birth, and social security number, to the credit bureau. If you order by phone or online you will need to use a credit card to pay for your report. The report usually costs something, but the fee varies, depending on your state of residence.

Contact information is as follows:

> Experian Consumer Assistance Center
> PO Box 2104
> Allen, TX 75013-2104
> Phone: +1-972-390-3000 or 888-397-3742
> Website: http://www.experian.com
> At the time of this writing you cannot order your credit report online. The cost for residents of most states is $8
>
> Equifax Inc.
> PO Box 740241
> Atlanta, GA 30374-0214
> Phone: +1-770-375-3050 or 800-997-2493
> Website: http://www.equifax.com
> You can order your credit report online at this website

Trans Union
1561 E. Orangethorpe Ave
Fullerton, CA 92631-5207
Phone: 800-858-8336
Website: http://www.tuc.com
You can order your credit report online at this
website

The best way to keep a good credit rating is to pay off your loans on time. Using loans occasionally for major purchases such as automobiles, and using credit cards wisely give the credit bureaus a way to measure your credit performance and reliability.

9. FINANCIAL RISK MANAGEMENT– INSURANCE

Just as you cannot separate your financial life from other aspects of your life, many risks you face have financial implications. In this chapter, we discuss how to deal with the financial implications of several risks, but not investment risk. Investment risk is discussed in Chapter 11, Investment Management.

Part of achieving your goals is avoiding catastrophic financial loss when disaster strikes. Some of the more obvious financial dangers we must protect ourselves against are the death of the major income producer in a family, a prolonged or expensive illness, and loss of our belongings because of their destruction or theft. Insurance is an effective, and in some cases cost efficient, means of protecting yourself from the financial consequences of such disasters. However, you must choose and buy your insurance carefully to be properly protected, and to avoid paying more than necessary. Insurance is not a panacea for financial risks. Protecting yourself with enough long-term care and disability insurance to guarantee an unchanged lifestyle for your family is too expensive for most people. If we protected ourselves from every conceivable misfortune, many of us would not have enough money left, after paying all the insurance bills, to live a comfortable life and achieve our goals. You need to buy enough insurance to protect yourself from major financial loss. However, buying more insurance than you need, or paying too much for your coverage, costs you money you could use elsewhere.

It is impossible to eliminate risk in our lives, but there are steps we can take to reduce the risks we face and to manage those that remain. Many of us are responsible in daily life. We do not drive after drinking, avoid dangerous areas and situations when possible, eat right and get sufficient exercise to improve our chances of living long and healthy lives. If we approach financial issues with the same attitude we find many similarities. There are financial tools available to deal with the financial aspects of some risks that are not available in other aspects of life.

Insurance cannot protect you from some financial disasters. Spending that does not allow you to save the money you need for the future is an insidious threat that can rob your children of a college education or you of a comfortable retirement. Not understanding the details and conditions of your retirement plan early in life has caused financial disaster late in life for many people. Acquiring excessive debt and not using debt wisely have driven many people to bankruptcy. Insurance is not effective in guarding against any of these financial disasters, but all of them can be avoided, sometimes at little or no monetary cost, by using good financial planning practices.

The three primary tools in financial risk management are planning ahead, maintaining enough self-insurance funds to cover unforeseen or emergency expenses, and properly using insurance. By simply having a financial plan you are already using the first of the financial risk management tools. By planning ahead you are less likely to face unwelcome surprises. One common mistake is not planning for retirement. You need to begin planning for retirement many years ahead to avoid a situation in which you must accept a lower standard of living in retirement or continue to work to simply put food on the table. If you ignore such eventualities until they are almost upon you, you will find it is too late to resolve them without drastically altering your way of life.

As thorough as your financial planning may be, nobody can foresee every possibility. Keeping a self-insurance fund protects you from moderate financial emergencies that could not be foreseen. This buffer of readily available cash held in a money market account with your bank or discount broker should be equal to three to six months of take-home pay. Six months of your take-home pay will cover the average period of unemployment (3–4 months) or the five months until social security disability payments begin should you become disabled. Without self-insurance funds an unforeseen crisis, such as an unexpected trip to the U.S. to deal with a family emergency, could force you to liquidate some of your long-term investments. In a situation where you are forced to liquidate a long-term investment at an inopportune time, you may lose a significant amount of money, which can have a profound negative impact on the long-term financial goals you were trying to achieve with that investment. By building a reasonable self-insurance fund you can protect yourself from many financial dangers. In addition, you can save money on insurance by purchasing policies with higher deductibles and using money from your self-insurance fund to pay the deductibles as needed.

INSURANCE

Insurance reduces your financial loss if a major catastrophe befalls you. The goal of this chapter is to help you get the most from each dollar you spend on insurance and to make sure the hard choices you make are educated decisions.

If you fully insure yourself against every possible risk you will probably find your insurance bills are more than you can afford. Most of us must make hard choices about whether to leave ourselves under-insured against some risks or shortchange our financial futures by not saving and investing enough to meet future financial needs.

When buying insurance, it is important to remember why you are buying the insurance. Insurance protects you from large financial losses if disaster strikes, not from the risk of that disaster occurring. By insuring yourself against small potential expenses you actually lose money over the long-term by paying higher premiums to the insurance company. The insurance industry is much like the casino industry. By serving a large number of people, insurance companies and casinos are able to use statistics to ensure that, on average, they make money. The insurance premium you pay on your homeowner's policy is calculated to make the insurance company money. Premiums from your policy and many others, plus the money the insurance company earns by investing those premiums, is (in an average year) sufficient to pay for the property damage that occurs to all homes insured by that company. Premium levels are set not just to cover the costs of expected claims, but to also cover the operating and administrative costs of the insurance company and provide a margin of profit.

When you buy insurance you should buy it to protect yourself from a catastrophic financial loss, such as you would face if your house burned to the ground. To do this you must carry enough insurance so that the insurance company would pay for you to build an equivalent house and replace your lost belongings. On the other hand, if your deductible is so low the insurance company pays to replace the living room window after a baseball comes through it, you can be sure the additional money you pay in premiums will, over time, reward the insurance company—not you. Use the money in your self-insurance fund to replace the living room window. Buy insurance policies with the highest deductibles you can easily afford to pay out of your self-insurance fund. By opting for a higher deductible you save money, over the long-term, on your insurance premiums. Buying insurance for protection from small expenses is sometimes referred to as trading dollars with the insurance company. You rarely get as many dollars back as you pay in such an arrangement.

BUYING INSURANCE

Insurance companies sell their products in a number of ways. The least expensive insurance is usually sold direct from the insurance company, rather than through a network of insurance agents. The most expensive insurance is usually sold by independent insurance agents or brokers who represent and sell insurance from many companies. When you first learn of an upcoming foreign assignment check immediately with your current insurance companies to learn if they will be able to continue your coverage in that country. The cost of your insurance may increase and some insurance may not be available, depending on your country of assignment and the insurance company your are using.

You should limit your choice in insurance companies to those that are financially strong. Should you need to make a claim 10 or 20 years from now, you want to be sure the company can make good on its promise to meet your claim. Thankfully there are several good independent insurance rating services. Five of the best-known are A.M. Best, Moody's, Weiss Ratings, Standard and Poor's, and Duff and Phelps. The rankings from these services reflect the ability of insurance companies to pay claims and the soundness of their financial condition. A.M. Best's top three rankings for a company—in descending order—are A++, A+, and A. Their scale descends to F, but you should stay with a company that rates no lower than A. The top three rankings for Moody's are Aaa, Aa1, and Aa2. For Weiss the top two rankings are A and B. For Standard and Poor's the top three rankings are AAA, AA+, and AA. For Duff & Phelps the top three ratings are AAA, AA+ and AA. Any insurance company you are seriously considering should be ranked somewhere in the top two or three categories by at least two of these five rating companies. These companies rate many international insurance companies as well as American companies.

Contact information for these rating companies follows:

A.M. Best Company
Ambest Road
Oldwick, NJ 08858
Phone: +1-908-439-2200.
Website: http://www.ambest.com

Moody's Investor Services
99 Church St.
New York, NY 10007
Phone: +1-212-553-0377
Website: http://www.moodys.com

Weiss Research
4176 Burns Road
Palm Beach Gardens, FL 33410
Phone: +1-561-627-3300 or 800-289-9222
Fax: +1-561-625-6685

E-mail: wr@weissinc.com
Website: http://www.weissratings.com

Standard & Poors
55 Water Street
New York, NY 10041
Phone: +1-212-208-1527 or +1-212-438-7280
Fax: +1-212-438-7290
E-mail: ratings@mcgraw-hill.com
Website: http://www.standardandpoors.com

Duff & Phelps
55 E. Monroe Street, Suite 3500
Chicago, IL 60603
Phone: +1-312-368-3198
or +1-312-368-3100
Fax: +1-312-1032
E-mail: hotline@dcrco.com
Website: http://www.dcrco.com

Many of these ratings services have simple letter ratings of many insurance companies available on line for free; some do not. A.M. Best is the biggest insurance rating service; their ratings cost $4.95 each. Weiss Research sells reports on the financial safety of banks, brokerage firms, and insurance companies. Costs are $15 per rating, $25 for a one-page report. Weiss also sells a list of recommended banks, insurers and brokers for $55.

Some insurance, such as property insurance, is only available individually. Other types of insurance, such as health insurance and some life insurance, are often available to larger groups of people. If it is available, insurance that is not an individual policy is usually the better deal.

Group Insurance

Group insurance is usually the least expensive and so is the first place to look for insurance coverage. The group often consists of employees who work for the same company. Group policies guarantee the insurance company a larger number of policies, so insurance for individuals in the group is usually less expensive. Group policies are also the least restrictive in terms of proving insurability and covering pre-existing conditions. The preferential treatment such a group receives usually varies with the size of the group. The cost savings are best for groups of fifty or more people; groups as small as ten people may not be eligible for group insurance at all. If you work for a small company, group insurance may not be an option.

Association Insurance

This is similar to group insurance, but instead of a group that shares an employer, these people have something else in common. Members of a credit union or professional organization may, for example, be eligible for association insurance. The cost savings and reduced restrictions on association insurance are usually not as good a deal as group insurance, but are usually better than for individual policies. Many companies that are too small to obtain group insurance can offer insurance for employees through membership in a trade association.

Individual insurance

If you are not eligible for group or association insurance, or if the policies available to you in group or association form are inadequate for your needs, or are offered by a company that does not meet your quality standards; you may need an individual policy. These are usually the most expensive and restrictive policies and the variation in cost and restrictions available from top quality insurance companies make comparison-shopping important. If you use an individual policy to supplement a group or association policy purchase additional coverage selectively to cover those needs not covered under your primary policy.

Insurance from Foreign Insurance Companies

The quality of insurance around the world varies drastically from country to country. The independent rating companies that review U.S. insurance companies frequently do not have counterparts abroad. The five major rating companies listed above rate several foreign insurance companies as well as American companies. Some of the ratings are free, other rating companies charge for ratings. Standard and Poors financial strength ratings for some foreign insurance companies are available free on line from http://www.insure.com. Shop around before you buy local insurance in a country where you live. Learn which American insurance companies, preferably companies that sell directly by mail, offer similar policies in the country where you live. Before you buy the local insurance, request a comparable policy from a reliable U.S. insurance company that will sell insurance overseas and compare the coverage and premiums to those offered locally. If you cannot find an evaluation of the foreign insurance company from the insurance rating companies listed above ask the foreign insurance company for references, preferably including Americans or expatriates from other countries who hold policies with that company. Talk to these people and learn how long they have been customers, how much they shopped around before buying this insurance, and what their experiences have been when they have submitted claims. Ask them for names of other expatriate customers (not provided to you by the insurance company), who also hold policies with this company and ask them the same questions. To learn something about the financial strength of the company, check with local banks and research the company with Dun & Bradstreet.

This is one instance in which it may actually make sense to employ an independent insurance broker or agent who specializes in insurance for expatriates. There are a number of such firms. Do not simply accept what such a broker tells you; verify the facts about the strength of the companies recommended, and explore the other options that may be available to you. If you find an independent insurance broker who is knowledgeable, the best insurance that broker can provide may fit you better than insurance you could find from any other source.

Several companies in the United Kingdom provide insurance coverage in foreign countries. One advantage of dealing with these companies rather than buying in the country in which you live is that the policy will be written in English. Another advantage is that in the event of a dispute with the insurance company, any legal action will be resolved in a British court.

Keep in mind that if you have a legal dispute with your foreign insurance company, that dispute will be subject to the laws of that country rather than U.S. law. Depending on where you are, you may or may not have options for recourse that U.S. courts allow you in disputing a claim. If you are not a citizen of the country, your rights under that country's system of civil law may be restricted.

Most local insurance policies are written in the currency of the country in which the insurance company is located. If you are insuring something purchased in the local currency that may be all right, but if you are insuring an item available only for dollars you face an additional exchange rate risk when buying insurance from a foreign company.

PROPERTY AND CASUALTY INSURANCE

Examples of property and casualty insurance include automobile, homeowners, and personal property insurance. Since this insurance protects you from costs associated with the loss of physical things, as well as protection from liability lawsuits, the question of how much insurance protection you need is straightforward. You need enough insurance to replace the physical property you might lose, and enough liability protection to protect you against any legal actions that may be brought against you. Since liability insurance is inexpensive for most people, and legal damages awarded in recent years have continued to rise, it makes sense to carry several hundred thousand dollars in liability insurance.

One important point related to property and casualty insurance is the difference between *cash value* and *replacement cost*. A cash value insurance policy depreciates the insured item over its theoretical useful life. This means, for example, that if your three-year-old television is stolen the insurance company pays you roughly what a three-year-old TV like yours costs in a used electronics store. A replacement cost policy would pay you approximately what it would cost for you to replace your old television today with an equivalent television, purchased new.

Be careful that your property and casualty insurance protects any property you have in the United States, any property located with you abroad, and your property when it is being transported from one assignment to another.

Automobile Insurance

Automobile insurance is composed of four elements:

> Liability coverage for bodily injury and damage to other people's property
>
> Medical payments coverage
>
> Uninsured motorist coverage
>
> Coverage for damage to your vehicle

A typical automobile insurance policy might provide liability coverage to $300,000, medical payments coverage to $10,000 for any individual injured in an accident, uninsured motorist coverage of $20,000 per accident, and cash value coverage for damage to your vehicle.

Automobile liability coverage protects you from lawsuits resulting from an automobile accident. In the past, liability coverage limits were often split—in some policies they still are. A typical liability policy might contain numbers like 25/50/10. Such a policy would cover a maximum of $25,000 in liability payments per individual injured, a total of $50,000 for all individuals injured in an accident, and a total of $10,000 for property liability resulting from an accident. Many policies today have moved away from this practice and simply place limits on the total liability coverage per accident. To be sufficiently insured you should carry liability coverage of at least several hundred thousand dollars. Automobile liability coverage may be safely reduced to minimum legal levels if you have liability coverage under an *umbrella* liability policy, described below.

Medical payments coverage pays medical expenses resulting from an accident for the policyholder and people riding in the policyholder's vehicle at the time of the accident. Uninsured motorists coverage covers injury resulting from an accident in which an uninsured (or under-insured), motorist was at fault. To collect this insurance you must prove that another motorist was at fault, that he/she had no applicable insurance, and that damages were actually incurred. If these are proven your insurer will pay what would have been paid by the uninsured motorist's liability coverage, up to the limits of your policy.

Coverage for damage to the insured vehicle pays for physical damage to that vehicle. The two types of coverage available are *collision* and *comprehensive*. Collision coverage insures against damage from a collision in which the vehicle is involved, regardless of who is at fault. Comprehensive coverage insures against most other things that could happen to the vehicle (such as theft or vandalism), but does not cover collisions. Personal property that was in the vehicle at the time and was lost or damaged is not usually covered by such policies. If the entire vehicle is stolen or totaled these forms of coverage will pay the (depreciated) cash value of the vehicle, minus the deductible.

Foreign countries often require you to purchase your automobile liability insurance from a company in that country. Remember that you may not be obligated to buy all of your insurance from that company, only the liability insurance. On the other hand, it may be cheaper to buy all of your insurance from that company than to split your coverage by buying your medical, uninsured motorist, and damage insurance from another company. Few American companies offer international automobile insurance. One of the few that does is American International Group through their International Services division. Another such company is United Services Automobile Association (USAA), but insurance from this company is only available to members. Membership in USAA is only open to people with certain past or present positions in the United States federal government. Another resource is the insurance broker Clements & Company.

Contact information follows:

> American International Underwriters
> 70 Pine Street
> New York, New York 10270
> Phone: +1-212-770-6087
> Fax: +1-212-480-3941
> E-mail: andrew.warren@aig.com
> Website: http://www.aig.com
>
> USAA
> 9800 Fredericksburg Road
> San Antonio, TX 78288-0001
> Phone: +1-210-498-8080 or 800-531-8080
> Website: http://www.usaa.com
>
> Clements & Company
> 1660 L Street, NW, 9th Floor
> Washington, DC 20036
> Phone: +1-202-872-0060 or 800-872-0067
> Fax: +1-202-466-9064
> Website: http://www.clements.com

When buying automobile insurance shop around. Check with several companies, particularly direct writers who sell by mail, and compare prices. Ask about any discounts you may be entitled to.

These discounts might include:

> Good driver discount
>
> Discount for students away at school
>
> Discount for insuring more than one vehicle with the same company
>
> Discount for safety features such as air bags

Discount for using anti-theft devices

Car-pool discount

Good student discount for teenage drivers

Drivers training discount for teenage drivers

Discount for vehicles driven infrequently

Discount for having taken a defensive driving course

If you are insuring an old vehicle with a low resale value, consider carrying no comprehensive or collision coverage. Every few years shop around again; you may find a better bargain. Buy insurance with the highest possible deductible—assuming you are maintaining a self-insurance fund—and only buy insurance from a solid company with a reliable history of payment.

Homeowner's Insurance

Mortgage lenders require homeowners to carry sufficient homeowner's insurance coverage. Most mortgage lenders like to ensure that the insurance premiums are paid regularly by making the insurance payments from an escrow account. A basic homeowner's policy insures a home and personal property against fire, lightning, vandalism, theft, glass breakage for dwelling buildings and personal property. It also provides comprehensive personal liability coverage. Some broader forms of homeowners insurance also cover dangers such as the weight of ice and snow, water damage from breaking or frozen plumbing, falling objects, damage from burglars, building collapse, and damage from malfunctioning heating and hot water systems. Special form insurance, which is even more comprehensive, covers loss from all causes except those specified in the policy. These policies typically exclude damage from floods, earthquakes, nuclear accidents, acts of war, and normal wear and tear such as rust, mechanical breakdown and deterioration. In areas prone to flooding, separate government underwritten flood insurance is usually available. For an additional premium, coverage for earthquake and landslide damage can usually be added.

A homeowner's policy usually covers damage to the following:

> The residence dwelling
>
> Other structures on the property
>
> The insured person's personal property at the insured site, with a provision to insure some part of that person's personal property anywhere in the world
>
> Loss of use, including the cost of staying in a hotel and eating in restaurants while the home is again made habitable
>
> Personal liability protection
>
> Medical payments to others, regardless of who is at fault and whether or not negligence was involved

The *insured* in a homeowners policy usually refers not only to the person who bought the policy, but also that person's relatives (if members of that person's household), and any other person under 21 years of age who is in the care of the insured.

Insurance against damage to the dwelling is usually replacement cost insurance. That is, the insurance company will pay to replace or repair the damage that occurred at current prices. It is important that your insurance provides replacement cost rather than cash value coverage for such claims. Cash value coverage depreciates the value of your home over the expected life of the building, providing you with insufficient money to repair the damage if it occurs.

Homeowner's insurance usually carries a provision that the dwelling must be insured for at least 80% of its replacement cost to receive actual replacement cost for any partial and repairable damage to the dwelling. If your home is not insured for at least 80% of its replacement value, the company will reimburse you at a rate lower than full replacement cost, meaning you are not sufficiently insured. Just because you insured your house for 80% of what you paid for it several years ago does not mean you now meet the minimum 80% requirement. Building costs go up and every few years you need to re-evaluate whether you are carrying enough homeowner's insurance.

Many homeowners' policies carry a provision that suspends or reduces your coverage if the property is unoccupied or vacant for some period—often thirty consecutive days. If you live overseas and leave your home in the U.S. unoccupied, or rent it out, make sure your homeowner's policy has a provision to insure your home and property when it is unoccupied.

Personal property insurance associated with homeowner's insurance is typically cash value coverage. For a larger premium, you can change this to replacement cost coverage. For people who live abroad and move frequently the additional expense of replacement cost coverage is money well spent. Typically, the personal property provision of your homeowners insurance protects your property anywhere in the world, but a few companies do have specific restrictions on property in certain countries and a few may not cover your property while it is in transit to an overseas location. Check any such provisions before you buy your insurance. For many policies the only exception to the worldwide coverage of personal property is for property kept in a second or vacation home. Property in such a home is usually only insured up to a maximum value of 10% of the total policy. If you keep a home in the United States, but live abroad, you may need to purchase a separate renter's insurance policy to protect the full value of the personal belongings you have with you abroad if your foreign home could be construed as a second or vacation home. If you have any doubts about this point check with your insurance company for a decision before you need to file a claim. Get the response from your insurance company in writing.

Personal property insurance usually places limits on the value of certain kinds of property that are covered under the policy. Typical examples are coverage of artwork to a maximum of $1,000, a $1,000 limit on watercraft, $1,000 limit on theft of jewelry, watches, and furs, $2,500 limit on the theft of silverware. If you own expensive individual items, or large numbers of such things so that the total value of such items exceeds your policy limits you should insure those items specifically under a personal property endorsement in your homeowners policy, or by buying separate policy floaters on those particular items. Motor vehicles, aircraft, business property, and automobile sound systems are excluded from coverage under personal property insurance.

To protect your personal property effectively you must accurately record what you own, when, where, and for how much you bought it, and keep these records—including the sales receipts for major purchases—in some safe location away from the insured goods. Keeping good records of purchases is a nuisance, but if you ever incur a major loss and need to file a claim you will be glad you made the effort. Video cameras and photocopiers have made the task of creating a documented inventory of your property less cumbersome. When living abroad make multiple copies of your personal property inventory. Leave one in a safety deposit box in the United States, another at a secure location outside your home, perhaps locked in your office in the country where you live. In the event something happens and you need to file a claim, you will have a personal inventory safe and available, whether you are in the United States or the country where you live. If you own and use a personal computer there are personal inventory programs to help you track what you own, when and where you bought it, and what you paid for it. These are available both as stand-alone programs and integrated into personal finance programs.

A *loss of use* provision can cover either your additional living costs while your home is uninhabitable, as long as the dwelling is your principal place of residence, or the fair rental value of the dwelling. This fair rental value covers any portion of the dwelling rented to others. Thus if your house in the United States is still your principal place of residence, but you have it rented while living overseas, you may design your homeowners policy to provide fair rental value for the property if an insured event occurs that makes your house uninhabitable.

Personal liability protection under a homeowner's policy is often referred to as Comprehensive Personal Liability (CPL) protection. It protects you from a broad range of legal liability, up to the limits of the policy.

CPL coverage pays on behalf of the insured, up to the limits of the policy, all sums the insured becomes legally obligated to pay as a result of bodily injury and/or property damage. The insurance company agrees to defend the insured against any suit that would be covered by the policy, whether or not that suit is groundless or even fraudulent. The insurance company's obligation to defend the insured ends when the limit of liability coverage has been paid in his/her defense. For this reason it is important to carry enough personal liability insurance coverage.

Coverage for medical payments to others under a homeowner's policy usually has a limit that applies per person injured. It pays, up to the limit of the policy, the medical expenses of somebody injured while on your property, who is there with your permission, regardless of who is at fault. Thus, if your neighbor falls down your stairs this coverage would pay the neighbor's medical expenses, up to the limit of the policy. If the stairs were icy at the time and the neighbor decides to sue you, the CPL insurance in your homeowner's policy pays for your legal defense and any damages you are obligated to pay.

The medical payments protection in your homeowner's policy may also pay for medical costs of others injured away from your residence if you caused the accident. This also covers actions by your pets and usually any household help, if it occurs while they are working for you.

When shopping for homeowner's insurance, ask if discounts are available for fitting your home with smoke detectors, burglar alarms, and/or fire extinguishers. Many companies offer such discounts these days, as well as offering lower premiums for newer homes and those located close to fire hydrants.

Umbrella Liability Insurance

In modern American society liability insurance is a necessity of life. Automobile insurance contains a liability component, as does homeowner's insurance, boating/yacht insurance, private aircraft insurance, and other such insurance. The liability coverage in these policies protects you, up to the limit of the policy, against legal liability for actions that fall within the scope of that policy. Increasing legal costs and damage settlements resulting from lawsuits has prompted the creation of umbrella, also known as excess, liability insurance to provide liability protection beyond the limits of other insurance. There is no industry standard for these policies, but they are typically written for a minimum of one million dollars in liability coverage. Umbrella liability policies cover all possible liabilities unless the policy specifically excludes them.

In addition to extending your liability protection, umbrella liability coverage insures you against liability not covered by any other type of policy. Examples of liability not usually covered by other policies include coverage against liability for damaging another person's property that was in your custody, worldwide liability coverage—important for Americans living abroad—and coverage for personal injury claims that might include libel, slander, invasion of privacy, or other such accusations.

As an example, consider what would happen if your neighbor slipped and fell on the icy steps in front of your house, was badly injured, and sued you. If the legal fees and penalties resulting from the suit totaled $800,000 and your homeowner's policy carried a CPL component of $500,000, you would still be personally liable for the $300,000 not covered by your homeowner's policy. If, on the other hand, you had an umbrella liability policy, that policy would then pay the $300,000 not covered by your homeowners insurance.

As with all insurance coverage, it pays to shop around for the best deal from a top rated company. Umbrella liability insurance has not yet been standardized, so compare policy provisions and the fine print carefully. One way to reduce the net cost of umbrella liability coverage is to reduce your liability coverage under other insurance policies (auto and homeowners insurance, for example) and so save money on those premiums.

In selecting a company to provide an umbrella liability policy, it may pay to check the company's history in paying large liability claims. In the past, some insurance companies have defaulted on such a policy when faced with a huge liability payment. In doing so, the insurance company is betting that the policyholder, already facing at least one lawsuit, will simply declare bankruptcy. The chance the insurance company is taking is that the policyholder will file a successful suit against the insurance company, forcing the company to honor the provisions of the policy they sold. In doing so, the company calculates that the damage to their business reputation will cost them less than it would have cost the company to simply pay the claim.

HEALTH AND DISABILITY INSURANCE

Insurance against the financial costs of health problems comes in three basic forms: Health insurance, also called medical insurance, covers the cost of acute medical care. Disability insurance replaces income you may lose during a long illness. Long-term care insurance pays the cost of a long convalescence in a nursing home, assisted living facility, or your own home

In addition to these, medical evacuation insurance is necessary for people living in countries that lack first world medical care. Emergency medical evacuation in a private ambulance jet can be extremely expensive. When faced with a serious medical emergency in a third world country it can also save your life.

Medical insurance capable of covering hundreds of thousands of dollars in medical expense is extremely important for Americans, whether living abroad or in the United States. Disability insurance may also be important if a long debilitating illness or injury strikes you. Long-term care insurance can potentially save you or your family a great deal of money if you ever face a convalescence of a year or more. Nonetheless, many people find they are willing to forego long-term care insurance until they are much older, and more likely to need it. Some people are also comfortable without disability insurance. These are purely personal choices about the kind of risk you want to take. If you were to purchase all the insurance you might want, chances are that you would not have enough money left to put toward your other goals. You must decide which insurance is the most critical and do without insurance in less critical areas if buying that insurance means you must forego important future goals. The choices are not easy and they involve tradeoffs, but it is important to make these decisions with full information and your eyes open.

When shopping for health, disability and long-term care insurance, find out first if you are eligible for group coverage. If group coverage is not an option, explore coverage as part of an association before buying a policy as an individual.

Health Insurance

The two kinds of health insurance commonly available today are fee-for-service insurance that reimburses you for medical expenses and health maintenance organizations (HMOs) that cover everything from measles shots to a heart transplant for one yearly fee. Most health maintenance organizations cannot provide coverage or care for Americans living outside the United States. Unlike HMOs, traditional insurance typically has many levels and types of coverage, and often has maximum amounts they will pay for particular medical procedures. One variation on fee-for-service coverage is the preferred provider organization (PPO). Within the network of health care providers belonging to a particular PPO, each member has agreed to accept a fixed fee from the insurance company for a given medical procedure. Some networks provide almost worldwide coverage. If you are in a location where there is no preferred provider, this insurance functions like a traditional fee-for-service plan.

Fee-for-service health insurance typically pays reasonable and customary expenses for specific procedures. Some medical procedures are not covered under such plans. Sometimes the insurance company's idea of reasonable and customary may differ considerably from what the treatment actually costs. The procedure of receiving a bill for your medical care and then seeking reimbursement from your insurance provider can be a lengthy and complicated one. Many health insurance policies will make arrangements to pay the hospital directly for any in-patient care you receive, reimbursing you only for outpatient care. If it is available this is a nice feature.

Health insurance typically has a deductible, may have a co-insurance provision, and often has a maximum benefit that may be as high as one million dollars or more. Health insurance with no deductible, also known as first dollar insurance, that has a low maximum benefit does not protect you effectively against a catastrophic loss and amounts to trading dollars with the insurance company. If your self-insurance fund is large enough, you can save money in the long run by choosing a health insurance plan with a high deductible. Many plans offer a choice of deductibles, with your premium getting smaller as the deductible gets larger.

Deductibles vary widely between health insurance policies. Most are calendar year all-inclusive deductibles, meaning your total out-of-pocket medical expenses add up all year long and are applied directly against the policy deductible. Some policies carry deductibles that apply to your entire family; others are per-person deductibles. Some deductibles are applied on a per-accident or per-illness basis; meaning that if you suffer several unrelated health problems during the year, you may pay several times the deductible out-of-pocket before your insurance coverage takes effect. Some calendar year deductibles have a carry-over provision so that medical expenses in the last three months of a calendar year can be applied to either that calendar year, or the next one.

You need a health insurance policy with a maximum benefit of at least several hundred thousand dollars. Note that maximum benefits come in various forms, some are lifetime total maximum benefits, and some are annual maximum benefits. Some are maximum benefits per person, and some are maximum benefits per family.

Co-insurance, also known as participation, means that the insurance company pays some percentage of your medical expenses, after the deductible—you pay the rest. Typically, the insurance company pays about 80% of the bill and you pay 20%. Most health insurance plans with co-insurance contain a stop-loss provision, so that the total you are required to pay is limited. Co-insurance is less common with international health insurance than it is with health insurance in the United States, but there are several international health insurance policies with co-insurance provisions.

Consider, as an example, insurance coverage of a major illness that costs $50,000. Assume the policy has a $500 deductible, a 20% co-insurance requirement, and a $1,000 stop-loss provision. First, you would pay the $500 dollar deductible out of your self-insurance fund. From that point the insurance company would pay 80% of additional costs; you would pay 20%. After $5,000 the stop-loss provision kicks in. At that point the insurance company has paid $4,000, you have paid $1,000, and of course you paid the initial $500. That leaves $44,500, which the insurance company pays in full because you have reached your $1,000 stop loss limit. In sum, you paid $1,500; the insurance company paid $48,500. If treatment of the illness had cost $150,000 the cost to you would have been the same, $1,500, but the insurance company would have paid $148,500, as long as you had the foresight to carry enough insurance to cover $150,000 in medical expenses.

Note that since some insurance companies are able to negotiate lower total prices for medical treatment than is reflected in the bill you actually see, you may end up paying more than 20% of the cost of your care. If, for example, you receive medical care that your bill states cost $5,000 and you have a 20% co-insurance provision, you would be obliged to pay $1,000 toward your medical expenses. If, however, the company negotiated the cost of that care down to $3,000—you would typically not be told. You would still pay 20% of the list price of the treatment, while the insurance company pays only $2,000. Rather than 20% of the actual cost of the treatment, you would unknowingly pay 33% in this case.

If your health insurance has a co-insurance component, it is important that your policy include a stop-loss provision. Without a stop loss provision, a $100,000 illness covered by major medical insurance with 20% in co-insurance could cost you $20,000 out-of-pocket.

Internal limits, also known as inside limits, are a feature of some health insurance policies that limit specific types of expenses, such as private nursing care, extended care facility expenses, hospital room and board charges. The fewer inside limits in a policy and the higher any limits are the better.

Some health insurance policies insure only the policyholder; others insure that person's immediate family. Some international policies cover younger children for free, as long as the parents have health insurance policies with that company. If you have dependent children reaching adulthood you must consider how they will be covered after they outgrow the protection your policy provides.

Most U.S. health insurance policies will not cover you if you are outside the United States for an extended period of time. They also lack the international expertise and contacts needed to effectively administer international health insurance. Some international health insurance policies have options that cover customers in certain parts of the world, typically charging more if the policyholder needs true worldwide coverage. Make sure the health insurance you buy covers you everywhere in the world you expect to travel. Many international policies exclude coverage in the United States or all of North America, because of the high cost of medical care in those locations.

If you have any ties to North America, you will need a policy that covers your medical treatment there. Some international policies that provide coverage in North America limit that coverage to 30 or 90 days of residence in North America per year and exclude coverage if you traveled to North America specifically to seek medical treatment. While such policies are often less expensive than other international alternatives, they have very serious drawbacks for anybody with family or business in the United States and anybody who wants the freedom to seek the best treatment possible if facing a life threatening illness or injury.

Some policies have a provision that allows the insurance company to cancel them at any time. Other policies give the insurance company the option to renew, or not renew, the policy at the end of the policy year. Make sure the policy you buy contains a provision that specifically states that the insurance company cannot cancel your insurance as long as the premiums are paid. This is particularly important if you may be moving to a country where your policy will cover you, but where your insurance company will not write new policies.

A guaranteed renewable policy is one you are guaranteed to be able to renew for some period of time, often until age 65 or for the rest of your life. Your policy premiums can increase, but the insurance company is not allowed to increase the premium on just your policy; they can only increase the premiums for a certain class or group of policies. Non-cancelable policies are guaranteed renewable, but also contain a provision that fixes the premium so that it cannot increase during the life of the policy.

Many international health insurance policies require pre-approval before medical treatment is given, particularly before admission to a hospital. This provision can be a nuisance, but is so common that it is hard to avoid.

Some policies cover the costs of rehabilitation as well as care for acute conditions. Such coverage is a nice feature if available at reasonable cost. Particularly if you plan to have children, examine the maternity provisions of the insurance policy carefully. Some are extensive, others non-existent.

Many policies will not insure you against any medical condition you had before buying that policy; such conditions are referred to as pre-existing conditions. Individual policies are more likely to exclude or restrict pre-existing conditions than group policies. Some policies simply do not cover pre-existing conditions; others do not cover such conditions for some period, but will then cover them if the condition has not recurred. Yet other policies cover pre-existing conditions, but limit lifetime insurance benefits related to the treatment of that condition to some amount far less than the normal maximum policy benefit. Remember that any changes in coverage of pre-existing conditions that may result from new legislation in the United States are unlikely to apply to international insurance policies, particularly those offered by foreign insurance companies.

One serious problem faced by Americans living abroad is converting back to U.S. medical coverage when they return to the United States. As stated earlier, most international health insurance policies do not provide coverage to people living in North America. Only a few insurance companies that provide international health insurance offer coverage to U.S. and Canadian citizens living in North America. Those few that do are probably not the best insurance deals available to Americans in America. This means that in most cases you will need to leave your current American insurer when moving overseas—and will face the pre-existing conditions issue when applying for a new insurance policy. You will have to convert to an American health insurance policy upon returning to America—encountering the pre-existing condition issue again. If you contract a serious illness while abroad and return permanently to North America as a result, this problem will be much more acute. You may find yourself uninsurable by most American health insurers and pay a horrific premium if you do succeed in buying coverage. This is a problem your employer may be able to help you with. One option is to stay enrolled in a company provided health insurance plan while you are abroad. You could also explore whether your employer would be willing to make some agreement to protect you financially to some extent if you find yourself back in the United States, without health insurance, and seriously ill as a result of having taken an overseas assignment for them.

Although it only applies in the United States, it is worth knowing about COBRA. COBRA, officially called the Consolidated Omnibus Budget Reconciliation Act of 1985, forces most U.S. employers—those with twenty or more employees—to offer continued group health insurance coverage to former employees (if they offer it to current employees) for a period of time. Retirees and those who leave employment with a company are eligible to continue coverage for up to 18 months. If a person loses coverage because of the death of a family member or divorce, they can continue coverage for 36 months. Coverage under this act is not automatic. The eligible person must elect to continue coverage and must pay for the continued coverage at up to 102% of the total cost—both the part paid by the employee and the part paid by the employer. Insurance coverage continued in this way is not subject to any requirement that the eligible person is insurable, and all pre-existing conditions are covered by the continued insurance. When the continued coverage expires, the eligible person must be given the option of enrolling in any conversion health plan available. COBRA also applies to those who retire from an employer, but COBRA continued coverage ends when a person becomes eligible for Medicare.

Currently Medicare, which is U.S. federal government health insurance for older people, does not cover Americans living overseas. In these days of Medicare cost cutting it is doubtful that Medicare will ever be expanded to cover Americans abroad.

One particular type of health insurance important for Americans living and working abroad is medical evacuation, or medevac insurance. A medical evacuation, usually by specially equipped private ambulance jet, to a country with first world medical facilities is extremely expensive. A single evacuation often costs $30,000 to $100,000. Medical evacuation is not covered by most U.S. insurance policies, except those from companies with specialized international policies. Medical evacuation coverage is often included in international health insurance policies. A person's employer often provides medevac insurance when Americans are sent to work and live in countries with substandard medical facilities. If you live in or travel to such a place, or think you may in the future, examine your coverage for medical evacuation. Also make sure that the medical facilities the medical evacuation insurance company considers adequate meet your own standards. Private medevac insurance is available from some companies if the coverage provided by your employer does not meet your personal standards.

Long-Term Care Insurance

Private insurance against the expense of long-term care, either in a nursing home or in your own home, is a relatively recent development in the insurance industry. As of this writing long-term care insurance is only available in the United States. Long-term care protection abroad, if available, is usually a facet of a country's social security or government provided medical care system. If you are eligible to participate in the socialized medical system of a foreign country you are probably also covered by their long-term care provisions. If you are not covered by another country's socialized medical care system you will have to return to the United States for long-term care if you want any insurance protection from the expense of long-term care. Long-term care insurance is sometimes referred to as LTC insurance.

Since LTC policies are not yet standardized, they vary widely. Many people choose to live without LTC insurance, or if they do purchase it, they do so only as they reach their senior years, when they are more likely to need it. In the early 1990s those selling long-term care insurance developed a reputation for heavy-handed sales tactics. While LTC insurance gives one peace of mind the question of whether or when you should buy LTC insurance is a complex one, since LTC insurance is expensive. Because of the expense, those who buy LTC policies abandon them more frequently than is common for other forms of insurance. The cost of LTC insurance goes up with the age at which you begin coverage because the chances you will need the benefits of the LTC policy rise as you age. For those who need LTC insurance, buying a policy while in your fifties or sixties may be a reasonable compromise between policy expense and the length of time you are likely to pay premiums without receiving any benefits. If you buy a LTC policy while in your fifties or sixties make sure the policy contains good inflation protection.

Medicare and regular health insurance will not cover long-term care. The Health Insurance Portability and Accountability Act of 1996 is aimed at discouraging people from deliberately spending down their assets in old age with the goal of qualifying for Medicaid, which is the only form of U.S. Government provided assistance that covers the cost of long-term care. (Medicaid, like Medicare, is not available to U.S. citizens living overseas.) This law also made it possible for some people to deduct the cost of LTC insurance premiums from their federal income taxes. Long-term care premiums, up to a limit that increases with your age, can be included with medical expense for tax deduction purposes. The fine print in this deal is that you can only deduct medical expenses that exceed 7.5% of your adjusted gross income. This means those of us without expensive medical conditions are rarely able to make use of this tax deduction, even with LTC premiums included. The good news is that reimbursements paid by tax-qualified LTC policies—and most LTC policies are now tax-qualified—are not subject to federal income tax.

The financial danger from long-term care comes in two forms. If an illness or accident that requires a long rehabilitation (more than a year) strikes you while you are young, disability insurance will replace some of your lost income, but the cost of any needed long-term care in your home, a nursing home, or an assisted living facility must be covered by LTC insurance or come out of your pocket. The second threat comes in later years as a danger to your estate and your children's financial well being. If you eventually require long-term care because of old age infirmity, the financial strain will quickly reduce the estate you leave to your heirs. Many children take on the financial as well as the personal burden of caring for aging parents. You can reduce the risk to your estate and the potential financial burden on your children by insuring yourself against the financial costs of long-term care. The average stay in a nursing home is one and a half years, so choose a policy with a duration of benefits of at least two years—three is better.

If you decide that you need LTC insurance, compare policy provisions carefully and read the fine print. Nursing home care typically costs $100–$140 per day ($36,000–$51,000 per year), varying widely with geographic location, so the prospect of paying for long-term care represents a serious potential financial threat.

Most LTC policies determine whether a person is eligible to receive benefits based on the person's inability to perform some number of Activities of Daily Living (ADLs), as defined in the policy. Typical ADLs include bathing, walking, eating, dressing, getting into and out of bed, taking one's medicine, and using the toilet. Typically a policy will require that the insured cannot perform two to three of the specified ADLs before they are eligible to be reimbursed for long-term care costs.

Some long-term care insurance only covers nursing home costs. Other policies only pay for services delivered in the policyholder's home. Since most people prefer to recuperate in their own home or an assisted living facility when that is possible—and doing so is less expensive—a policy that provides for both options is the best choice. Such a policy typically provides some maximum daily benefit for nursing home care with a fraction of that amount available for long-term health care in your own home. A policy that covers nursing home, assisted living, and home health care is called an integrated policy. They are usually more expensive than nursing home only policies, but are often worth it.

One confusing feature of LTC coverage is the duration of benefits provision. The so-called duration of benefits of a LTC policy is not really the amount of time the policy will pay for your long-term care. It is the amount of time the policy will pay the maximum benefit covered by your policy. The total amount of money the insurance company would have to pay if it paid your maximum benefit for the duration of benefits is the means by which the limits of a LTC policy are measured. For example, if you had an integrated LTC policy with three year duration of benefits that paid a maximum daily benefit of $100 per day for nursing home care, $75 per day for assisted living care, and $50 per day for home care, that policy would cover $100 per day for three years if you were in a nursing home, $75 per day for four years in an assisted living facility, or $50 per day for six years of long-term care in your home.

Some LTC policies limit their coverage to certain types of care. The level of care is distinguished as skilled, intermediate, and custodial. Some policies provide for services such as adult day care, and some do not. Make sure you choose a policy that provides for skilled, intermediate, and custodial care. Some policies cover the cost of cleaning your home or making necessary modifications to it if required for home health care, some do not.

LTC policies require a waiting period during which the insured meets eligibility requirements, but pays for long-term care from his/her own pocket before the insurance company begins to make payments. Typical waiting periods range from a month to 100 days. Policies with longer waiting periods are less expensive. The waiting period functions exactly like a deductible for other forms of insurance. Unlike other forms of insurance the policy with the longer waiting period is not always the best deal. Examine the costs of policies with different waiting periods carefully and remember that the cost of long-term care paid out of your pocket during the waiting period will probably increase—maybe dramatically—during the life of your policy.

Avoid LTC policies that require you be hospitalized immediately before long-term care begins. Likewise, avoid policies that require you to receive care in a nursing home before you can receive care in your own home or assisted living facility.

Some policies exclude benefits if long-term care is necessary because of a mental disorder. If you choose such a policy, be sure that brain disorders, such as Alzheimer's, are not among the excluded mental disorders.

Some policies contain provisions to guard against the effects of inflation. Some of these inflation protection features compound at a specified rate continuously, others compound with simple interest, still others are tied to inflation measures like the consumer price index. You should buy a policy that contains some provision to protect you against the effects of inflation.

As with health insurance, choose a policy that is guaranteed renewable and avoid any with an optional renewability clause that makes it renewable at the option of the insurer. Non-cancelable LTC policies (where the premium is guaranteed not to increase for the life of the policy) are not commonly available at this time.

Policy premiums vary widely with this kind of insurance, so shop around. Generally, it is best to look for a policy with level or issue age rate premiums. Because of the importance of fine print in comparing LTC policies, LTC insurance may be one of the few areas where working with a good independent insurance broker may actually be worth the additional expense.

Disability Income Insurance

While health insurance and long-term care insurance protect you from the costs of medical care, disability insurance protects you from loss of income during a long illness. To be effective, a disability policy must protect you in the event of both accident and illness. Statistically the chance you will be disabled for at least three months at some point in your life is far greater than the chance you will die prematurely.

As with long-term care insurance, disability insurance is rarely available for people living outside their country of citizenship. Unless you are eligible to receive disability benefits from the social security system of another country you should plan to return to the United States to live if faced with a long-term disability, to benefit from any disability insurance you may purchase. Any expenses you encounter in such a move, whether permanent or for a few months while you recover, will not be covered by any form of insurance.

To be properly protected against a financial catastrophe from lost income during a long disability, your disability protection from all sources should provide 75%–100% of the aftertax income you live on. Most payments from disability insurance are not taxable. With your income needs covered, you can leave your long-term investments in place, as well as the income you receive from those investments. To be safe, this replacement income should be capable of continuing until you reach retirement age—if your pension plan would provide for your retirement if you were permanently disabled.

In estimating how much disability income insurance you need, only include sources of income that will continue either until your retirement or for the rest of your life. A disability income insurance provision from your employer that would provide benefits for a few months should not be included in this calculation, neither should disability payments from workers' compensation, since that only covers injuries related to your work.

To estimate how much disability income insurance you need, start with your monthly take-home pay. From this subtract the amount of income replacement you would receive each month from the sources of income listed below:

> Social security disability benefits from your Social Security Statement
>
> Any permanent disability benefits your pension plan provides
>
> Disability benefits from individual and group life insurance policies
>
> Any long-term group disability insurance or wage continuation plans provided automatically by your employer

Check with your employer and pension plan administrator to learn whether your pension plan provides any permanent disability benefits. Disability benefits from life insurance policies are not as common as they once were. Note also that disability benefits will be taxable if your employer has paid the premiums for the disability insurance plan.

Any shortfall from the above sources can be covered by disability income insurance that you buy as part of a group or association plan, or individually. Disability insurance purchased as part of a group plan will typically provide a benefit calculated as some percentage (often about 60%) of your net base pay. An individual disability income policy will usually state the benefit as a fixed monthly dollar amount.

KEY FEATURES OF DISABILITY INCOME INSURANCE

Different plans define disability differently. The most common definitions are any occupation, own occupation, and a split definition. Any occupation, the definition used by social security, is the most restrictive. By any occupation standards you are only disabled when you are incapable of any type of gainful employment. If you are able to sweep floors you are not disabled by this definition, even if before the onset of your health problem you were a pilot. By the own occupation definition you are considered disabled if you can no longer perform the occupation you had before developing your disabling health condition. A split definition applies the own occupation standard for some amount of time, typically two to five years, before applying the any occupation standard. The theory behind the split definition is that the period for which own occupation standards are applied gives you time to adjust to your disability and retrain for another occupation you find personally rewarding. The optional residual benefits provision in some disability plans, described below, combined with an any occupation policy may provide essentially the same protection as an own occupation policy, but sometimes at lower cost.

Some policies carry a presumed disability clause in addition to the own occupation or any occupation disability definitions. Under a presumed disability clause, conditions specified in the policy will be considered a disability without having to be measured against the any occupation standard. Typical conditions that meet this condition include complete deafness and total blindness.

Most disability policies contain a probationary period, typically one month, between the time the policy is purchased and the time it takes effect. Disability policies also contain a waiting period, also known as an elimination period. As in long-term care policies, the waiting period is the amount of time a person must be disabled according to the policy definition, before the insurance company begins to pay benefits. Waiting periods vary from one week to a year or more. Choosing a policy with a longer waiting period reduces the policy premium dramatically, since short duration disabilities are much more common than long-term or permanent disabilities. In deciding which waiting period to choose, consider factors such as any temporary sick pay benefits or short-term disability coverage provided by your employer. Also consider the liquid assets you have saved in your self-insurance fund. Keep in mind the other demands that may be made on your reserves during this time by the deductible and co-insurance payments for your medical insurance. Disability policies with waiting periods of three months are typically only about half as expensive as policies with two-week waiting periods. You can save many thousands of dollars in premium costs over the long-term by choosing a policy with a longer waiting period. If your employer covers you for short-term disability you can save this money at no risk and no cost.

Some disability policies offer adjustable rates. As you get older the chances you will suffer a long-term disability increase. Thus the cost to insure against a disability also increases. Like life insurance, adjustable rate disability premiums go up as you age. Also like life insurance, companies offer level premium policies that average the premium you pay over the long run. In this way you pay higher premiums than required while you are young, but pay relatively lower premiums (still level in dollar amount) when you are older and more at risk. Some companies offer disability policies that are adjustable, but convertible to a level premium policy in the future.

Under current tax law any disability insurance benefits you receive from a policy you bought with aftertax dollars are tax-free. If your employer pays the disability insurance premiums for you, those payments are a pretax benefit to you, so any benefit payments you receive from that insurance are taxable as ordinary income.

One small benefit of many policies is that they waive your disability insurance premium for some period of time—typically two to three months—after you become disabled. Some disability policies offer a residual benefit that allows you to continue to receive some fraction of your disability benefit even after you go back to work, if the work you perform after becoming disabled pays you less than you earned before the disability. Such a clause can be added to an any occupation policy to provide substantially the same benefits an own occupation policy would provide. The any occupation provision protects you if you become totally disabled and cannot work at all. If you recover to the point that you can go back to work, but must take a lower paying job because of residual effects of your disability, the residual benefit clause would make you eligible to continue to receive some disability benefits to supplement the income from your new work.

Since disability insurance is a long-term prospect you should build some mechanism into the policy to protect it from the eventual effects of inflation. One way to do this is to buy a policy with a cost of living allowance provision that increases the benefit paid according to some formula, usually tied to an inflation measure such as the consumer price index. Another way to do this is to include a guaranteed insurability option in the policy. Such an option guarantees you will be able to buy additional disability coverage at any time in the future. Some such options are written to guarantee that you can buy this additional coverage at the prices in effect when you first bought your original disability policy. This feature guarantees you the right to buy additional disability insurance in the future without any need to prove you are still insurable.

Guaranteed insurability can also be useful as you advance in your career. Benefits sufficient to replace 75%–100% of your aftertax income today may leave you underinsured 20 years from now, when your career may have advanced considerably and your salary as well. Once you stop working you no longer need disability insurance.

As with other types of health related insurance, be sure to choose a policy that the insurance company cannot cancel at its discretion.

LIFE INSURANCE

Because of traditionally high commissions on life insurance sales, life insurance policies have long been a favorite of insurance salesmen. When shopping for life insurance you are more likely to encounter high-pressure sales tactics than with any other kind of insurance; disability and long-term care insurance probably tie for second place. Those who sell it have hailed life insurance as a financial panacea. This is not the case. Life insurance should not be used as an investment vehicle, but only as a way to compensate for the lost income a family would suffer should one of its major earners die prematurely. The one other reasonable—if obscure—use for life insurance is as an estate-planning tool for high networth individuals. To use life insurance in this way you should rely on the advice of a competent tax attorney—never an insurance salesperson or an ordinary financial planner.

Broadly speaking, there are two kinds of life insurance, term insurance and cash value insurance. Term life insurance provides a payment in the event of the death of the person insured by the policy. Cash value policies, which come in several varieties including whole life, universal life and variable universal life, amount to life insurance connected to a highly restricted savings and investment account. Insurance salespeople earn the largest commissions for cash value policies because these policies make the most money for the insurance company—and are the worst deal for the policyholder. Life insurance policies do enjoy certain tax benefits under current U.S. tax laws, but those tax benefits are not sufficient to outweigh the drawbacks inherent in using life insurance as an investment tool. In addition, there is no guarantee the tax advantage life insurance currently enjoys will still be in place by the time you or your heirs can benefit from them. If you need life insurance, purchase term life insurance.

If you are single, or if you are part of a two-career family, and have no children, you probably do not need life insurance. If you have children, and especially if one family member provides most of the family's income, then you probably do need life insurance. If you need life insurance you probably need a great deal of it, since investment of the money the policy would pay upon the death of the insured person must be sufficient to replace the income the deceased family member would have earned over the years to come.

Term Life Insurance

Term life insurance policies are issued for a fixed duration, or term. Any term life insurance policy you buy should be guaranteed renewable. If you buy a guaranteed renewable policy you will not have to prove that you are in good health, and hence insurable, every time you renew your policy. Many term policies contain provisions that guarantee the policyholder the right to renew for some number of years or until some age.

As you age the chance of death increases, so the cost of the term life insurance goes up. Term life insurance for the elderly is very expensive, if it is available at all. Thankfully, by the time we reach our twilight years we usually have fewer people depending on the income we produce, hence we have less need for life insurance. If you have a defined benefit pension make certain you choose the distribution method that allows for your spouse to continue to receive some pension benefits after your death.

Term insurance policies that provide a constant death benefit for the life of the policy are called straight term or level term policies. With these the death benefit is set at some level for the duration of the policy, the premiums the customer pays increase as the insured person gets older. One alternative to this is decreasing term insurance. With decreasing term insurance the premium you pay remains the same, but the size of the death benefit decreases, as you grow older. Decreasing term insurance is useful when the amount of life insurance you need declines over the years—as when the policy exists to cover the outstanding principal on a home mortgage.

LIFE INSURANCE KEY POINTS

Buy Only Term Life Insurance—Insurance companies and insurance agents try very hard to sell other forms of life insurance because they make more money from them. Recently many sales commissions on cash value policies have dropped because of competitive pressure. Whether no-load, low-load, or a policy that provides a full commission for the sales person, you should avoid everything except term life insurance.

In trying to sell cash value life insurance, sales representatives use policy illustrations that invariably show a huge cash value for the policy that develops tax-free over the long-term. When the interest earned on the cash value in such a policy grows large enough to pay the premium, you no longer need to pay the premiums. Some policy illustrations show this happening after ten or fewer years. These policy illustrations are nothing more than an illustration of the power of compounding. They show an outcome based on long-range assumptions for inflation and interest rates that are carefully chosen to help sell insurance policies.

If you already own a cash value policy be aware that some insurance sales representatives try very hard to get people to switch cash value policies every few years. Most of the salesperson's commission on a cash value policy is paid in the first ten years. If a person switches cash value insurance every few years he/she will constantly pay new sales commissions, making the sales person rich and building nothing in the cash value account of the policy. Instead of switching to a new cash value policy, consider replacing your cash value policy with term life insurance.

If you already own a cash value policy you should carefully evaluate your situation, rather than simply continuing to make payments on your existing policy. You probably would be better off without your cash value policy. How you extricate yourself from the policy to your best advantage depends on many factors. If you have owned the cash value policy for five or fewer years your best course is probably to simply drop the cash value policy for its surrender value—if any. Count the money you lost paying high premiums toward tuition in the school of hard knocks. If you need life insurance protection, buy term life insurance.

If you have been paying for a cash value policy for many years your options are more complex. State nonforfeiture laws require cash value life insurance policies to carry provisions that allow you to get out of your policy without losing all the money you have paid into it. The best way to leave your cash value policy depends on the details of your policy and whether, upon examination, you find that you still need life insurance protection. If you do not need life insurance protection, or need much less than your old cash value policy provided, consider surrendering your policy for its current cash value. If you do this, the insurance company will pay you the cash value you have in your policy and drop your insurance coverage. If your policy's cash value exceeds the net premiums you have paid for the policy you will be liable to pay U.S. income tax on the excess amount.

If you still need life insurance protection you have two other options. You may be able to declare your policy reduced and paid-up. In doing so, you stop making payments on this policy, but leave the current cash value of the policy intact. You accept a lower death benefit on your policy in return for paying no further premiums. The new death benefit will be based on the premiums paid by the interest the current cash value earns. If you need additional life insurance beyond this amount buy a term life insurance policy to supplement this policy.

Another option may be extended term insurance, in which you exchange the cash value of the policy for a term life insurance policy paying the full death benefit provided by the cash value policy. The length of time this term policy is in force depends on the price of term insurance when you exercise this option and the cash value in your insurance policy.

Buy only a term life insurance policy that is guaranteed renewable—
The term of the policy is usually less important than the fact that
the policy is guaranteed renewable for the entire time you need
life insurance. Your health, habits, age, and family health history
when you first purchase a life insurance policy greatly affect what
you will pay for the policy. If you are in bad health you may not be
insurable at all. If you hold a renewable term policy and develop a
health problem that would otherwise affect your rates, the guaranteed renewable clause will protect you from increased costs or
loss of insurance. Once you have a policy with such a provision,
you do not need to prove you are insurable to renew your policy
under the same terms. Any medical condition you develop will
not be factored into the pricing for such a renewed policy.

*Buy your life insurance from one solid company—*Like many things,
the cost of life insurance often goes down when purchased in bulk.
It is usually less expensive, and certainly less cumbersome, to
buy all of your life insurance from one company. The corollary is
that you must be sure that company is financially sound and remains financially sound so that it can pay the benefits if needed.
Term life insurance at reduced rates is often available as group or
association insurance. Explore these options and compare rates
and features for such insurance before you buy life insurance as
an individual.

*Do not pay for a multiple indemnity clause—*Most often this is a
double indemnity clause, that pays twice the death benefit if the
insured dies in certain ways. Paying for such a clause is nothing
more than placing a bet on how a person will die; it fulfills no
useful insurance function.

*Suicide clause—*A suicide clause frees the insurance company from
its obligation to pay a benefit if the insured person commits suicide within some period (usually two to three years) of purchasing the policy.

*Incontestability clause—*Life insurance policies contain a clause
that gives the insurance company one to two years to investigate
the information provided by the insured in applying for the policy.
If the insured lied in the application process and the insurance

company determines this within this period they can nullify the policy. After this period the insurance company can no longer challenge the validity of the policy.

Avoid credit life insurance—Credit life insurance pays off an outstanding loan upon the death of the policyholder. You can usually buy an additional decreasing term life insurance policy more cheaply than buying credit insurance from a company associated with the lender.

Policy dividends—A policy that can pay dividends to policyholders from the excess earnings of the insurance company is called a participating policy. A non-participating policy pays no dividends. This is a minor selling point. A non-participating policy with a smaller premium is usually better than paying a higher premium in the hope that you may get some of it back at the end of the year.

Policy premium payment—Insurance can be paid on an annual, quarterly, or monthly basis. Annual premiums are usually the least expensive, since they involve lower administrative costs for the insurance company. You can usually arrange for the insurance company to be paid directly from your bank account every time the premium comes due. Some term insurance policies offer discounts for the pre-payment of premiums.

Guaranteed rate structures—A term policy with a guaranteed rate structure fixes the initial premium when the policy is first purchased and the rate at which premiums will increase in the future. As the insured person ages the premiums go up, but the customer knows when the policy is first purchased exactly what premiums he/she will be paying at a given age. An indeterminate premium policy may change the rate schedule every time the policy is renewed. Such policies are usually initially less expensive than those with guaranteed rate structures, since they give the insurance company more flexibility to raise premiums to offset inflation or unexpected losses.

Lower rates for better risks—Some insurance companies offer lower rates to people who are better risks. You may be a better risk if you are not overweight, do not smoke, and do not have a family history of serious disease. If you have such characteristics you may save money by buying a policy from a company offering these rate reductions. If you are not in this low risk group you may find better prices with companies that do not offer preferred risk rates since those companies group everybody together when pricing their policies.

Ability to reduce the amount of insurance—Some term policies allow you to reduce the amount of insurance you carry. Since people often need less life insurance later in life, and since life insurance rates go up as people age, this can be an important feature.

HOW MUCH LIFE INSURANCE DO YOU NEED?

The amount of life insurance you need depends on your circumstances. If you are single and have no children you probably do not need life insurance. If you are retired and your retirement income will continue for your spouse, you probably do not need life insurance. If you are married with no children and your spouse earns enough money to continue his/her lifestyle without you, you probably need either no life insurance, or perhaps enough to pay off all or part of your home mortgage. If you have children to support, particularly young children, or have a spouse who does not work and could not be expected to earn enough to continue the family's present lifestyle, you may need quite a lot of life insurance. Life insurance needs decrease as your children grow up and leave home. That need for insurance vanishes once you retire and make provisions for your spouse to continue receiving retirement income after your death.

If you need life insurance to insure against a particular expense—such as an outstanding balance on a home mortgage—then the amount of life insurance you need is simple. Buy enough life insurance to cover the current costs you want to insure against.

If you need life insurance to replace all or part of the earnings of a major income producer for the family the calculation is more complicated. One well-known—but not always accurate—rule of thumb is to buy life insurance with a benefit equal to ten times your annual earnings. A detailed analysis of your financial situation to approximate the amount your heirs will need is another approach. A practical approach is to estimate the size of the life insurance benefit that would be needed to replace the earnings that the insured person brings to the family, once that insurance benefit is invested.

To estimate the size of the insurance benefit you need, begin with the yearly take-home earnings of the insured person. This is the amount that will have to be replaced by investment of the life insurance benefit if the person were to die. We assume other investment income, alimony payments to the surviving spouse from previous marriages, rental income, and other such income will remain unaffected if the insured person dies. From the yearly take home earnings subtract the annual amount your family would receive from social security as survivor benefits, based on the Social Security Statement you receive each year from the U.S. Social Security Administration. If your pension plan contains a premature death provision that pays survivors pension benefits if you die while employed, subtract that yearly sum as well. If the insured person, or the insured person's spouse, qualifies for benefits from the social security system of another country, and that system would offer survivor benefits to the family of the deceased, subtract that amount as well. To replace the rest of the money the insured person would have earned every year the life insurance benefit needs to be invested.

In addition to income replacement, the life insurance benefit should cover final expenses. A reasonable allowance for final expenses is one third to half a year of annual take-home income. Most international health insurance policies contain provisions for repatriation of remains if you die overseas. If your policy does not contain such a provision, your family will need to cover this expense out of your self-insurance fund.

An insurance benefit cannot be invested in a tax-free account such as a Roth IRA, so investment returns on the benefit will be subject to taxation. In our example, we assume an aftertax investment return of 8.5%. Using your assumed aftertax return and the duration for which replacement income is needed, use Table 4, Lump Sum Factors, in Appendix C, to calculate the size of the life insurance benefit needed to replace the lost yearly income. Inflation will increase the income that needs to be replaced each year and Table 4 incorporates an inflation rate of 3%, the historical average.

A worksheet follows to guide you through the estimate of the amount of life insurance you need to replace an insured person's income.

Life Insurance Needs

EXAMPLE

A couple, both aged 35 with a five-year-old child. One person is working and earns $40,000 per year aftertax.

INCOME

They begin the estimate with the take home income of the person they want to insure. Get this number from last year's records, probably off of the end of the year pay stub. This is the amount of income you will need to replace if the insured person dies.

SOCIAL SECURITY

The best estimate of the social security survivor benefit comes from the Social Security Statement you receive from the Social Security Administration. If you don't yet have that number you can use a rougher approximation based on the average social security benefit for your family size and age. This is available in Chapter 10, Financial Risk Management–Social Security. Social security benefits are given as a monthly number so multiply the benefit by 12 to get a yearly estimate. In this example, a check of their Social Security Statement indicates the surviving parent and child could expect to receive $1800 per month ($21,600 per year), until the child turns 16. At that point the parent would lose social security benefits, but the child would continue to receive $900 per month until age 18. The family decides that after the child is in high school, the surviving parent could take a job and probably earn $21,000 aftertax to replace the loss of social security benefits. In this example, they decide to use $21,000 as the social security survivor benefit.

PENSIONS

This refers to any pension benefits that would be paid to survivors if the person died while employed. It also includes any social security survivor benefits from a social security system other than that provided by the United States social security system. If you have such benefits you can learn the details from your employer or the foreign country. If this is a monthly amount multiply it by 12 to get a yearly benefit amount. In this example, the employed person's company pension plan offers no death or survivor benefits, but will pay the surviving spouse a pension when he/she reaches retirement age. The only social security this family qualifies for is from the United States government, and the surviving family members plan to return to the United States to live if the main income producer dies.

INCOME REPLACEMENT NEEDED

This is the amount of annual income that would not be replaced by social security and pension benefits. In this example, subtracting the social security benefit from the take-home income leaves $19,000 per year that will have to be replaced by life insurance, so that the surviving parent could maintain the family lifestyle until eligible to receive social security and retirement benefits.

DURATION OF INCOME

Calculate the number of years you would need to depend on income from a life insurance benefit before the surviving spouse becomes eligible for retirement benefits, or for that spouse's remaining life expectancy. In this example, they will need to maintain that income until age 65—30 years from now—so they enter 30 on line 5 of the worksheet.

AFTERTAX RATE OF RETURN

Your aftertax rate of return is the total investment return minus the taxes your owe on that return. Since the insurance benefit will be invested over a long time frame, you can invest the insurance benefit in stock mutual funds where your expected rate of return may be 11%, the historical average. You may wish to favor large capitalization and value investment styles of stock mutual funds when investing an insurance benefit. (You can read more on this topic in Chapter 11, Investment Management.) With a long-term horizon for your investments, much of your return may be in the form of long-term capital gains, which are currently taxed at 20% in the United States. In this example, we assume a U.S. long-term capital gains tax rate of 20% plus 1% to account for distributions that will be taxed at your marginal tax rate. If you are in a high tax bracket (greater than 35%) you should add two or three percent rather than one percent to your 20% effective tax rate. Using the one percent correction, an estimate of the aftertax annual rate of return from stock investments is 8.5% (11% × [100% - 21%] ÷ 100%, rounded down to the nearest 0.5%).

INSURANCE BENEFIT TO REPLACE INCOME

Since investment of the life insurance benefit will need to replace the lost income for 30 years, in this example, they use Table 4, Lump Sum Factors, in Appendix C, to find the number corresponding to an aftertax return of 8.5% for 30 years. This number is 14.5372. Multiplying this number times the amount of income that needs to be replaced—$19,000 in this case—yields $276,000, which is an estimate of the life insurance benefit needed to replace that income for that length of time.

FINAL EXPENSES

Allowing half a year's annual take home income for final expenses, we enter an estimate of $20,000 in this example.

INSURANCE BENEFIT REQUIRED

Adding the final expenses ($20,000) to the insurance benefit needed to replace income ($276,000) gives an estimate of the total insurance benefit required. In this example, they come up with a total of about $296,000. Term insurance coverage for a healthy 35-year-old male might cost $3.75 per year per $1000. For a female this might cost $2.90 per year per $1000. If the father was the principal breadwinner $296,000 of term life insurance might cost about $1,110 per year ($3.75 times 296). This same amount of insurance for the mother would cost $860.

LIFE INSURANCE BENEFIT WORKSHEET

1. TAKE-HOME EARNINGS

Enter the total yearly take-home earnings
of the person you need to insure $40,000

2. SOCIAL SECURITY SURIVOR BENEFIT

Get this from your Social Security
Statement $21,000

3. PENSION BENEFITS

Survivor benefits from company pension
system or foreign social security   0

4. UNCOVERED EARNINGS

Subtract the amounts on lines 2 and 3
from the amount on line 1 $19,000

5. DURATION OF INCOME

Number of years the replacement earnings
will be required   30

6. AFTERTAX RATE OF RETURN   8.5%

7. LUMP SUM FACTOR

Enter the number from Table 4, Lump Sum
Factors, based on a your aftertax return in line 6
and the duration listed on line 5   14.5372

8. BENEFIT TO REPLACE EARNINGS

Multiply the number on line 7 by the sum
on line 4 $276,207

9. FINAL EXPENSES

Enter an estimate for final expenses $20,000

10. REQUIRED BENEFIT

Add the numbers on lines 8 and 9 $296,207

Insurance needs change as conditions in a family change. If we re-examined the family in this example 20 years later the results would look quite different. Now 55 years old with aftertax earnings of $60,000 per year and $15,000 per year of investment income, their child would be 25 and living independently. They might decide the surviving non-working spouse could get by comfortably on $30,000 per year aftertax. The $15,000 in investment income would continue unaffected, which leaves $15,000 of income to be replaced by life insurance. Since the surviving spouse is eligible to receive a pension and full social security retirement benefits in ten years, the insurance benefit need only supply the $15,000 per year for ten years. Using the Lump Sum Factor for ten years at 8.5% we see this calls for an insurance benefit of $115,470. ($15,000 × 7.6979). To this we add $20,000 to cover final expenses, to come up with about $135,470 of life insurance needed. Although this is less than half the insurance the family needed at age 35, term life insurance for a 55 year old male would cost about $19 per $1000, for a total life insurance bill of $2,570 per year.

10. FINANCIAL RISK MANAGEMENT– SOCIAL SECURITY

The United States social security system was established in 1935 and was originally intended to be a government administered mandatory insurance system to provide a minimum guaranteed retirement income for Americans. In 1939 the plan for social security to function as insurance was scrapped and the current pay-as-you-go system was adopted. This means that rather than social security recipients receiving money derived from the invest ment of payments they and their employers made during thei working years, the money they receive comes directly from pay ments made by others who are now working. This system allowec the government to expand the scope of social security in 1939 tc include payments to dependents and survivors of social security recipients, regardless of whether they had ever contributed to the social security system themselves.

Social security, officially known as Old Age, Survivors, and Disability Insurance (OASDI) is mandatory for most Americans, although some civilian federal government employees covered under the Civil Service Retirement System are exempt, as are employees of U.S. state and local governments who choose not to participate.

The future of social security is uncertain because of political issues and demographics. As the baby-boom generation retires and begins to collect social security, their payments will come from contributions made by a much smaller workforce. Many experts expect the social security system to collapse under the strain. Nonetheless, you may want to factor the benefits from social security into your retirement, life insurance and disability insurance planning. To help you in this process, this chapter presents general eligibility requirements and benefits. In addition, it outlines particular treaty agreements and other regulations that affect U.S. citizens living outside the United States.

ELIGIBILITY AND BENEFITS

The best way to learn about your eligibility and potential benefits from social security is to request a copy of your Social Security Statement from the Social Security Administration. (The Social Security Statement replaces the Personal Earnings and Benefit Estimate Statement. Starting October 1, 1999, Social Security Statements will be mailed annually to each contributor to U.S. social security approximately three months before their birthday.) You can receive this statement by contacting the Social Security Administration in the United States by mail, phone, or via their Website. This statement will include the Social Security Administration's record of your earnings and social security taxes paid to date. It is worthwhile checking these numbers against your own records, keeping in mind that only earnings on which you have paid U.S. social security taxes will be reported. The statement will also indicate your eligibility for the various social security benefits and, where eligible, your estimated retirement, survivors, and disability benefits. These figures are a good foundation to use in your financial planning calculations.

You can contact the Social Security Administration at:

Social Security Administration
PO Box 20
Wilkes Barre, PA 18767-0020
Phone: 800-772-1213
Website: http://www.ssa.gov

Because it takes some time to receive your estimates from the Social Security Administration, national average benefit amounts are provided below for your use in preliminary planning. When you receive personalized estimates, from your Social Security Statement, replace the national average benefits with the Social Security Administration's estimates in your financial planning.

General Eligibility Information

In general, you are entitled to social security benefits after working and contributing to the social security system for a total of 40 quarters, ten years. Those who have contributed to social security for 40 quarters are fully insured. Should you die, your survivors—spouse and dependents—may be eligible to receive survivor benefits. A person without the requisite ten years of contributions will be considered insured and survivor benefits may be paid if the person had six quarters of coverage during the 3-year period preceeding the date of death. Eligibility for disability coverage varies. There is no simple formula to determine if you are eligible for disability benefits from social security, it depends on your age, and the number of months you have paid social security taxes since you were 21 years of age.

Retirement Benefits

The age at which you can retire and receive social security retirement benefits also varies, depending on when you were born. As originally envisioned, the social security system provided retirement benefits when participants reached 65 years of age. People can elect to begin receiving social security retirement benefits at 62 years of age, but these benefits are reduced by 20% from what they would be if the person waited until age 65 to begin collecting. Social security amendments, passed in 1983, are gradually pushing the standard social security retirement age up to age 67—from age 65—between 2005 and 2027. This change is aimed at helping the social security system stay solvent while it pays benefits to the baby-boom generation. The reduction in benefits for those choosing to begin receiving benefits at age 62 will also increase. In 2027 a person electing to begin receiving social security benefits at age 62 will receive 70%—a reduction of 30%—of what they would receive if they waited until age 67 to begin collecting payments.

The calculation of U.S. social security retirement benefits involves several steps, which are described in SSA Publication No. 05-100700, *How Your Retirement Benefit is Figured.* Here is a brief description. First, your actual earnings (up to a given maximum) are indexed to inflation. (The index factor and maximum earnings for each year are given in SSA Publication No. 05-100700.) Second, the average of your monthly indexed earnings is calculated based on the 35 years in which you had the highest earnings. Next, your monthly average earnings are divided into three amounts, which are multiplied by three different factors to determine your social security benefit. The first $505 of your average monthly indexed earnings are multiplied by 90%. The next $2,538 are multiplied by 32% and any remaining earnings are multiplied by 15%.

The Social Security Administration has a program on its website that allows you to calculate your own retirement benefit, but you will still need to request a Social Security Statement to learn what your survivors and disability benefits would be. To give you a general idea, in 1997 the minimum full retirement benefit was about $745 per month, and the average full retirement benefit for a couple that year was $1,256. These amounts vary (usually increase slowly) with time, since a cost of living adjustment is automatically applied to social security benefits to help protect the recipients from inflation.

The spouse of a social security retirement benefit recipient is entitled to a benefit equal to one half of the benefit paid to the spouse who is covered by social security. If that spouse is entitled to a social security retirement him/herself, they have the option of taking the larger of their own benefit or one half of their spouse's benefit.

If a person receiving social security retirement benefits has a child under 18 years of age, or under 19 years of age and still attending high school, or has a child that became permanently disabled before reaching 22 years of age, then that child is entitled to receive a benefit equal to one half of the recipient's retirement benefit.

A divorced person can receive social security benefits like a spouse, widow, or widower as long as the marriage lasted for ten years, the ex-spouse was fully insured under social security, and has retired, died, or become disabled. The divorced person need not have contributed to social security. As with a spouse, widow, or widower, the benefit to the divorced person depends on the earnings of the ex-spouse.

There is a maximum retirement benefit that can be paid to any family, which in 1997 was about $1,989 per month. An average couple with only one person contributing to social security might expect to collect a full retirement benefit of $1,256, based on the 1997 average. If that couple decided to retire at age 62 rather than age 65–67, they would receive roughly $880–$1,005 per month (70%–80% of $1,256, depending on the year in which they were born).

Remember that these figures are only rough approximations: You may receive more reliable estimates from the Social Security Administration. There is not even any guarantee the social security system will still exist by the time you are in a position to receive any benefits. Nonetheless, you may want to factor social security retirement benefits into your retirement planning; few of us are likely to turn down $500–$1,000 per month in retirement if it is available and we are entitled to it.

Survivor Benefits

Since most people need life insurance before reaching an eligible age to collect retirement benefits, social security survivor benefits are at least as relevant to your life insurance planning as social security retirement benefits are for your retirement planning. As with retirement benefits, the only way to get reliable information about your status in the system, and the benefits your survivors would be eligible to receive, is to ask the Social Security Administration for your Social Security Statement. Survivor benefits are calculated as a percentage of a figure known as the social security contributor's primary insurance amount (PIA).

Social security survivor benefits currently include:

>A one-time cash payment of $255

>For each child under 18 years of age, or 19 years of age and attending high school full time, or disabled before reaching 22 years of age, a benefit equal to 75% of the PIA

>For a surviving spouse with children less than 16 years of age or disabled and "in care" a benefit equal to 75% of the PIA

>A widow or widowers benefit for the surviving spouse once they reach age 60

>A surviving dependent parent benefit for parents of the deceased, under some circumstances

Benefits for a surviving spouse stop once all the children reach 16 years of age, although each child's benefits continue until age 18. If the surviving spouse chooses to begin receiving survivor benefits at age 60 they will receive an amount less than the PIA. If the widow or widower elects to begin receiving these benefits at age 65 (or age 67 depending on their date of birth) they will receive the full PIA benefit.

Dependent surviving parent benefits are extremely complicated. Under some circumstances dependent parents who received at least half of their support from their deceased offspring may be eligible to receive up to 75%, or more, of the PIA benefit.

In 1997 a widow or widower received an average survivor benefit of $687 per month. A young widow or widower with two children received an average family benefit of $1,478 per month. The maximum survivor benefit a family can receive is usually 150%–180% of the PIA—approximately $2,614 per month in 1997.

As an example, consider a family of four, with two children aged five and seven. Assume a PIA of $800. If the working parent who is eligible for social security survivor benefits died, the surviving parent and each of the children would receive a monthly survivor benefit of $600 (75% of $800). The family would receive a one-time payment of $255 and thereafter benefits totaling $1800 per month until the youngest child reached the age of 16. That year, with the oldest child reaching 18 years of age and the youngest 16, the family's benefits would be reduced twice. The surviving parent would lose his/her benefit for being the parent of a child under 16 years of age, and the oldest child (assuming he/she was not still in high school) would lose his/her benefit. In this year the family's social security benefits would drop from $1800 per month to $600, with the only remaining benefit belonging to the youngest child. That benefit would continue until that child reached 18. The children would be entitled to no further social security benefits based on their parents' earnings, and the surviving spouse would receive no further social security benefits until he/she reached 60 years of age (65–67 to receive the full $800 per month).

Disability Benefits

As with survivor benefits, you are likely to need disability insurance before retirement, so social security plays a role in disability insurance planning. Eligibility for disability benefits under social security is particularly complicated; it depends on the age of the insured at the time of the disability, the number of quarters the insured has paid social security taxes, and the nature and extent of the disability. Most people working in jobs where they contribute to social security are covered by the disability benefits provision.

To be considered disabled for the purpose of social security benefits you must be either blind or unable to engage in any substantial activity because of a medically identifiable physical or mental impairment which is expected to last for 12 continuous months or can be expected to result in death. Note that if you cannot do your regular job, but can perform other substantial gainful work, you will not be considered disabled by social security.

Social security disability benefits can be paid to the disabled person; that person's children, if under 18 years of age, or under 19 and attending high school, or disabled before reaching age 22; that person's spouse if he/she has children under 16 years of age; or that person's spouse if he/she is 62 years of age or older.

The following are some features of social security disability benefits:

Benefits only begin after a full five-month waiting period following the disability, i.e., they begin six months after the disability

Each child under 18 receives 50% of the basic benefit

A spouse with children under 16 receives 50% of the basic benefit

In 1997 average disability benefits were $704 per month for a disabled social security contributor and $1,169 per month for a family consisting of a disabled social security contributor, a spouse, and two children

Maximum benefits in 1997 were roughly $1,508 per month for the disabled person and about $2,262 per month for his/her complete family

Any dependent receiving social security disability benefits, who earns more than a certain amount ($8,640 in 1997) may have their benefits reduced

The only reliable estimate of what you may expect in disability benefits from social security will appear on your Social Security Statement from the Social Security Administration.

As an example, consider a family of four with children aged five and eight and the primary income provider eligible for a basic disability benefit of $900 per month. If the primary provider becomes permanently disabled the family will receive no disability benefits from social security for the first five full months. On the sixth month the disabled person would begin receiving monthly benefits of $900 per month. Also on this date, the other parent (because he/she has a child under 16) would begin receiving a benefit of $450, and each of the children would begin to receive a benefit of $450 per month, for a total potential family benefit of $2,250 per month. In ten years, when the oldest child turns 18 and the youngest turns 15, the family's monthly benefit would drop to $1800 ($900 for the disabled parent, $450 for the other parent because of the 15-year-old, and $450 for the 15-year-old). The 18-year-old child would lose benefits. A year later, the other parent would lose benefits, because the youngest child turned 16. The disabled person would continue to receive $900 and the 16-year-old child $450. These benefits would drop to $900 two years later when the youngest child turned 18. The $900 per month disability benefit would continue until social security retirement benefits begin at age 65–67.

SOCIAL SECURITY BENEFITS UNDER TOTALIZATION AGREEMENTS

The United States has established bilateral agreements with 17 countries that help Americans working overseas avoid paying both U.S. social security taxes and the equivalent taxes in any of the agreement countries. These totalization agreements also help you to qualify for social security benefits. The countries and the effective date of their totalization agreements with the United States are:

Austria	November 1, 1991
Belgium	July 1, 1984
Canada	August 1, 1984
Finland	November 1, 1992
France	July 1, 1988
Germany	December 1, 1979
Greece	September 1, 1994
Ireland	September 1, 1993
Italy	November 1, 1978
Luxembourg	November 1, 1993
Netherlands	November 1, 1990

Norway	July 1, 1984
Portugal	August 1, 1989
Spain	April 1, 1988
Sweden	January 1, 1987
Switzerland	November 1, 1980
United Kingdom	January 1, 1985

To qualify for U.S. social security retirement benefits you must have accumulated 40 credits (40 quarters—ten years—of work history paying U.S. social security taxes). If you have worked outside the United States for much of your career you may not have the requisite credits. If you have earned a minimum of six credits in the United States you can add credits earned in one of the above 17 countries to reach the required 40 credits. You can use only one country—these agreements are bilateral, not multilateral—but you can choose the country where you have garnered the most credits. The effective date indicates when U.S. citizens working in one of the bilateral treaty countries could avoid paying two sets of social security taxes. Before the effective date, U.S. citizens, living and working in one of the countries listed above, had to pay social security taxes to that country just as they would to any country that did not have a totalization agreement with the United States. When those taxes were paid, credits were accrued in that country, but U.S. citizens could not use the credits to qualify for U.S. social security benefits. Credits accrued in any of the above 17 countries—whether those credits were accrued before or after the effective date of the totalization agreement—can now be applied toward qualifying for U.S. social security benefits.

These are reciprocal agreements, meaning U.S. social security credits can be applied toward qualifying for social security benefits in any of the 17 countries where you have accumulated social security credits. The number of years you need to pay into the social security system of one of the above 17 countries varies from three to 40 years, with most requiring an earnings history (payment of their social security taxes) of 10–15 years. In addition, several countries have a two-tiered system, requiring you to meet certain residence tests, as well as the earnings requirements.

If you have worked outside the United States but not in any of the 17 agreement countries you will not be able to add credits earned outside the United States to any credits you have earned inside the United States or visa versa. Your eligibility for social security benefits will be based solely on your earnings record in each country separately. Further, if you have paid social security taxes to the country where you live and work and also to the United States you will receive social security credits in the country where you reside, not in the United States.

Credits and earnings histories are not transferable: They remain in the country where they were earned. Credits in a treaty country only help you to qualify for social security benefits; they do not contribute to the amount of your benefit. The amount of your benefit is based solely on your earnings history in the country where you qualify for benefits—not your combined earnings histories from both countries. For example, if you have earned six credits in the United States and 34 credits from one of the totalization agreement countries, you have the required 40 credits to qualify for U.S. social security benefits. The amount of your U.S. benefit will be based solely on your earnings during the six quarters you worked in the United States. None of your earnings from the other country will be considered in calculating your U.S. benefits.

If you have earned a minimum of 40 credits in the United States you qualify for U.S. social security benefits—in your own right. Credits earned in another country are not considered. If you also qualify for social security benefits in one of the totalization agreement countries—without the aid of your U.S. credits—you fall under the Windfall Elimination Provision (WEP) and your benefits will be reduced.

SSA Publication No. 05-10045, *A Pension From Work Not Covered By Social Security: How It Affects Your Social Security Retirement or Disability Benefits,* explains, in detail, how your U.S. social security benefits will be reduced if you fall under WEP. Here is a brief description of how your U.S. benefits will be reduced. Your monthly social security benefit is based on your average monthly indexed earnings. Your monthly average indexed earnings are divided into three amounts, which are multiplied by three different factors to determine your social security retirement benefit as described in the Retirement Benefits section earlier in this chapter. Normally, the first $505 of your average monthly indexed earnings is multiplied by 90%. WEP reduces the 90% factor based on the number of years of U.S. earnings you have accumulated. If your U.S. work history spans 30 years or more, your factor remains at 90%. With less than 20 years, the factor is reduced to 40%. Between 29 and 21 years of work in the United States, the factor is gradually reduced to 45%. If you worked in the United States early in your career your average monthly indexed earnings may be $500 or less. In turn, your monthly social security retirement benefit may be $200 or less per month.

In addition, social security benefits from one of the totalization agreement countries where you qualify in your own right may also be reduced. You will have to contact the appropriate governmental body in that country to determine your benefits. Links to many of these offices are available at the U.S. Social Security Administration website. In addition, copies of any of the totalization agreements are available in full or in brief at their website. You can also contact the U.S. embassy in your host country or write or call the Social Security Administration Office of International Programs at:

> Social Security Administration
> Office of International Programs
> P.O. Box 17741
> Baltimore, MD 21235-7741
> Phone: +1-410-965-3548
> or +1-410-965-3554
> Website: http://www.ssa.gov/international

ANNUAL EXEMPTION AMOUNTS

If you are receiving U.S. social security benefits they can be reduced if you work and your earnings exceed certain levels. Beneficiaries under 65 years of age, earning more than $10,080 a year ($840 per month) will see a reduction of one dollar in social security benefits for every two dollars they earn over this amount.

Beneficiaries aged 65–69, will lose one dollar in benefits for every three dollars they earn over $17,000 a year ($1,416.66 per month). An annual exemption amount is not applied to the earnings of beneficiaries aged 70 or older.

The above discussion only applies to earnings that are subject to U.S. social security taxation. If you are working overseas your earnings may not be subject to U.S. social security taxes. Unless you are working for a U.S. firm or one of its affiliates in one of the 17 totalization agreement countries, you are most likely paying social security taxes to your host country's government. (For further details on which country's social security taxes you will pay if working overseas in one of the 17 totalization agreement countries, see Chapter 12, Tax Management.)

If you work and pay social security taxes to your host country, while receiving U.S. social security benefits, the U.S. social security *Foreign Work Test* applies to you. Put simply, you cannot work more than 45 hours a month without losing your entire monthly U.S. social security benefit. The 45-hour limit applies whether you are self-employed, work for someone else, or even if you took leave equivalent to more than 45 hours and did not actually work. Not only do you lose your benefits, but other family members receiving benefits on your record (called the Master Beneficiary Record) lose their benefits as well. However, work they perform does not count toward the 45-hour work limit. For details see SSA Publication No. 05-10137, *Social Security—Your Payments While You Are Outside The United States* Part 8-B.) Once you reach age 70 you are no longer subject to the foreign work test and your U.S. social security benefit will not be reduced regardless of how many hours you work.

The foreign work test has an additional facet to it. SSA Publication No. 05-10137 states: "A person is considered to be working on any day he or she: ... is the owner or part owner of a trade or business even if he or she does not actually work in the trade or business or receive any income from it." This seems to be aimed at U.S. citizens who own businesses overseas. The above statement indicates that U.S. citizens who own businesses overseas will forfeit their social security benefits, whether or not they pay themselves a salary or the business is making money. Once you reach age 70, you can own a business overseas and still receive your social security benefits.

Before leaving the foreign work test, here is one other question. Do you fail the foreign work test if you own shares in a publicly traded foreign company? Owning shares in a company legally makes you a part owner of that company. Since you do not have to work for or receive income from a company you partly own you could, in principle, fail the foreign work test. According to a social security spokesperson, the business ownership may be either private or public. Work is defined as any day the business is open, even if no business is conducted. The spokesperson stated that the intent is not to penalize U.S. citizens holding foreign stock as an investment. It is not clear how you would prove that a small residual ownership in a company you started overseas, retired from and then sold (except for the small residual holding) is an investment.

Should you pass the foreign work test and receive your benefits, they may be subject to taxation by either the United States or your host country or both. (See Chapter 12, Tax Management for further details.)

RECEIVING U.S. SOCIAL SECURITY BENEFITS WHILE OVERSEAS

Although you can not receive Medicare benefits while living outside of the United States, you can receive social security benefits, as can your survivors, even if they are not U.S. citizens.

How do you get your U.S. social security benefit overseas? One option is to have your U.S. social security check mailed to your overseas address. Foreign postal systems generally are reliable, but some are not. Assuming the postal system is secure, the banking system in your host country will not be able to process a U.S. check on its own. When you take your U.S. Treasury check to a local bank it will be returned to the United States for clearance. After the U.S. check clearing system has processed your check, it will be mailed back to your host country bank to go through that country's clearing system. The whole process can easily take three weeks and can cost you as much as if you had wired the money to yourself from the United States. In addition, you will still have foreign exchange charges.

Another option is to have your social security check deposited directly to a U.S. financial institution and transfer the money to your local bank account as needed. If you do this you will have easy access to your money. Your charges will include a wire transfer fee plus the cost of converting U.S. dollars to your host country's currency.

The U.S. Federal Reserve Bank of New York and several central banks around the world have agreed to provide an international direct deposit service. This service allows the transfer and conversion of U.S. social security benefits to a foreign bank free of the various charges. The countries that currently subscribe to this international direct deposit service (also called electronic benefit transfer) are:

Argentina
Australia
Canada
France
Germany
Ireland
Italy
Norway
Portugal
Spain
Sweden
United Kingdom

You cannot receive your U.S. social security payments in certain countries, namely Cambodia, Cuba, and North Korea. If you live in one of these countries payments will be withheld, but you can receive them once you move to a non-restricted country.

The specific details regarding receipt of social security benefits outside the United States vary from country to country, depending on bilateral treaties between the United States and various countries around the globe. For details about social security payments while you are outside the United States, obtain a copy of SSA Publication No. 05-10137, ICN 480085 by mail from the Social Security Administration, at your nearest U.S. Embassy or Consulate, or from a social security office in the United States. The document is available in English, French, German, Greek, Italian, and Spanish. A summary of this document is also available online at the Social Security Administration's website at http://www.ssa.gov. This website contains a wealth of information.

Medicare Premiums

While you cannot receive Medicare benefits overseas, you can choose to not pay Medicare insurance premiums. (Normally, Medicare insurance premiums are deducted from your U.S. social security payments.) If you live overseas for an extended period of time and then return to the United States, you can again pay Medicare insurance premiums by having them deducted from your social security benefits at that time. However, your premiums will be 10% higher for each 12-month period you were not enrolled in the Medicare program. You also have the option to remain enrolled in the Medicare program while living overseas and to have Medicare insurance premiums deducted from your social security payments.

11. INVESTMENT MANAGEMENT

To manage your investments you must first understand the basic principles of investing. These include an understanding of compounding, investment returns, and investment risks. These topics are covered in the first section of this chapter, Basic Investment Principles. Once you are grounded in these concepts, you are ready to begin the investment process with an understanding of the three most important investment tools you will use: your cash management account, Treasury bills, and stock mutual funds. The second section of this chapter, The Investment Process, covers these topics and discusses building a portfolio of mutual funds, different types of investors, and different approaches to investing.

BASIC INVESTMENT PRINCIPLES

In this section, you will learn how compounding dramatically impacts the amount you need to save to achieve a goal. You will also gain a basic understanding of how you can earn a return using each of the three most common types of investments: stocks, bonds, and mutual funds. Most importantly, you will gain a thorough understanding of investment risks and how to minimize your exposure to them.

Compounding

When your investments earn money, that money can also be invested, compounding the total return you earn on your original investment. The familiar example is that of a savings account. The interest you are paid also earns money as long as you leave it in the account.

This is a simple idea, but the mathematics behind it are powerful. As an example, if you invested $1,000 so that it earned 10% annually and simply left it alone for 30 years it would grow to $17,449. If it were invested at 20% instead of 10% it would grow to $237,376 in the same time, far more than double the amount from investing at the 10% rate. If the $1,000 were invested at 10% for 15 years rather than 30 it would be worth $4,177. This is much less than half the $17,449 it would reach in twice the time.

Another way to look at this is to examine how compounding affects how much you have to save each month to meet a particular goal. Say you have determined that you will need a $250,000 nest egg to maintain your current life style in retirement. You are comfortable investing your money to earn an average annual return of 10% and you have 20 years until you retire. You are considering postponing saving for retirement for ten years. If you wait, you will need to save $1,220 each month for the ten years just before you retire. In all, you will have to save $146,400 of your income during this period, more than half of the $250,000. If instead you start now, saving and investing for 20 years to reach your goal, you will need to save only $330 each month, one quarter of what you will need if you postpone saving for your retirement. Your total cost to reach your goal of $250,000 will be $79,200, only a third of the total. Of the $171,000 your $79,200 investment would earn you, almost half would be earned on money you invested during the first five years. Start early so your money has more time to work for you.

Stocks, Bonds and Mutual Funds

Your investment returns are determined in part by the type of financial security you buy. When you buy stock in a company, you become a part owner of the company. How much of the company you own—your equity in the company—is based on the number of shares you purchase. Owning shares in a company can be profitable in two ways. First, the company may pay some of its profits to shareholders in the form of a dividend. Dividends can be increased, decreased, or stopped at the discretion of company management. Second, investors can sell their shares to someone else for more than they paid for them. When people think ownership in a particular company is more desirable than ownership in other companies, they will pay more to own part of that company, and the company's stock price increases. Conversely, when others think a company is not as desirable they will not pay as much to buy it and the stock price goes down. You can lose money by owning stock if you are forced to sell your shares when the stock price has fallen below what you paid for your shares, or if you buy stock in a company that goes bankrupt, making your shares worthless.

When you purchase a bond you are lending that money to the bond issuer, which is usually a company or government. The bond issuer pays the bondholder interest, and agrees to repay the principal when the bond comes due. Bonds can be bought and sold on public exchanges and fluctuate in price depending on changes in interest rates and people's view of the bond issuer's ability to repay the loan. The most popular long-term loan to the U.S. government is the 30-year Treasury bond and is referred to as the government long bond. Short-term loans to the U.S. government lasting three, six, or twelve months are called Treasury bills or just T-bills.

Mutual funds are investment companies that pool together the money of their investors to buy stocks, bonds, or a combination of the two. Open-ended mutual funds, the most common type, sell for their net asset value (NAV). This NAV is the total value of all investments held by a mutual fund divided by the number of mutual fund shares outstanding. Owning shares in a mutual fund allows individual investors to own a diversified collection of securities with a relatively small investment because their money is pooled with that of other investors. Any interest and dividend payments, as well as net gains on the sale of assets are distributed to the mutual fund's shareholders each year.

Risks

A savings account is one of the safest places to put your money, but because the risk of losing your investment is nearly zero, its return is one of the lowest. Conventional wisdom argues that to obtain higher returns on money we must invest in riskier securities. This is not strictly correct. At the low end of risk, conventional wisdom usually applies, but at the high end of risk there are no guarantees you will get a higher return and in fact, you can lose all of your investment. A prime example of this is Internet stocks. While a few of these stocks may provide exceptional returns to investors, the majority of them will eventually fail as companies and as investments. It is impossible to avoid all risks when investing, but it is possible to reduce your exposure to risk. To do that you need to understand the different types of investment risks: loss of capital, loss of purchasing power and lost opportunity. Liquidity risk and volatility are also issues. We explain how to minimize your exposure to investment risks by matching investments to your time horizon.

LOSS OF CAPITAL

You want to avoid losing any of your initial investment, referred to as capital. Because your goals have different time horizons, you are interested in the risk of losing part of your initial investment over a variety of holding periods. Because you will invest your savings in a number of different investments, you are interested in the risk of losing your initial capital when investing in these various securities. The major securities are stocks and bonds. Governments and corporations are the major issuers of bonds. The U.S. government backs U.S. Treasury bills and bonds, so unless the federal government defaults on its debt, you will get your money back when it is due. This guarantee does not free you from the risk of losing part of your original savings even if you invest it in U.S. bonds. For example, if you chose to invest your savings in U.S. government 30-year bonds and need to cash out your investment five years later, you could expose yourself to the risk of losing some of your original savings. This could happen if interest rates rise after you purchase your bonds making your 30-year bond worth less on the bond market than you paid for it originally.

To better understand the potential for loss of capital with stocks and bonds, we examined the returns for the S&P Stock Composite, U.S. government 30-year long bonds, U.S. government T-bills, and corporate bonds for the years 1900–1998 as provided by Global Financial Data. We examined the returns for each type of security over a number of holding periods (5-year, 10-year, 15-year, and 20-year). Between 1900–1998 these securities where affected by the Panic of 1907 (which led to the formation of the Federal Reserve in 1913), the Great Depression, World Wars I and II, the Vietnam War, several periods of deflation, high inflation, and several Federal Reserve policy changes. The percentage of holding periods for which the various investments lost money is given below.

Percentage of Holding Periods Ending in a Loss

Holding Periods	5-year	10-year	15-year	20-year
S&P Stock Composite	13%	3%	0%	0%
30-Year Long Bond	3	0	0	0
T-bills	0	0	0	0
Corporate Bonds	9	1	1	1

From this data it is clear T-bills are an effective way to avoid loss of capital even over short holding periods. (In fact, T-bills ended every year between 1900 and 1998 with a gain.) Long bonds have managed to occasionally lose value over short holding periods. All of the S&P Stock Composite 10-year holding periods—and most of the 5-year holding periods—that ended in a loss occurred during the Depression.

Over longer periods, investments in the S&P Stock Composite preserved invested capital. As you see, the best way to minimize the risk of losing part of your invested capital is to have a long time horizon.

If your time horizon is shorter than six years you should stick to investments, such as U.S. government T-bills, CDs, or cash management accounts. The same holds true when you near the end of your time horizon for achieving a goal.

Two to three years before the end of your time horizon, you should begin to shift any long-term stock mutual fund investments—and all new savings—into short-term CDs, U.S. government T-bills, or your cash management account. In this way, you preserve your capital, rather than risk it when your time horizon is short. Chapter 5, Targeting Your Goals, incorporates this basic idea of tailoring your investment choices to match your time horizon. In the process of doing this you reduce your exposure to the risk of losing your original capital investment—your savings. The time horizons, less than six years, six to ten years and over ten years, for our short-, medium-, and long-term worksheets were chosen based on the historical record above.

LOSS OF PURCHASING POWER

Inflation presents another risk to your investments. Inflation increases the price of almost everything we buy. Chapter 5, Targeting Your Goals, generally assumes the future cost of your goal will be today's cost plus an increase due to the effects of inflation over your time horizon. Historically, the inflation rate in the United States from 1900 to 1998 averaged 3% per year. During that period bank savings accounts produced average annual returns of less than 3%. A "careful" person leaving $10,000 for 30 years in a government insured bank account paying 3% would end up with $24,273. After taking inflation of 3% into account, that investment would be worth only $10,000 in purchasing power. A person who took the effort to invest the $10,000 in U.S. long-term bonds, also guaranteed by the government, but which returned an average of 5% during this period, would end up with $43,219 after 30 years. After taking inflation of 3% into account, that sum would buy

$18,114 worth of goods. A person who invested $10,000 in the stock market for 30 years earning an average common stock return of 11% would end up with $228,923 in dollar terms and $100,627 worth of purchasing power. The table below shows how effectively the various securities have beaten inflation over various holding periods.

Percentage of Holding Periods Beating Inflation

Holding Periods	5-year	10-year	15-year	20-year
S&P Stock Composite	79%	86%	91%	99%
30-Year Long Bond	57	56	53	51
T-bills	67	62	73	73
Corporate Bonds	55	49	49	53

Based on historical data, stocks are the best way to ensure your investment returns beat inflation, particularly over the long-term. Long-term bonds, whether government or corporate, are the least effective at beating inflation. T-bills are actually more effective at beating inflation than long-term bonds. In 1979, Federal Reserve policy was changed to emphasize controlling inflation. Since then, returns on T-bills have regularly beaten inflation by a small margin. For this reason, T-bills are a good short-term investment that preserves your purchasing power. Stocks are the most effective at beating inflation and their effectiveness increases as the holding period lengthens. From the Loss of Capital section, it is clear that stocks also preserve capital during long holding periods. For these reasons, stocks are a good long-term investment.

LOST OPPORTUNITY

When investing you want to do more than maintain the purchasing power of your savings, particularly when saving for a long-term goal such as retirement. In the section on compounding above, the example given demonstrated the importance of starting to invest early. Another advantage of starting early is that you do not need to restrict your investments to low-risk securities such as U.S. Treasuries. Historically, 1900–1998, the annual return for U.S. government Treasury bills was 4%, for U.S. government 30-year bonds 5%, and for common stocks 11%. In our previous example, you would need to save $330 each month for 20 years and invest it to earn 10% a year (via stock mutual funds) to have $250,000 for retirement. If you chose to play it safe and invest in U.S. long bonds instead, earning only 5% a year, you would have to save $608 each month. That additional $278 a month of savings is not available for other goals or regular spending. If your budget will only allow $330 to go toward retirement and you still play it safe, investing it at 5%, you will have only $136,000 for retirement. You may miss your opportunity to retire as planned and may need to continue working for several more years.

You want your money to work as effectively as possible. One way to gauge the effectiveness of different types of investments is to examine how often each investment was the best performer or the worst performer, for a variety of holding periods.

Percentage of Holding Periods Best Performer

Holding Periods	5-year	10-year	15-year	20-year
S&P Stock Composite	67%	71%	73%	78%
30-Year Long Bond	1	0	0	0
T-bills	17	14	13	4
Corporate Bonds	15	14	14	19

Percentage of Holding Periods Worst Performer

Holding Periods	5-year	10-year	15-year	20-year
S&P Stock Composite	15%	7%	4%	3%
30-Year Long Bond	17	22	20	18
T-bills	41	42	44	50
Corporate Bonds	27	29	33	30

For holding periods of ten years or longer, the figures clearly indicate stocks are the best performing asset far more frequently than bonds. Stocks are rarely the worst performing asset over long holding periods. It is tempting to interpret the percentages above for stocks as the best performer during 5-year periods as an argument to invest in stocks for 5-year holding periods. However, from the Loss of Capital section earlier, we know that these investments too often end in a loss after a 5-year holding period and are therefore not appropriate for short time horizons. For longer holding periods, your best opportunity is investing in stocks—via mutual funds. If you limit yourself to safe government bonds you will lose the opportunity to achieve more of your goals and you may not increase your personal wealth.

LIQUIDITY RISK

The more easily an investment can be converted to cash, the more liquid it is. Money in a checking account is completely liquid. Money invested in fixed assets such as art or real estate is not liquid: It may take months to find a buyer for such items. A number of financial instruments are illiquid; owners of these securities may experience difficulty finding a buyer when they choose to sell them. Common stocks and common stock mutual funds, also called equity mutual funds, are widely traded and can be easily bought or sold. When the time comes to use the money that you have invested, that money has to be in a form that is easily converted to cash. It is best to stick with widely traded liquid investments such as common stock mutual funds, U.S. government T-bills, CDs, or your cash management account with your broker. These investments can be sold easily to raise cash when you choose to do so.

THE DIFFERENCE BETWEEN RISK AND VOLATILITY

There is a widespread misconception in the financial community that volatility in the price of an investment is the same thing as risk. Investment risk is the potential loss of capital, loss of purchasing power, lost opportunity, or the inability to convert your investment into cash when needed. Volatility is the amount of fluctuation in the price of an investment over a given time period. A sound but volatile investment is only risky if the investment is too volatile for that investor's time horizon. In the short term, prices for stocks fluctuate wildly. The 52-week low price for many stocks is often half of the stock's 52-week high price. It is entirely possible that a sound investment in stocks may be worth only half as much as was originally invested after just one year. That same investment might go on to earn an 11% average annual return over the next ten years. Stocks, and stock mutual funds are appropriate investments for long time horizons, but not short time horizons.

Another risk associated with volatility is psychological. We all value predictability. We prefer to see our investments increase 10% each and every year, rather than have a decline in one year followed by an above average return the next. A person unwilling or unable to watch the value of his or her investment fall to half of its original value may wish to avoid common stock mutual funds with their double digit average annual returns and be content with single digit returns from less volatile investments. Unfortunately, earnings from less volatile investments may not be sufficient to achieve your long-term goals. The apparent middle road of investing in corporate and municipal bonds looks deceptively safe. They provide a highly predictable, fixed annual income to their owners and return the original investment at the end of the agreed term. However, there are risks involved in owning bonds as well. The company issuing the bond could default on their loan; they could pay the loan off early by calling the bond and repaying you your principal, but without having paid you much interest. The interest rate you locked in when you bought the bond can also trap you in an investment paying a lower return relative to what you could be making if interest rates increase after you buy the bond. If such a situation occurs you will lose a portion of your investment if you sell the bond before it comes due.

Finally, keep in mind the experiences of many investors during the October 1987 stock market crash. In one day the stock market lost 22% of its value, but in less then one and a half years the stock market was again at its pre-October level. Those who did not sell out saw their investments regain all of their paper losses. It often takes the market longer than a few months to recover from downturns, but if you have a long time horizon, you are in a position to ride out the storm, making—rather than losing—money in the long term.

DETERMINING THE APPROPRIATE AMOUNT OF RISK

The discussions above have given you an idea of the risks involved in various investments over various holding periods. The investments you make, and therefore the risks you choose to take, should be appropriate for your time horizon. In Chapter 5, Targeting Your Goals, we discuss the types of investments appropriate for each time horizon. For time horizons of less than six years, safe and liquid investments such as CDs, T-bills, and your cash management account with your discount broker should be used. For time horizons of six years or more, you can invest some or most of your savings in stock mutual funds. Regardless of which time horizon you start with, when you are two to three years from reaching your goal, your remaining time horizon is short-term. At that point, you should start to move previous investments that were in stock mutual funds, as well as all new savings, into safe investments such as CDs, T-bills, or your cash management account.

Time Horizon

Your time horizon will be determined largely by when you hope to achieve your goals. With some goals you may be able to adjust your timing. For example, you may choose to buy a new car every ten years rather than every seven. Other goals, such as providing a college education for your child, cannot be delayed so easily.

As you see from the discussion above, the earlier you begin to save and invest, the more compounding can work for you and the more you can minimize your exposure to the risks of lost capital, lost purchasing power, and lost opportunity. Start early. You do not have to wait until you are tired of renting to begin saving for a down payment on a house. Nor do you need to wait for your first child to be born to start putting money aside to cover his or her college education. The sooner you begin saving and investing, the greater will be the wealth you build.

Deciding when to liquidate your long-term holdings as you near the end of your time horizon is difficult. If you wait until the last year you run the risk that your long-term holdings will decline in value just before you need to spend the money. If you liquidate too soon, you run the risk of missing out on an opportunity to earn more money should your investments do well during the last two to three years before you need the money.

We advocate being conservative. Consider this example. Say you have $50,000 accumulated toward your goal and you have two years until you need to spend the money for your goal. Would you be further ahead to leave your long-term investments in place or move them into safe investments such as CDs? Suppose your mutual fund investments earn 10% during the next to the last year of your time horizon, but in the final year they lose 10%. Your $50,000 would increase to $55,000 in the penultimate year, but during the final year you would lose $5,500, leaving you with $49,500.

If you had moved your long-term investments into CDs earning 5% per year two years before needing the money you would have your $50,000 plus $5,125 or a total of $55,125. What if instead of earning only 10% during the next to last year, you earn 20%, before losing 10% in the final year? You would end up with $54,000, still $1,125 short of your total had you moved into safe investments two years earlier. The results are the same if during the penultimate year you lose 10%, but earn 10% (or 20%) in your final year. You would still have only $49,500 (or $54,000). It is better to err on the conservative side during the final few years of your time horizon.

THE INVESTMENT PROCESS

The goal of investing is to make money, but it takes money to make money. Through good money management and spending only according to your plan, you are setting aside the money you need to invest. Your primary investment tools are your cash management account with a discount broker (with its money market mutual funds), U.S. T-bills, CDs, and stock mutual funds. Each of these has a required minimum initial purchase. You will build up savings until you have the minimum required. Once you have made your initial purchase, subsequent purchases can often be made with much smaller sums of money. As you approach the end of the time horizon for your goal, you will want to convert these investments into ready cash, timing the purchase of any CDs and T-bills so that they mature shortly before the end of your time horizon. Cash management accounts do not have a maturation date. If the return is good, all short-term savings and the proceeds from the sale of long-term investments can be placed in your cash management account until you are ready to spend the money for your goal.

A brief analogy may help explain the process. Think of financial planning as taking a road trip. First, you decide where you want to go: Set your goals. Then, consider the route you want to take to get there: Match your investment choices to your time horizon. And finally, determine the resources needed to make the trip: Determine how much savings you need to set aside each month. With your planning done, you head out toward your goal. To continue the analogy, your brokerage account is your vehicle. Money market mutual funds associated with your cash management account, CDs and U.S. T-bills are back roads. Stock mutual funds are a high-speed limited access highway. The financial planning you have done to this point has developed your map. You know your goals, how much you need to save to get there, and how to match different types of investments with your time horizon. If your time horizon is under six years, restrict your travels to back roads (CDs, T-bills, your cash management account). If your time horizon is six years or more you will get onto the highway. Stay on the highway until you are two to three years from the end of your time horizon. At that point, you will start to look for an exit and make the rest of your journey on back roads.

The rest of this chapter explains in more detail how to use your cash management account, T-bills and stock mutual funds as you travel toward your goals. The chapter ends with discussions about different types of investors and different approaches to investing.

Your Cash Management Account

Your cash management account with your discount broker is where money management meets investment. For short time horizons, your cash management account, supplemented with U.S. T-bills, may provide a reasonable and safe return as you work toward your goal.

For longer time horizons you want your savings to accumulate to the minimum size needed to make specific investments. Most mutual funds require minimum initial investments of over $1,000; some require much larger initial investments. If you are saving $250 per month in your account you must let that sum build, earning money market rates until you have enough money in your account to make your initial mutual fund investment. Thereafter, additional purchases may be made with as little as $50 in many cases.

When you purchase a U.S. T-bill, CD, or mutual fund through your discount broker, leave that security on deposit in your discount brokerage account. You will receive regular consolidated statements from the broker summarizing all of your investment transactions, and can use money from the sale of those securities quickly and conveniently. Remember money and securities you have in your brokerage account are insured against default by the brokerage firm for up to $500,000 by the SIPC, but if you have chosen your broker carefully there is little chance you will need this insurance.

Treasury Bills

Treasury bills with maturities of three to six months are the safest of investments. Because they are issued directly by the U.S. federal government, the risk of default is practically zero. Unlike most bonds, they are not callable, which means that the debt cannot be paid off early, which would deny you interest. Because they have short times to maturity they have little interest rate risk. Interest rate risk is a lost opportunity should interest rates rise after you purchase the bond. In that situation, you could make more if you had the money to buy a new bond at the new higher interest rate, but your current bond is now worth less and you can only sell it at a loss. Treasury bills require a minimum initial investment of $1,000. Because the return on Treasury bills is commensurate with their perceived risk, they consistently pay interest only slightly better than money market funds. For this reason, they are not suitable for most people as an investment tool to build toward long-term goals. They are, however, very well suited to hold money from liquidated long-term investments for six months to three years before the money is spent. For a waiting period of less than six months the money should be in the money market mutual fund of your cash management account. For a time horizon of six years or more, the money can earn a greater return in a well-chosen mutual fund.

Mutual Fund Basics

Mutual funds are investment companies that buy and sell securities, most often common stocks. Different mutual fund managers invest in stocks in different ways, but every mutual fund has a set of guidelines that determines that fund's style of investing and fund managers must follow these guidelines. In addition, diversified mutual funds must invest within certain guidelines set by the Securities and Exchange Commission. No diversified mutual fund can have more than 5% of its money in the stock of any one company, nor can it own more than 10% of the voting stock of any publicly traded company. The first rule means that the mutual fund holds a diversified set of investments. The second rule keeps mutual fund managers focused on investing money rather than amassing a controlling stake in a company.

All of the money a U.S. mutual fund makes during the course of a year, whether profit made by selling stock or from dividends paid by stocks the fund owns, must be distributed to the mutual fund shareholders that year. The shareholders, not the mutual fund, are responsible for paying tax on the money the mutual fund earned and has distributed to them. When you invest in a mutual fund you buy shares in that mutual fund. Most mutual funds are open-ended, which means they continue to grow as new people invest in them (or shrink as people take their money out). When a person invests in an open-end mutual fund the fund issues new shares to that investor. The number of shares the investor receives is determined by dividing his or her investment by the net asset value (NAV) of the mutual fund.

When the amount of money a mutual fund contains (total assets) gets too large it becomes more difficult for managers to find appropriate investments. To avoid owning more than 10% of any one company, fund managers must restrict their investments to large corporations or they must own an increasing number of companies. In such a situation, the mutual fund may choose to close its doors to new shareholders. If you already own shares in the mutual fund you usually can continue to invest additional money in that mutual fund, but on occasion a mutual fund may close its doors to all new money.

Closed-end mutual funds have a limited number of shares, like the stock of most companies. The fixed number of shares means the shares of closed-end mutual funds often trade at a premium or discount to the fund's NAV. Closed-end funds are now not as common in the United States as open-end funds and many closed-end funds are facing pressure from their shareholders to convert to open-end funds.

There are some unusual investment restrictions imposed on U.S. citizens living overseas by the United States and foreign governments that you need to know. U.S. mutual funds are prohibited from marketing their funds outside of the United States. To sell a mutual fund within the United States, the mutual fund must be registered with the state where their potential customers live. To sell the fund nationally the fund must register with all fifty states; this takes time. International tax treaties complicate the situation further. In sum, the rules governing whether a particular U.S. citizen living in a particular foreign country is technically allowed to buy a particular mutual fund is extremely complicated.

Different mutual funds and brokers interpret the prohibition on overseas marketing differently. Some U.S. brokers are so strict in their interpretation that they will not mail a mutual fund prospectus to an overseas address. There are various ways around this problem, but the most effective is to keep an address in the United States to use for correspondence with your broker and fund companies. The least expensive way to do this is to have the mail sent to you at the address of a stateside friend or relative. If you do not want to impose on friends or relatives you might ask your employer if they would forward your mail from a stateside office to your overseas address. Other alternatives include asking your lawyer or accountant to forward correspondence to you for a small fee, or renting a box at one of the small packing and mailing service firms that now exist in every corner of America. If you choose this option, check with your broker to see if they have any problem mailing your correspondence to a post office box. A few brokers refuse to mail to a post office box, but many mail service firms allow you to use your box number as a suite number at their street address, so your address does not look like a post office box. The mail service firm will charge you a yearly fee for the service, as well as postage and handling fees for each piece of mail forwarded to you. Since you only need this service for correspondence from your broker the total cost for this service should remain reasonable. Many firms will sort your mail for a fee and forward only important items, throwing away the junk mail. You can have your name removed from the lists of direct marketers by writing to:

> Mail Preference Service
> PO Box 9008
> Farmingdale, NY 11735-9008

You will need to contact them every few years to keep your mailbox clear of junk mail.

In addition to U.S. mutual funds, some fund companies offer offshore funds to non-U.S. customers. Because of tax complications U.S. citizens living overseas are generally prohibited from buying these funds. Offshore funds do not receive the same regulatory oversight as U.S. mutual funds, they charge substantially higher fees, and these fees are frequently hidden from the investor.

U.S. mutual funds have several types of fees and investment styles that you need to be aware of.

LOADS, FEES AND EXPENSES

Some mutual funds charge sales fees when you first invest in the fund, such fees are called loads and are typically a few percent of the total of your investment. The load is a sales commission that goes to the company that sold you the mutual fund. No-load mutual funds have no such sales fees. If you buy a no-load fund direct from the mutual fund company you pay no load or commission. Many discount brokerage firms now offer large numbers of no-load mutual funds free of any up front sales charges. Instead, the funds pay a fee to the brokerage firm in exchange for the marketing advantage they gain by offering their funds to investors in these mutual fund supermarkets. This fee may be absorbed by the fund or it may be passed onto you through a 12b-1 fee; more about this fee later.

A load paid when you buy a fund is called a front-end load. Front-end loads are only paid once, so if you hold the mutual fund for a long time the effect of that load on your total return is reduced. A front-end load does have a more profound effect on your long-term total return than you might expect, because the size of your initial investment is reduced by the amount of the load. Thus, not only do you pay the load, but you also lose any earnings that money would have earned had it been invested in the mutual fund instead of paying the mutual fund load.

In addition to sales charges when you buy a mutual fund, some funds contain provisions that require you to pay a fee if you buy and then sell the mutual fund within some period of time. Such back-end loads or deferred loads are to discourage market timers and others from trading in and out of mutual funds frequently. Most back-end loads drop to zero if you hold the mutual fund for a sufficient number of years before selling. When investors trade in and out of a mutual fund that trading creates difficulties for the fund manager and creates expenses for the remaining fund investors. If the fund does not have sufficient cash, on any given day to pay the NAV of the shares sold, the fund manager will have to sell some of the fund's investments early, interfering with the fund's investment strategy. Most brokerage firms that offer a supermarket of no-load mutual funds to their customers place limitations on frequent trading in and out of mutual funds to preserve the fund's investment strategy and reduce costs to long standing shareholders.

The 12b-1 fee covers the cost of marketing the mutual fund. Money paid to discount brokers to offer a fund in a mutual fund supermarket as a no transaction fee (NTF) fund are paid from the fund's 12b-1 fee and hence ultimately by the fund's investors. The fee is typically 0.25% of the fund's NAV and is assessed yearly. Some funds offered through a mutual fund supermarket require a one-time transaction fee when purchased, rather than charge a 12b-1 fee. For long-term investments, you may be better off paying a one-time transaction fee to purchase a mutual fund through a discount broker, rather than paying 0.25% each year on your holding. Over the course of ten years, an initial $1,000 investment growing at 10% per year will cost you $43.83 in 12b-1 fees. If your initial investment is $2,500, over the course of ten years, you will pay $109.57 in 12b-1 fees. The one-time transaction fee at most discount brokers is less than $35.00. Once you have narrowed your mutual fund selections down to a few, you may be better off buying a mutual fund through a broker that charges a one-time transaction fee, not a yearly 12b-1 fee.

In addition to loads and marketing fees, mutual funds charge annual operating fees. The sum of all the operating fees for a U.S. mutual fund is referred to as its expense ratio. Operating fees include management, administrative, and brokerage fees. These fees are subtracted from the mutual fund's total earnings (or losses) before those earnings are reported and distributed to the shareholders. Returns quoted by U.S. mutual funds are net of operating expenses. Sales loads and marketing expenses are not subtracting from these reported earnings.

MUTUAL FUND INVESTING—BUILDING YOUR PORTFOLIO

To make long-term investments in mutual funds you should have a time horizon of at least six years. Initially, you will own one mutual fund, but over long time horizons you should eventually have your money invested in four to six mutual funds with differing investment styles. Only invest in mutual funds with a good long-term record, preferably of ten years or longer. Once invested in a good mutual fund, do not leave that fund to invest in another fund unless there is a fundamental change in the fund. Examples of such changes include fund policy changes, merging with another mutual fund, selling the mutual fund to another company, or replacing the mutual fund manager. Such an event may not be bad for the fund's long-term performance, but you will need to assess the impact the change may have on the fund's performance going forward. For example, you can examine the track record of the new manager or company to see if it matches the fund's past performance.

Different mutual funds invest in companies of different sizes, referred to as market capitalization. (Market capitalization is a company's stock price times the number of shares of stock outstanding in the market.) Funds that invest in stocks of small companies (called small-cap stocks) tend to perform better in some markets than others; the same is true for medium sized companies (mid-cap stocks) or large companies (large-cap stocks). Investments in small companies are generally riskier than investments in medium or large companies, which usually have more business experience. In some economic environments—recessions, for example—funds that invest in large-cap stocks tend to outperform small-cap funds. For proper diversification, you should own one to two mutual funds that invest in small-cap stocks, and one to two funds that invest in large-cap stocks. A fund investing in mid-cap stocks is a nice addition, but not required for diversification in your portfolio of mutual funds. If you have a higher tolerance for risk you may want to have more money in small-cap stock mutual funds than in large cap stock mutual funds.

Size is only one aspect of how a mutual fund manager invests your money. Different mutual funds use different investment styles categorized as growth or value or a blend of the two. Growth oriented funds invest in the stocks of fast growing companies; value funds look for stocks that are undervalued, which is often considered a more conservative investment approach. The relative performance of growth and value investing depends on many factors including the current economic environment. It is impossible to say whether growth or value funds will be more successful over your time horizon. Your best strategy is to own one or two mutual funds with each investment style.

Mutual funds can be described using a combination of the size of the companies they invest in and the style of investing they use (growth or value). For example, your portfolio of mutual funds may include a large-cap value fund, a large-cap growth fund, a small-cap value fund and a small-cap growth fund. Or you could choose to have two large-cap value funds and two small-cap growth funds. Either way, you would have some money in each of the four major segments: large, small, value, and growth. How much money you have in each segment depends on your tolerance for risk. The more comfortable you are with the investment risks associated with stocks, the more money you should invest in growth or in small-cap oriented mutual funds. If you are a more conservative investor, you should invest more in value or large-cap oriented mutual funds.

There are two other mutual fund investment styles you should be aware of. One investment style specializes in a particular industry or even just a segment of an industry. Mutual funds with this strategy are called sector funds and they are a more risky investment than other funds. They carry more risk because they invest in only one or a few industries and so are not diversified against factors that may have a profound impact on that one industry. A good sector fund might be a reasonable investment for a small portion of a risk tolerant investor's portfolio.

Another mutual fund investment style is the international or foreign fund. These funds invest mostly or exclusively in the stock of companies outside the United States. Adding a good international fund to your portfolio may even out your portfolio's total return, since an economic downturn in the United States may not affect stocks in other countries as severely as those of American companies. Likewise, an international fund would not benefit to the same extent as domestic funds from an economic boom in the United States. One type of international fund we recommend you avoid, is the single country or regional sector fund. Such funds invest in the securities of one foreign country or geographic region. In general, they are risky investments and do not belong in most portfolios as a general-purpose investment. Your international or foreign fund exposure should be limited to a small portion of your total long-term investments.

Investors, Traders, and Speculators

It is important to distinguish between three groups of people who participate in the equities markets. There is a trend in the financial press to refer to everybody buying and selling securities as investors. Using traditional definitions, this is not the case. Understanding the difference between the various groups—who have differing goals and interests—will go a long way toward helping you sort through the constant barrage of largely irrelevant financial information coming from the news media.

SPECULATORS

Speculators try to make a great deal of money in a short time by taking enormous risks. They are rarely successful. Speculators are likely to sell stocks short, buy on margin, and buy and sell options, warrants, and various other financial derivatives. Speculators employ a variety of strategies, each hoping to find a system that will consistently earn enormous returns quickly. This is not to say that there is anything wrong with speculating; if you have a small sum of money you would not mind losing, you may do at least as well intelligently speculating on the equities markets as you would gambling in Las Vegas. Speculating with any money that you need to reach a goal is as irresponsible as betting that money at a roulette wheel.

TRADERS

Traders move in and out of the market, holding positions for very short times. Most traders who actually make money work for professional financial firms. When it is well done, trading can make money, but it is rarely a successful strategy for individuals. This is because the instantaneous sources of accurate information needed are expensive and successful traders spend several hours a day perusing this information. In addition, brokerage commissions, which are much higher for an individual than for a professional, greatly reduce any profits. To trade successfully a trader needs a constant flow of information. Professional traders have many up-to-the-minute information sources specially designed for them. In addition, many "finance and investment" television shows seem to be aimed at the needs of the trader. The constant barrage of instant information that is essential for a trader is a distraction for an investor, who needs more in-depth information when selecting a mutual fund as a long-term holding.

So-called day traders are a recent phenomenon. They are usually individuals who acquire their trading information at little or no cost via the Internet. This kind of trading is particularly risky, because the sources of information are of unknown reliability and are extremely easily manipulated by those who want to manipulate short-term moves of market prices for their own gain. Such market manipulation is illegal, and the Securities and Exchange Commission recognizes the threat to individuals posed by those manipulating this information, but the safest course is to simply avoid this extremely risky and unproven stock market activity.

INVESTORS

Investors try to achieve long-term growth of their investments. They do not take the enormous risks or have "get rich quick" schemes that typify speculators. While investors with different time horizons hold their investments for relatively shorter or longer periods, none constantly darts in and out of equities the way a trader does. Investors require accurate in-depth information and must be adept at analyzing and using that information. Different types of market participants have different approaches to investing.

Approaches to Investing

Investment approaches can be divided into two basic groups. This difference in approach applies not only to those who buy stocks and mutual funds, but also to mutual fund managers who buy stocks for their mutual funds.

MARKET TIMERS

Market timers try to make money by understanding and predicting the action of the stock market, or pieces of the market. To market timers, stocks are the medium of exchange. To them the action, history, and psychology of the market are the keys to success. When somebody asks, "Where do you think the market is going?" or, "What do you think interest rates or inflation will do in the next year?" they are asking market timing questions. No one has consistently succeeded at timing the market. To do so, would require predicting the actions of tens of thousands of investors. Profitable market timing would require you to not only gauge when to get into a market, but also when to get out. The American Association of Individual Investors did a survey, based on data from Lipper Analytical Services, of the return an investor would have received had they not been in the market during the best performing months between 1977–1997. For investors remaining in the market during the entire 240 months, their return would have been 16.65 %. Had they missed the best month, their return would have dropped to 16.00%. Investors who missed the five best individual months would have seen their return fall to 13.66% and for those who missed the ten best individual months, their return would have been only 11.66%. Instead of market timing, focus on your timing. When your time horizon allows you to invest in stock mutual funds, remain invested until you near the end of your time horizon—two to three years before the money is needed.

STOCK PICKERS

Stock pickers, also known as fundamental investors, represent the other investment approach. A stock picker thinks of stocks as part ownership of a company. To a stock picker the stock market is simply a means to buy pieces of companies. Sometimes the market has companies available at a fair price; sometimes a company is a bargain; at other times it may be vastly overpriced. Stock pickers focus on identifying good businesses, believing that over the long run, the money a good business earns will be reflected in a higher price for the stock of that company. When applied to mutual funds, this approach compares and examines the performance and quality of individual mutual funds and fund managers over a long period of time, seeking those that will outperform similar funds in the future.

Not all investors fall neatly into these two categories, of course. Some investment approaches are blends of these two philosophies. Another theory, modern portfolio theory, maintains that nobody can beat the broad market over the long run, and so limits investments to index funds designed to mirror the market as a whole. Index funds may be the only option available in your 401(k) plan. We do not adhere to the modern portfolio theory. A number of mutual funds do consistently beat their competition. We look for, and encourage you to look for, those mutual funds that outperform the market over the long term.

12. TAX MANANGEMENT

TAXES AND INVESTING

The goal of investing is not to minimize taxes, but to maximize your aftertax return. The key to judging whether a tax-free investment is better than a taxable one is to compare the tax-free return of the tax-free investment with the aftertax return of the taxable investment. For example, if you are considering investing in a tax-free municipal bond fund with an average annual historical return of 6%, can you do better by investing your money in a taxable stock index fund with an average annual historical return of 11%? To answer this question you need to determine the aftertax rate of return for the taxable investment and compare it to the rate of return for the tax-free municipal bond fund.

The first step is to estimate your effective tax rate on investment returns. Your U.S. tax rate on investment returns in stock mutual funds should be the long-term capital gains tax rate of 20% plus 1% to account for dividends that are taxed at your marginal tax rate. (If you are in a high tax bracket, greater than 35%, you should add two or three percent to 20% to estimate your effective investment tax rate.) The next step is to determine how much of your taxable return you get to keep after paying taxes to Uncle Sam. You do this by subtracting your effective investment tax rate from 100% and multiplying the result by your taxable rate of return. The result is your aftertax rate of return, which in this case is 8.7% (11% × [100% - 21%]). An aftertax return of 8.7% beats a tax-free return of 6%: You would be better off investing in the stock index fund, with a taxable historical rate of return of 11%.

While a U.S. municipal bond mutual fund may be free of U.S. taxes, its returns may be taxable by your host country, as may other investments you hold. If the effective tax rate in your host country is 50% on investments the aftertax rate of return on your U.S. tax-free investment is 3% (6% × [100% - 50%]). Because you did not pay U.S. taxes in your U.S. tax-free investment return you cannot take a foreign tax credit for your host country's taxes. (Please see the next section of this chapter for more details on foreign tax credits.) Each country has different policies concerning taxation of investments outside their borders. Consult your host country's tax authority or a tax professional that practices in your host country for more information.

U.S. taxation of U.S. mutual fund distributions depends on the source of the fund's earnings. Generally, there are three broad categories of earnings: interest, dividends, and capital gains. If the fund holds CDs, government treasuries, or bonds the fund earns interest income. If a fund holds stocks that pay a dividend the fund earns dividend income. When a fund manager sells an investment the gain or loss on that sale impacts the fund's return. At least once a year, mutual fund companies are required to tally interest and dividend payments, any capital gains net of capital losses, and subtract from that sum the fund's expenses. When the result is positive, the mutual fund must distribute all the proceeds to its shareholders. Shareholders—not the mutual fund—are responsible for paying taxes on those distributions.

Interest, dividends, and short-term capital gains are taxed at your marginal tax rate. A capital gain (or loss) is short-term when an investment is held for one year or less before being sold. The proceeds from the sale of investments held for more than a year are categorized as long-term and are currently taxed at 20% (for tax payers in the 28% marginal tax bracket or higher).

When you sell mutual fund shares you will owe taxes on any gain from the sale. Again, if you held the shares for more than a year your gains are taxed at the lower long-term capital gains tax rate. Otherwise, gains are short-term and taxed at your marginal tax rate. Long-term capital gains can be offset by long-term capital losses if you have any; the same applies to short-term capital gains and losses.

Your gain or loss on the sale of a mutual fund share is determined by subtracting your acquisition cost—your tax basis—from the selling price of the share (minus any sales commission). If you reinvested mutual fund distributions then your tax basis is different. Your tax basis is the acquisition cost of your original mutual fund shares plus the cost of additional shares you acquired by reinvesting distributions. This increases your total acquisition cost, which reduces your capital gain and so your tax liability.

Awards of company stock by an employer represent a special case investment. Generally, you will not be able to sell or dispose of the stock for some number of years, as stipulated by your employer. Under the U.S. tax code section 83(b) you can elect to include this stock in your income for that year, at its market value on the day your received it. From the day you receive the stock you have only 30 days to elect to do this. If you do not your reported income, at the end of the stipulated period, must reflect the market value of the stock on the day you are free to sell the stock.

For example, assume you receive an award of company stock valued at $5,000, which you are free to sell in five years. If you elect to include the market value of this stock in your income within the 30 days, you will owe income taxes on an additional $5,000 of compensation. Assuming you are in the 28% tax bracket, you will owe $1,400 in additional taxes that year. From a tax perspective, your tax basis—your acquisition cost—for this stock is $5,000. If after the stipulated period of five years the market value of the stock has appreciated to $20,000 and you sell it you will have a capital gain of $15,000 ($20,000 - $5,000), which will be taxed at the long-term capital gains tax rate of 20%. You will owe capital gains tax of $3,000 (20% × $15,000 ÷ 100%). In total you will have paid $4,400 in taxes. If instead the stock falls to $1,000 and you sell it you can use the capital loss to offset capital gains from the sale of other profitable long-term investments. Excess capital losses, up to $3,000, can be used to reduce your taxable income.

If you do not take the election within 30 days the market value of the stock at the end of the stipulated period (five years in this case) will be included as compensation and taxed as income at your regular tax rate. If the stock value appreciates to $20,000 you will owe $5,600 in additional taxes if you are still in the 28% tax bracket five years later. If the stock declines in value to $1,000 you will owe $280 in additional income taxes. If you believe your company and its stock will increase in value in the future you should take the election.

Stock options are treated a little differently. If you dispose of the stock less than two years after the option was granted to you, or less than one year after you converted the options to stock, part of the gain on the sale will be treated as earned income. This will be taxed at your regular tax rate rather than as capital gains. (See IRS Publication 525, *Taxable and Non-taxable Income* for further details.) Many other countries treat stock options as compensation and you may have to pay income taxes on the options when they are granted to you or when you exercise them.

Finally, U.S. brokerage firms, banks, and other financial institutions are required to withhold tax at a flat 30% rate—or, in some cases, at a lower treaty rate—on dividend and interest income for account holders with foreign addresses. This regulation is meant for non-U.S. citizens who reside outside the United States. As a U.S. citizen you can stop the withholding by sending a written statement in duplicate to the financial institution indicating you are a U.S. citizen and not subject to the withholding. Include a copy of the first two pages of your passport to expedite the processing. (You also have the option of using a stateside address and having someone forward your mail to you to avoid this problem.)

INCOME TAXES

The United States, unlike all other countries except the Philippines and Eritrea, tax worldwide earnings on the basis of citizenship. Americans (U.S. citizens and resident aliens) have to pay U.S. tax on their worldwide income no matter where they live.

Most other countries apply the principle of residence-based taxation (as did the United States prior to 1962) meaning taxes are paid solely to the country in which the person resides irrespective of where the person earns the income. This explains why some countries tax investment income that is earned outside their borders. Americans working overseas face the prospect of double taxation on their foreign earned income. To mitigate this double taxation, Section 911 of the U.S. Internal Revenue Code excludes certain foreign earned income from U.S. taxation. In tax year 1999, U.S. citizens could exclude up to $74,000 of foreign earned income from federal income taxation under certain conditions. The maximum exclusion amount will increase by $2,000 a year until 2002, when the limit will reach $80,000. Starting in 2008, the $80,000 limit will be indexed to inflation. Your employer is not required to withhold U.S. income taxes on foreign income equal to the exclusion amount. If your employer is withholding U.S. income taxes on the exclusion amount, you can use IRS form 673 to stop the withholding.

You can take advantage of the Section 911 exclusion through IRS form 2555 if you have lived in your host country for at least 330 days or meet other residency requirements. Form 2555 also allows you to exclude certain housing expenses that exceed a base amount. In 1998, that base housing amount was $9,643. (See IRS publication 54, *Tax Guide for U.S. Citizens and Resident Aliens Abroad* for more information.)

If you do not qualify to use form 2555 you can take a credit for the foreign taxes you have paid by filing IRS form 1116. In addition, you can use form 1116 to take a credit for foreign taxes you have paid on foreign earned income that exceeds the exclusion limit. You will need to file a separate form 1116 to take credit for foreign taxes paid on foreign investment income and capital gains. (Different types of foreign income must be reported on separate form 1116s.) IRS Publication 514, *Foreign Tax Credit for Individuals* explains in detail the various types of foreign tax and the amount of tax that can and cannot be taken as a credit against your U.S. income tax liability.

You can take a credit for foreign taxes up to a limit. That limit is based on the fraction of your income that is derived from foreign sources versus your total income from all sources. You also have the option of taking a deduction rather than a credit. The tradeoffs are money saved in taxes versus time spent filling out the forms. A deduction reduces your taxable income; for each dollar deducted from your income, your tax bill is reduced by the tax you would have owed on that income. If your marginal tax rate is 28% a dollar in deductions reduces your tax bill by $0.28. For each dollar of foreign tax credit you are eligible to take, you reduce your tax bill by a full dollar, but the form 1116 needed to claim this credit takes considerably longer to fill out. If you are paying a professional to do your taxes you will have to weigh their fee to prepare all the necessary form 1116s against your expected tax savings.

If you are single and your total income is greater than $112,000 ($150,000 if married and filing jointly) you are required to file form 6251, *Alternative Minimum Tax–Individuals.* If you took a foreign tax credit you will have to file an additional form 1116, using an alternative minimum tax rate rather than a regular tax rate, for each form 1116 you originally filed.

Filing your U.S. taxes on foreign earnings is quite involved. Fortunately, Americans residing overseas qualify for an automatic two-month extension to file their U.S. income tax return by filing form 2350. If you need more time you can request an additional two-month extension by filing form 4868. You also have the option to request a four-month extension to file your taxes by filing form 4868 initially. In either case, you are required to pay a fair estimate of any U.S. federal taxes you expect to owe. The extension gives you additional time to file your taxes, but not to pay them. It is best to overestimate the taxes you might owe. If you underestimate the tax you owe when filing form 4868 over several years the IRS will penalize you at the rate of 5% per month, up to a maximum of 25%, on the tax due.

Your occupation will affect how you file your federal return. Americans working overseas for the U.S. government pay U.S. taxes, not foreign taxes and do not qualify for any exclusion of their income. Americans who are self-employed overseas can use the foreign income exclusion, but the amount that can be excluded is based on complex calculations related to their salaries and their firms' earnings and expenses. When filing your federal taxes be sure to get IRS publication 54, *Tax Guide for U.S. Citizens and Resident Aliens Abroad*. It is available at the IRS website or you can request a copy by mail or by phone at:

> Eastern Area Distribution Center
> P.O. Box 85074
> Richmond, VA 23261-5074
> Phone: 800-829-3676
> Website: http://www.irs.ustreas.gov

This publication is not available by fax. If you live or work near a U.S. Embassy, you may be able to obtain a copy there. However, embassies sometimes experience delays in receiving forms and publications.

Keep your address updated with the IRS by filing form 8822 each time you move. This form (and many other forms and instructions you will need) is available by fax at: +1-703-368-9694.

Where possible you should negotiate a tax equalization package with your employer. Typically, you should expect to pay "normal" U.S. taxes on your earnings, and you should expect your employer to cover any additional U.S. taxes beyond this amount as well as the host country taxes. Here normal refers to the federal and state taxes you would normally pay on your income if you earned it while living in the United States. Some employers offer a tax protection plan and only cover the foreign taxes.

Local hires typically receive no assistance with taxes and are paid in the local currency. Here, a local hire refers to an American who joined a firm only after moving overseas, as opposed to an American who agreed to go overseas on assignment before being transferred by their employer.

Your employer can compensate you in other ways. You may be able to arrange to have part of your compensation paid in the local currency and part in U.S. dollars. This will reduce your currency risk to the extent that your local currency earnings match your local currency expenses. Many expatriate packages include a housing allowance and an education allowance if you have children. In most countries, but not all, you can avoid taxation of these benefits if your employer pays these expenses directly. If your employer pays you an allowance for these expenses you may be taxed by both the United States and your host country on this amount. If you do not have a tax equalization package, you will have higher expenses and will probably pay more taxes on your income.

Just in case all the hassles of getting the necessary forms and filing them tempts you to give up and not file a U.S. tax return, be forewarned. The statute of limitations is ten years if you do not file a return. (Once a tax return is filed, the statute of limitations is three years.) If you plan to return to the United States to work, the IRS may notice the gap in your reporting and question your income during the years you did not file a return, prompting an audit. If you live out your years overseas and never return to the United States your heirs, both in the United States and abroad, may have to pay extensive U.S. taxes from your estate upon your death. You may have other plans for your estate. It is tempting to forego filing a U.S. tax return while living abroad, but consider the potential consequences. If caught, you may face criminal charges for tax evasion, possible imprisonment, and payment of penalties, interest, and back taxes.

If you do prepare a return, but it is lost in the mail, the IRS may classify you as a nonfiler for that year. To avoid this problem, you should send your return by registered or certified mail or by overnight express via one of the IRS approved private-delivery companies: Currently, these are Federal Express, DHL, and United Parcel Service.

To ease the chore of filing your taxes, keep your records organized. This will ease your work or the fee if you have a professional prepare your tax return. Be sure to keep records concerning the purchase of your home and investments and any transactions related to these items until three years after the sale of these items. If you plan to apply for foreign social security benefits you may wish to keep your foreign tax returns as proof of your earnings history.

Should you find you have overpaid your federal taxes, have your refund direct deposited to your U.S. bank, credit union, mutual fund, or brokerage account. You will receive your money sooner and avoid the hassle of sending the check back to the U.S. for deposit or the expense of finding a foreign bank that can process a U.S. check.

TAX TREATIES

With respect to its own citizens, the United States taxes on the basis of citizenship and not residence. Most countries tax on the basis of residence, irrespective of citizenship. If the United States taxed on the basis of citizenship alone, non-U.S. citizens could live in the United States and not pay taxes to the United States (because they are not U.S. citizens) nor would they have to pay taxes to their home country (because they are not resident there). The United States does not tax on the basis of citizenship alone. When a non-U.S. citizen resides in the United States, their worldwide income is subject to U.S. taxation. In effect, the principle of residence-based taxation is applied by the United States to residents who are not U.S. citizens.

How is the U.S. based income of non-U.S. citizens taxed when they live outside the United States? To address this question, the United States has established bilateral tax treaties with 48 countries. They are:

Australia	Japan
Austria	Kazakstan
Barbados	Korea, Republic of
Belgium	Luxembourg
Canada	Mexico
China, People's	Morocco
Republic of	Netherlands
Commonwealth of	New Zealand
Independent States	Norway

Cyprus	Pakistan
Czech Republic	Philippines
Denmark	Poland
Egypt	Portugal
Finland	Romania
France	Russia
Germany	Slovak Republic
Greece	South Africa
Hungary	Spain
Iceland	Sweden
India	Switzerland
Indonesia	Thailand
Ireland	Trinidad & Tobago
Israel	Tunisia
Italy	Turkey
Jamaica	United Kingdom

These treaties apply principally to resident citizens of the foreign countries listed above who receive certain types of income from sources within the United States. Typically, citizens of a treaty country who receive income from U.S. sources will be taxed at a reduced rate or will be exempt from U.S. income taxes. The treaties are all different, but a few general observations can be made about them.

In principle, the tax treaties are reciprocal. However, a Saving Clause is incorporated into each treaty, stipulating that the worldwide income of U.S. citizens remains subject to U.S. taxation. U.S. citizens must pay U.S. taxes on their worldwide income regardless of any bilateral tax treaty. When double taxation occurs, U.S. citizens abroad may be reimbursed through the use of a Section 911 foreign income exclusion or a foreign tax credit when they file their U.S. tax return. There may be cases in which they may not be reimbursed for foreign taxes paid. For example, distributions from a Roth IRA to a U.S. citizen resident overseas are not subject to U.S. taxes, but these distributions may be subject to taxation by the country where the U.S. citizen lives. In that case, double taxation has not occurred and a foreign tax credit cannot be taken. (Note: this could occur in a non-tax treaty country as well.)

The treaties apply to certain types of compensation categorized as:

Income from personal services (doctors, lawyers, engineers)

Salaries of teachers, professors, and researchers

Amounts received for studies and maintenance of students

Wages, salaries, and pensions paid by a foreign government

These treaties also apply to certain types of investment income such as bond interest, dividends, royalties, and capital gains on the sale of real property such as land. Generally, the payee in the source country withholds taxes. So for example, non-U.S. citizens resident outside the United States with certain U.S. investment income are subjected to a 30% tax withholding. Similarly, a U.S. citizen, residing in the United States with income from one of the treaty countries may be subject to tax withholding by the treaty country.

In addition, the treaties cover taxation of social security payments and other pensions. For example, a 30% withholding tax will be applied to 85% of the value of all social security payments made to non-U.S. citizens residing outside the United States. Some of the treaty countries tax U.S. social security benefits paid to U.S. citizens resident in their country.

IRS Publication 901, *U.S. Tax Treaties* discusses the treaties from the perspective of a citizen from each of the 48 treaty countries. Each of the four types of compensation is covered in this publication, as are the various other types of income discussed above. All the treaties are different and you are advised to get a copy of the treaty from the taxing authority in your host country. In addition, some of the treaties can be obtained by writing to:

Department of Treasury
Office of Public Liaison
1500 Pennsylvania Avenue NW Room 4418
Washington, DC 20220

The treaties are each unique and complicated. You may wish to consult a tax attorney with experience in dealing with the treaty if you believe you may have benefits under the treaty.

SOCIAL SECURITY TAXES

While the tax treaties above cover taxation of certain types of income, they do not address how social security taxes should be paid by Americans working overseas, nor how social security credits earned in one country can be applied to another. The United States has established bilateral social security (totalization) agreements with 17 countries to cover social security taxes. (How these totalization agreements affect your ability to qualify for social security benefits is discussed in Chapter 10, Financial Risk Management—Social Security.) The countries and the effective date of their totalization agreements with the United States are:

Austria	November 1, 1991
Belgium	July 1, 1984
Canada	August 1, 1984
Finland	November 1, 1992
France	July 1, 1988
Germany	December 1, 1979
Greece	September 1, 1994
Ireland	September 1, 1993
Italy	November 1, 1978
Luxembourg	November 1, 1993
Netherlands	November 1, 1990
Norway	July 1, 1984
Portugal	August 1, 1989
Spain	April 1, 1988
Sweden	January 1, 1987
Switzerland	November 1, 1980
United Kingdom	January 1, 1985

The totalization agreements determine whether you will pay U.S. or foreign social security taxes if you live in one of these countries. Each agreement has its own variations, but in general, if your

U.S. employer sent you to one of the above countries for five years or less you will have to pay U.S. social security taxes. If you become an employee of the U.S. foreign affiliate, rather than remaining an employee of the U.S. firm, your employer will need to have an agreement with the IRS under Section 3121(1) that allows all U.S. citizens employed by the affiliate to pay U.S. social security taxes. Your employer will need to obtain a certificate of coverage from the U.S. Social Security Administration rather than the foreign social security administration to indicate to the host country that you are exempt from that country's social security taxes.

If you work for more than five years in a totalization agreement country you will have to pay the social security taxes levied by your host country. If you are assigned to work in one of the above countries by a non-U.S. company you will be liable to pay foreign social security taxes. If you are a local hire you will pay local social security taxes regardless of the national affiliation of the employer. Your employer will need to obtain a certificate of coverage from the host country's social security administration to indicate to the U.S. Social Security Administration that you are exempt from U.S. social security taxes.

Self-employed people living overseas will be liable for the local social security taxes. You will need to obtain a certificate for self-employed persons from the appropriate authority in your host country to be exempt from U.S. social security taxes.

If you work in one of the 17 totalization agreement countries and pay foreign social security taxes you cannot take a foreign tax credit for those taxes. If you work in a non-totalization agreement country and pay both U.S. and host country social security taxes you can take a foreign tax credit for the host country social security taxes that you pay.

If you do not work for one of the 17 treaty countries you are liable to pay social security taxes in both the United States and your host country.

Copies of any of the totalization agreements are available in full or in brief online at: http://www.ssa.gov/international. You can also contact the U.S. embassy in your host country or write or call the Social Security Administrations Office of International Programs at:

> Social Security Administration
> Office of International Programs
> P.O. Box 17741
> Baltimore, MD 21235-7741
> Phone: +1-410-965-3548 or +1-410-965-3554
> Website: http://www.ssa.gov/international

TAXATION OF U.S. SOCIAL SECURITY BENEFITS

The totalization agreements discussed above also help you to qualify for U.S. social security benefits or similar benefits from one of the 17 countries. To learn more about qualifying for social security benefits see Chapter 10, Financial Risk Management— Social Security. Here we discuss taxation of your social security retirement benefits once you begin receiving them.

U.S. citizens or U.S. resident aliens receiving U.S. social security benefits face taxation of retirement benefits once their income exceeds certain levels. Currently, a married couple filing jointly, with a combined income of $32,000 to $44,000, face taxation of up to 50% of their social security benefits. (Beneficiaries filing individually face the same taxation if their income is between $25,000 and $34,000.) Combined income is defined as your adjusted gross income plus any nontaxable interest plus one half of your social security benefits. Once a couple's combined income exceeds $44,000, 85% of their social security benefits will be taxed. (Incomes exceeding $34,000 will trigger the same taxation for individual filers.)

For non-U.S. citizens residing outside the United States, the situation is different: Federal income taxes are withheld at a rate of 30% on 85% of your U.S. social security benefit, regardless of your income level. Thus, 25.5% (30% of 85%) of your social security benefits are withheld for income tax purposes.

If you are living overseas and receiving U.S. social security benefits they may also be taxed by your host country. This may be the case even if your host country has a tax treaty with the United States as discussed in the above section on tax treaties.

AFTERWORD

Rather than trying to spell out a formula to achieve financial success (however you define that term) as most personal finance books do, this book is about making the right financial choices for yourself. Nobody has your best interest, financial or otherwise, at heart as much as you do. This is not to say that there are not times when you need professional financial advice. Knowing enough about these issues lets you judge accurately when you need the help of a professional, and makes you better able to judge how competent that professional is.

This book is meant to be a long-term reference that gives you the information you need to make the right choices. As your life changes and you face fresh financial challenges refer back to this book. Sections that were previously uninteresting may be relevant to your new situation and contain the information you need to make the best choices.

All the publications of GIL Financial Press are written from this perspective. Our goal is to give you the tools you need to forge your own financial future. We would like to hear from you to learn how well this book met that goal. We would appreciate your ideas about ways we can improve future editions of this book. In addition, we would like to know what other financial matters you would like us to write about. To suggest topics for future books or to share your thoughts about this book send us a letter or an e-mail. Our e-mail address is info-gil@GILFinancialPress.com and our postal address is GIL Financial Press, 21055 Hawthorne Court, Sterling, VA, 20164 USA. Our website is www.GILFinancialPress.com and we encourage you to visit to see what new publications are available.

APPENDIX A
FINANCIAL
STATEMENTS

NET FINANCIAL WORTH STATEMENT[1,2]

DATE _____

Assets

CASH ASSETS[3]

Checking Accounts   _____

Savings Accounts   _____

Money Market Accounts   _____

Brokerage Accounts[4]   _____

Life Insurance Cash Value   _____

TOTAL   _____

INVESTMENTS

Stocks   _____

Mutual Funds   _____

Bonds and T-Bills   _____

CDs   _____

IRAs   _____

401(k) Pension Plans   _____

Other   _____

TOTAL   _____

REAL ESTATE[5]

Land   _____

Primary Home   _____

Second/Vacation Home   _____

TOTAL   _____

---

[1] This statement reflects the value of your possessions minus what you owe as of the date you enter. This differs from your net income statement, which reflects your average monthly income and expenses over the course of a year.

[2] Convert all local currency figures into dollar amounts based on the current exchange rate.

[3] These are assets you can access via check or can easily convert to cash. Your self-insurance fund may be held in any of these accounts, except life insurance.

[4] Include cash holdings only; investments are covered separately.

[5] Use market value. If that is not available use what you paid for the property.

PERSONAL PROPERTY

Automobiles (resale value) _____

Recreational Vehicles (resale) _____

Household Items[6] _____

Collections (antiques, etc.)[7] _____

Original Art[8] _____

Luxury Items[9] _____

Other _____

TOTAL _____

Total Assets _____

(Total Cash Assets, Investments,
Real Estate and Personal Property)

Liabilities[10]

Mortgage Balance _____

Bank Loans _____

Educational Loans _____

Auto Loans _____

Recreational Vehicle Loans _____

Life Insurance Policy Loans _____

401(k) Pension Plan Loans _____

Balance on Credit Cards _____

Other Loans _____

Total Liabilities _____

Net Worth _____

(Total Asset - Total Liabilities)

---

[6] Include only the more expensive items; use your best estimate of their resale value.

[7] Items such as stamp or coin collections should be professionally appraised. If that is not practical use what you paid for these items as an estimate. Include only the more expensive items.

[8] See footnote 7 for details.

[9] Items may include fur or jewelry. See footnote 7 for details.

[10] At least once a year you should receive a statement showing the amount of principal remaining on each of your loans, use that figure minus any payments of principal made after each statement's date.

MONTHLY NET INCOME STATEMENT[1]

Income

EARNINGS

Salary and Wages   _____

Self-employment Income   _____

Housing Allowance[2]   _____

Other Overseas Allowances[3]   _____

Bonuses   _____

TOTAL   _____

INVESTMENTS

Capital Gains[4]   _____

Interest Income   _____

Dividend Income   _____

Mutual Fund Distributions[5]   _____

TOTAL   _____

OTHER INCOME

Rental Income   _____

Social Security Benefits   _____

Alimony/Child Support   _____

Other   _____

TOTAL   _____

Total Income   _____

---

[1] Enter monthly figures. In many cases it will be necessary to estimate the monthly amount using yearly figures and dividing by 12. Convert all foreign currency figures into dollars using the current exchange rate.

[2] If your employer pays you a housing allowance, include the amount here. Housing paid directly by your employer should not be included.

[3] Include only those allowances paid directly to you by your employer.

[4] Only include capital gains net of capital losses on investments you sold during the year and divide by 12.

[5] As an estimate, you can use last year's figures from your federal tax return, Schedule D, and divide by 12.

TAXES[6]
U.S. Federal Income Taxes _____
U.S. State & Local Income Taxes _____
Other U.S. Taxes[7] _____
Host Country Income Taxes _____
Other Host Country Taxes _____
TOTAL _____

Total Net Income _____
(Total Income - Total Taxes)

Expenses

HOUSING
Mortgage/Rent (overseas home)[8] _____
Mortgage for U.S. Home[9] _____
Home Repairs, Improvements _____
Management Fees (U.S. home) _____
Home Owners Assoc. Fees _____
Real Estate Taxes _____
Other[10] _____
TOTAL _____

FOOD
Groceries _____
Dining Out _____
TOTAL _____

---

[6] Not all taxes apply. Some taxes may be due in both your host country and the United States. Use last year's tax returns as an estimate and divide by 12.

[7] For example, personal property taxes. Exclude real estate taxes. They are listed separately under housing expenses.

[8] If you pay your rent or a mortgage directly—even if your employer pays you a housing allowance—include that amount here. If your employer pays your rent or mortgage directly, do not include that amount here.

[9] Enter your mortgage payment (principal and interest only) here. Real estate taxes and homeowners insurance are listed separately under property taxes and homeowners/renters insurance respectively.

[10] This might include housing costs for a second home.

UTILITIES[11]
Phone (local)   _____
Phone (international)   _____
Electricity   _____
Gas   _____
Water/Sewage   _____
Garbage Removal   _____
Cable/Satellite TV   _____
On-line Computer Services   _____
Other   _____
TOTAL   _____

TRANSPORTATION
Car Loan Payment   _____
Auto Repairs   _____
Gasoline   _____
Public Transportation   _____
Other [12]   _____
TOTAL   _____

INSURANCE
Auto   _____
Homeowners/Renters   _____
Disability   _____
Health   _____
Life   _____
Long-term Care   _____
Other   _____
TOTAL   _____

CLOTHING   _____

---

[11] If covered by your employer, enter zero.
[12] Exclude travel for vacations and other recreational travel; recreation is covered separately. Include any other travel not covered by your employer.

HOUSEHOLD FURNISHINGS
Furniture and Appliances _____
Other Household Items _____
TOTAL _____

MISCELLANEOUS DEBTS
Educational Loans _____
Personal Loans _____
Credit Card Debt Payments _____
Other Loan Payments _____
TOTAL _____

HEALTH CARE[13]
Doctor Visits _____
Dentist Visits _____
Prescriptions _____
Hospital and Other Expenses _____
TOTAL _____

PERSONAL CARE
Dry Cleaning _____
Barber/Hair Dresser _____
Other _____
TOTAL _____

RECREATION
Vacation _____
Weekend Trips _____
Other Weekend Activities _____
Books, Music CDs _____
Movies/Theater/Concerts _____
Other _____
TOTAL _____

---

[13] Only include expenses not covered by your insurance policies.

OTHER

Daycare   _____

Alimony/Child Support   _____

Tuition   _____

Pet Care   _____

Magazines   _____

Gifts   _____

Other   _____

TOTAL   _____

Total Expenses   _____
(Total all expenses except taxes)

Savings   _____
(Total Net Income
- Total Expenses)

Savings Ratio   _____
(Savings ÷ Total Net Income,
see text for discussion)

Total Debt Payments   _____
(Mortgage Payments
+ Car Loan Payments
+ Total Miscellaneous Debts)

Debt Service Ratio   _____
(Total Debt Payments
÷ Total Income,
see text for discussion)

APPENDIX B
FINANCIAL
PLANNING
WORKSHEETS

SHORT-TERM FINANCIAL GOAL WORKSHEET

1. TIME HORIZON
How many years before you need the money?   _____

2. AMOUNT NEEDED
a. What does your goal cost now?   _____
b. How quickly are costs increasing on a
     yearly basis? Use 3.0%–4% for most goals.   _____
c. Determine the growth factor for your
     time horizon. Use Table 1 for the time
     horizon in line 1 and the rate in 2.b above.   _____
d. Calculate how much you will need to reach
    this goal. Multiply the growth factor in
    line 2.c by the amount in line 2.a above.   _____

3. PRETAX RATE OF RETURN
What is the expected rate of return for the
investments you will use?   _____

4. YOUR MARGINAL TAX RATE   _____

5. AFTERTAX RATE OF RETURN
line 3 × (100% - line 4) ÷ 100%   _____

6. SAVINGS FACTOR
Using Table 2, find the monthly savings factor
based on your time horizon in line 1 and the
aftertax rate of return in line 5.   _____

7. MONTHLY SAVINGS NEEDED
line 2.d × line 6   _____

MEDIUM-TERM FINANCIAL GOAL WORKSHEET

1. TIME HORIZON
How many years before the money is needed? _____

2. AMOUNT NEEDED
a. What does your goal cost now? _____
b. How quickly are costs increasing on a
    yearly basis? Use 3.0%–4% for most goals. _____
c. Determine the growth factor for your
    time horizon. Use Table 1 for the time
    horizon in line 1 and the rate in 2.b above. _____
d. Calculate how much you will need to reach
    this goal. Multiply the growth factor in line
    2.c by the amount in line 2.a above. _____

3. PRETAX RATE OF RETURN
What is the expected rate of return for the
investments you will use? _____

4. YOUR MARGINAL TAX RATE _____

5. AFTERTAX RATE OF RETURN
line 3 × (100% - line 4) ÷ 100% _____

6. REDUCTION IN RETURN
for the time your money is in short-term
investments _____

7. FINAL AFTERTAX RATE OF RETURN
line 5 - line 6 _____

8. SAVINGS FACTOR
Using Table 2, find the monthly savings factor
based on your time horizon in line 1 and the
aftertax rate of return in line 7. _____

9. MONTHLY SAVINGS NEEDED
line 2.d × line 8 _____

LONG-TERM FINANCIAL GOAL WORKSHEET

1. TIME HORIZON
How many years before you need the money?   _____

2. AMOUNT NEEDED
a. What does your goal cost now?   _____
b. How quickly are costs increasing on a
     yearly basis? (For college, the figures have
     been 5%–7% a year.) Use 3.0%–4% for
     most long-term goals.   _____
c. Determine the growth factor for your goal.
     Use Table 1 for the time horizon in line 1
     and the rate in 2.b above.   _____
d. Calculate how much you will need to reach
     this goal. Multiply this factor by the amount
     in line 2.a above. (Repeat this process for each
     additional year your child will attend college.) _____

3. PRETAX RATE OF RETURN
What is the expected rate of return for the
investments you will use?   _____

4. YOUR EFFECTIVE TAX RATE   _____

5. AFTERTAX RATE OF RETURN
line 3 × (100% - line 4) ÷ 100%   _____

6. REDUCTION IN RETURN
for time money is in short-term investments   _____

7. FINAL AFTERTAX RATE OF RETURN
line 5 - line 6   _____

8. SAVINGS FACTOR
Using Table 2, find the monthly savings factor
based on your time horizon in line 1 and
the aftertax rate of return in line 7.   _____

9. MONTHLY SAVINGS NEEDED
line 2.c total × line 8   _____

SAVING FOR RETIREMENT WORKSHEET

1. TIME HORIZON
How many years before you retire?   _____

2. YOUR CURRENT INCOME
How much are you currently making a year?   _____

3. DISCONTINUED EXPENSES
What expenses will be discontinued
in retirement? (Annual amount)   _____

4. DISCONTINUED SAVINGS
How much of current savings will be
discontinued in retirement? (Annual amount)   _____

5. INCOME REQUIREMENT
What percentage of your salary
do you need in retirement?
(line 2 - line 3 - line 4) ÷ line 2 × 100%   _____

6. INCOME FINANCED BY OTHERS IN RETIREMENT
a. How much of your income will be met through a
   defined benefit retirement plan with your employer?
   (no. of years of service × percentage
   - reduction for survivor benefit if appropriate) _____
b. Social security retirement benefits
   (expected benefits ÷ line 2 × 100%)   _____
c. Total financed by others
   line 6.a + line 6.b   _____

7. PORTION OF YOUR INCOME YOU MUST PROVIDE
line 5 - line 6.c   _____

8. AMOUNT OF CURRENT INCOME YOU NEED TO FINANCE
line 7 × line 2 ÷ 100%   _____

9. REDUCTION FOR TAXES IF YOU ARE USING A ROTH IRA

a. What was your total federal tax bill last year? _____

b. What was your total income last year? _____

c. What was your effective tax rate last year?
line 9.a ÷ line 9.b × 100% _____

d. The amount of taxes you will not owe is:
line 9.c × line 8 ÷ 100% _____

e. Adjusted current income you need to finance
line 8 - line 9.d _____

10. INFLATION RATE _____

11. GROWTH FACTOR
From Table 1, find the growth factor for
the number of years until you retire in
line 1 and the inflation rate in line 10. _____

12. RETIREMENT INCOME NEEDED IN THE FIRST YEAR
line 9.e × line 11 _____

13. YEARS IN RETIREMENT
Based on your life expectancy at retirement age
plus a buffer for good measure: How long must
your nest egg support you? _____

14. LUMP SUM RATE OF RETURN
The rate of return you expect your lump sum
to earn during retirement. _____

15. LUMP SUM FACTOR
From Table 4, find the lump sum factor for
the years in retirement in line 13 and
expected rate of return in line 14. _____

16. LUMP SUM NEEDED FOR RETIREMENT
line 12 × line 15 _____

17. AMOUNT YOU HAVE ALREADY SAVED _____

18. BEFORE AND AFTERTAX RATE OF RETURN
What is the expected rate of return for the
investments you will use?   _____

19. GROWTH FACTOR
From Table 1, find the growth factor for the
time horizon in line 1 and the
aftertax rate of return in line 18.   _____

20. AMOUNT OF LUMP SUM COVERED BY CURRENT SAVINGS
line 17 × line 19   _____

21. AMOUNT OF LUMP SUM YOU STILL NEED TO SAVE
line 16 - line 20   _____

22. SAVINGS FACTOR
Using Table 2, find the monthly savings factor
based on your time horizon in line 1 and
the aftertax rate of return in line 14.   _____

23. MONTHLY SAVINGS NEEDED
line 21 × line 22   _____

LIFE INSURANCE BENEFIT WORKSHEET

1. TAKE-HOME EARNINGS

Enter the total yearly take-home earnings
of the person you need to insure

_____

2. SOCIAL SECURITY SURIVOR BENEFIT

Get this from your Social Security
Statement

_____

3. PENSION BENEFITS

Survivor benefits from company pension
system or foreign social security

_____

4. UNCOVERED EARNINGS

Subtract the amounts on lines 2 and 3
from the amount on line 1

_____

5. DURATION OF INCOME

Number of years the replacement earnings
will be required

_____

6. AFTERTAX RATE OF RETURN

_____

7. LUMP SUM FACTOR

Enter the number from Table 4, Lump Sum
Factors, based on a your aftertax return in line 6
and the duration listed on line 5

_____

8. BENEFIT TO REPLACE EARNINGS

Multiply the number on line 7 by the sum
on line 4

_____

9. FINAL EXPENSES

Enter an estimate for final expenses

_____

10. REQUIRED BENEFIT

Add the numbers on lines 8 and 9

_____

APPENDIX C
FINANCIAL
TABLES

Time Horizon in Years	TABLE 1: GROWTH FACTORS Annual Rate of Return				
	3%	3.5%	4%	4.5%	5%
1	1.030	1.035	1.040	1.045	1.050
2	1.061	1.071	1.082	1.092	1.103
3	1.093	1.109	1.125	1.141	1.158
4	1.126	1.148	1.170	1.193	1.216
5	1.159	1.188	1.217	1.246	1.276
6	1.194	1.229	1.265	1.302	1.340
7	1.230	1.272	1.316	1.361	1.407
8	1.267	1.317	1.369	1.422	1.477
9	1.305	1.363	1.423	1.486	1.551
10	1.344	1.411	1.480	1.553	1.629
11	1.384	1.460	1.539	1.623	1.710
12	1.426	1.511	1.601	1.696	1.796
13	1.469	1.564	1.665	1.772	1.886
14	1.513	1.619	1.732	1.852	1.980
15	1.558	1.675	1.801	1.935	2.079
16	1.605	1.734	1.873	2.022	2.183
17	1.653	1.795	1.948	2.113	2.292
18	1.702	1.857	2.026	2.208	2.407
19	1.754	1.923	2.107	2.308	2.527
20	1.806	1.990	2.191	2.412	2.653
21	1.860	2.059	2.279	2.520	2.786
22	1.916	2.132	2.370	2.634	2.925
23	1.974	2.206	2.465	2.752	3.072
24	2.033	2.283	2.563	2.876	3.225
25	2.094	2.363	2.666	3.005	3.386
26	2.157	2.446	2.772	3.141	3.556
27	2.221	2.532	2.883	3.282	3.733
28	2.288	2.620	2.999	3.430	3.920
29	2.357	2.712	3.119	3.584	4.116
30	2.427	2.807	3.243	3.745	4.322
31	2.500	2.905	3.373	3.914	4.538
32	2.575	3.007	3.508	4.090	4.765
33	2.652	3.112	3.648	4.274	5.003
34	2.732	3.221	3.794	4.466	5.253
35	2.814	3.334	3.946	4.667	5.516
36	2.898	3.450	4.104	4.877	5.792
37	2.985	3.571	4.268	5.097	6.081
38	3.075	3.696	4.439	5.326	6.385
39	3.167	3.825	4.616	5.566	6.705
40	3.262	3.959	4.801	5.816	7.040

TABLE 1: GROWTH FACTORS Annual Rate of Return					Time Horizon in Years
5.5%	6%	6.5%	7%	7.5%	
1.055	1.060	1.065	1.070	1.075	1
1.113	1.124	1.134	1.145	1.156	2
1.174	1.191	1.208	1.225	1.242	3
1.239	1.262	1.286	1.311	1.335	4
1.307	1.338	1.370	1.403	1.436	5
1.379	1.419	1.459	1.501	1.543	6
1.455	1.504	1.554	1.606	1.659	7
1.535	1.594	1.655	1.718	1.783	8
1.619	1.689	1.763	1.838	1.917	9
1.708	1.791	1.877	1.967	2.061	10
1.802	1.898	1.999	2.105	2.216	11
1.901	2.012	2.129	2.252	2.382	12
2.006	2.133	2.267	2.410	2.560	13
2.116	2.261	2.415	2.579	2.752	14
2.232	2.397	2.572	2.759	2.959	15
2.355	2.540	2.739	2.952	3.181	16
2.485	2.693	2.917	3.159	3.419	17
2.621	2.854	3.107	3.380	3.676	18
2.766	3.026	3.309	3.617	3.951	19
2.918	3.207	3.524	3.870	4.248	20
3.078	3.400	3.753	4.141	4.566	21
3.248	3.604	3.997	4.430	4.909	22
3.426	3.820	4.256	4.741	5.277	23
3.615	4.049	4.533	5.072	5.673	24
3.813	4.292	4.828	5.427	6.098	25
4.023	4.549	5.141	5.807	6.556	26
4.244	4.822	5.476	6.214	7.047	27
4.478	5.112	5.832	6.649	7.576	28
4.724	5.418	6.211	7.114	8.144	29
4.984	5.743	6.614	7.612	8.755	30
5.258	6.088	7.044	8.145	9.412	31
5.547	6.453	7.502	8.715	10.117	32
5.852	6.841	7.990	9.325	10.876	33
6.174	7.251	8.509	9.978	11.692	34
6.514	7.686	9.062	10.677	12.569	35
6.872	8.147	9.651	11.424	13.512	36
7.250	8.636	10.279	12.224	14.525	37
7.649	9.154	10.947	13.079	15.614	38
8.069	9.704	11.658	13.995	16.785	39
8.513	10.286	12.416	14.974	18.044	40

Time Horizon in Years	TABLE 1: GROWTH FACTORS Annual Rate of Return				
	8%	8.5%	9%	9.5%	10%
1	1.080	1.085	1.090	1.095	1.100
2	1.166	1.177	1.188	1.199	1.210
3	1.260	1.277	1.295	1.313	1.331
4	1.360	1.386	1.412	1.438	1.464
5	1.469	1.504	1.539	1.574	1.611
6	1.587	1.631	1.677	1.724	1.772
7	1.714	1.770	1.828	1.888	1.949
8	1.851	1.921	1.993	2.067	2.144
9	1.999	2.084	2.172	2.263	2.358
10	2.159	2.261	2.367	2.478	2.594
11	2.332	2.453	2.580	2.714	2.853
12	2.518	2.662	2.813	2.971	3.138
13	2.720	2.888	3.066	3.254	3.452
14	2.937	3.133	3.342	3.563	3.797
15	3.172	3.400	3.642	3.901	4.177
16	3.426	3.689	3.970	4.272	4.595
17	3.700	4.002	4.328	4.678	5.054
18	3.996	4.342	4.717	5.122	5.560
19	4.316	4.712	5.142	5.609	6.116
20	4.661	5.112	5.604	6.142	6.727
21	5.034	5.547	6.109	6.725	7.400
22	5.437	6.018	6.659	7.364	8.140
23	5.871	6.530	7.258	8.064	8.954
24	6.341	7.085	7.911	8.830	9.850
25	6.848	7.687	8.623	9.668	10.835
26	7.396	8.340	9.399	10.587	11.918
27	7.988	9.049	10.245	11.593	13.110
28	8.627	9.818	11.167	12.694	14.421
29	9.317	10.653	12.172	13.900	15.863
30	10.063	11.558	13.268	15.220	17.449
31	10.868	12.541	14.462	16.666	19.194
32	11.737	13.607	15.763	18.250	21.114
33	12.676	14.763	17.182	19.983	23.225
34	13.690	16.018	18.728	21.882	25.548
35	14.785	17.380	20.414	23.960	28.102
36	15.968	18.857	22.251	26.237	30.913
37	17.246	20.460	24.254	28.729	34.004
38	18.625	22.199	26.437	31.458	37.404
39	20.115	24.086	28.816	34.447	41.145
40	21.725	26.133	31.409	37.719	45.259

| TABLE 1: GROWTH FACTORS | | | | | Time |
| Annual Rate of Return | | | | | Horizon |
10.5%	11%	11.5%	12%	12.5%	in Years
1.105	1.110	1.115	1.120	1.125	1
1.221	1.232	1.243	1.254	1.266	2
1.349	1.368	1.386	1.405	1.424	3
1.491	1.518	1.546	1.574	1.602	4
1.647	1.685	1.723	1.762	1.802	5
1.820	1.870	1.922	1.974	2.027	6
2.012	2.076	2.143	2.211	2.281	7
2.223	2.305	2.389	2.476	2.566	8
2.456	2.558	2.664	2.773	2.887	9
2.714	2.839	2.970	3.106	3.247	10
2.999	3.152	3.311	3.479	3.653	11
3.314	3.498	3.692	3.896	4.110	12
3.662	3.883	4.117	4.363	4.624	13
4.046	4.310	4.590	4.887	5.202	14
4.471	4.785	5.118	5.474	5.852	15
4.941	5.311	5.707	6.130	6.583	16
5.460	5.895	6.363	6.866	7.406	17
6.033	6.544	7.095	7.690	8.332	18
6.666	7.263	7.911	8.613	9.373	19
7.366	8.062	8.821	9.646	10.545	20
8.140	8.949	9.835	10.804	11.863	21
8.994	9.934	10.966	12.100	13.346	22
9.939	11.026	12.227	13.552	15.014	23
10.982	12.239	13.633	15.179	16.891	24
12.135	13.585	15.201	17.000	19.003	25
13.410	15.080	16.949	19.040	21.378	26
14.818	16.739	18.898	21.325	24.050	27
16.374	18.580	21.072	23.884	27.056	28
18.093	20.624	23.495	26.750	30.438	29
19.993	22.892	26.197	29.960	34.243	30
22.092	25.410	29.209	33.555	38.524	31
24.411	28.206	32.568	37.582	43.339	32
26.975	31.308	36.314	42.092	48.757	33
29.807	34.752	40.490	47.143	54.851	34
32.937	38.575	45.146	52.800	61.708	35
36.395	42.818	50.338	59.136	69.421	36
40.217	47.528	56.127	66.232	78.099	37
44.439	52.756	62.581	74.180	87.861	38
49.105	58.559	69.778	83.081	98.844	39
54.261	65.001	77.803	93.051	111.199	40

Time Horizon in Years	TABLE 2: MONTHLY SAVINGS FACTORS Annual Rate of Return				
	3%	3.5%	4%	4.5%	5%
1	0.08219	0.08200	0.08182	0.08163	0.08144
2	0.04048	0.04029	0.04009	0.03990	0.03970
3	0.02658	0.02639	0.02619	0.02600	0.02580
4	0.01963	0.01944	0.01925	0.01905	0.01886
5	0.01547	0.01528	0.01508	0.01489	0.01470
6	0.01269	0.01250	0.01231	0.01212	0.01194
7	0.01071	0.01052	0.01034	0.01015	0.00997
8	0.00923	0.00904	0.00886	0.00867	0.00849
9	0.00808	0.00789	0.00771	0.00753	0.00735
10	0.00716	0.00697	0.00679	0.00661	0.00644
11	0.00640	0.00622	0.00604	0.00587	0.00570
12	0.00578	0.00560	0.00542	0.00525	0.00508
13	0.00525	0.00507	0.00490	0.00473	0.00456
14	0.00480	0.00462	0.00445	0.00428	0.00412
15	0.00441	0.00423	0.00406	0.00390	0.00374
16	0.00406	0.00389	0.00373	0.00357	0.00341
17	0.00376	0.00359	0.00343	0.00327	0.00312
18	0.00350	0.00333	0.00317	0.00301	0.00286
19	0.00326	0.00309	0.00294	0.00278	0.00264
20	0.00305	0.00288	0.00273	0.00258	0.00243
21	0.00285	0.00269	0.00254	0.00239	0.00225
22	0.00268	0.00252	0.00237	0.00222	0.00209
23	0.00252	0.00236	0.00221	0.00207	0.00194
24	0.00238	0.00222	0.00207	0.00193	0.00180
25	0.00224	0.00209	0.00195	0.00181	0.00168
26	0.00212	0.00197	0.00183	0.00169	0.00157
27	0.00201	0.00186	0.00172	0.00159	0.00146
28	0.00190	0.00176	0.00162	0.00149	0.00137
29	0.00181	0.00166	0.00153	0.00140	0.00128
30	0.00172	0.00157	0.00144	0.00132	0.00120
31	0.00163	0.00149	0.00136	0.00124	0.00113
32	0.00155	0.00142	0.00129	0.00117	0.00106
33	0.00148	0.00134	0.00122	0.00110	0.00099
34	0.00141	0.00128	0.00115	0.00104	0.00094
35	0.00135	0.00122	0.00109	0.00098	0.00088
36	0.00129	0.00116	0.00104	0.00093	0.00083
37	0.00123	0.00110	0.00099	0.00088	0.00078
38	0.00118	0.00105	0.00094	0.00083	0.00074
39	0.00113	0.00100	0.00089	0.00079	0.00069
40	0.00108	0.00096	0.00085	0.00075	0.00066

TABLE 2: MONTHLY SAVINGS FACTORS					Time Horizon in Years
Annual Rate of Return					
5.5%	6%	6.5%	7%	7.5%	
0.08125	0.08107	0.08088	0.08069	0.08051	1
0.03951	0.03932	0.03913	0.03894	0.03875	2
0.02561	0.02542	0.02523	0.02504	0.02486	3
0.01867	0.01849	0.01830	0.01811	0.01793	4
0.01452	0.01433	0.01415	0.01397	0.01379	5
0.01175	0.01157	0.01139	0.01122	0.01104	6
0.00979	0.00961	0.00943	0.00926	0.00909	7
0.00832	0.00814	0.00797	0.00780	0.00763	8
0.00718	0.00701	0.00684	0.00667	0.00651	9
0.00627	0.00610	0.00594	0.00578	0.00562	10
0.00553	0.00537	0.00521	0.00505	0.00490	11
0.00492	0.00476	0.00460	0.00445	0.00430	12
0.00440	0.00425	0.00410	0.00395	0.00380	13
0.00396	0.00381	0.00366	0.00352	0.00338	14
0.00359	0.00344	0.00329	0.00315	0.00302	15
0.00326	0.00311	0.00297	0.00284	0.00271	16
0.00297	0.00283	0.00269	0.00256	0.00244	17
0.00272	0.00258	0.00245	0.00232	0.00220	18
0.00250	0.00236	0.00223	0.00211	0.00199	19
0.00230	0.00216	0.00204	0.00192	0.00181	20
0.00212	0.00199	0.00187	0.00175	0.00164	21
0.00196	0.00183	0.00171	0.00160	0.00150	22
0.00181	0.00169	0.00157	0.00147	0.00136	23
0.00168	0.00156	0.00145	0.00134	0.00125	24
0.00156	0.00144	0.00134	0.00123	0.00114	25
0.00145	0.00134	0.00123	0.00114	0.00104	26
0.00135	0.00124	0.00114	0.00104	0.00096	27
0.00126	0.00115	0.00105	0.00096	0.00088	28
0.00117	0.00107	0.00098	0.00089	0.00081	29
0.00109	0.00100	0.00090	0.00082	0.00074	30
0.00102	0.00093	0.00084	0.00076	0.00068	31
0.00096	0.00086	0.00078	0.00070	0.00063	32
0.00090	0.00081	0.00072	0.00065	0.00058	33
0.00084	0.00075	0.00067	0.00060	0.00053	34
0.00079	0.00070	0.00062	0.00056	0.00049	35
0.00074	0.00066	0.00058	0.00051	0.00045	36
0.00069	0.00061	0.00054	0.00048	0.00042	37
0.00065	0.00057	0.00050	0.00044	0.00039	38
0.00061	0.00054	0.00047	0.00041	0.00036	39
0.00057	0.00050	0.00044	0.00038	0.00033	40

Time Horizon in Years	TABLE 2: MONTHLY SAVINGS FACTORS Annual Rate of Return				
	8%	8.5%	9%	9.5%	10%
1	0.08032	0.08014	0.07995	0.07977	0.07958
2	0.03856	0.03837	0.03818	0.03800	0.03781
3	0.02467	0.02448	0.02430	0.02412	0.02393
4	0.01775	0.01756	0.01739	0.01721	0.01703
5	0.01361	0.01343	0.01326	0.01309	0.01291
6	0.01087	0.01070	0.01053	0.01036	0.01019
7	0.00892	0.00875	0.00859	0.00843	0.00827
8	0.00747	0.00731	0.00715	0.00699	0.00684
9	0.00635	0.00620	0.00604	0.00589	0.00575
10	0.00547	0.00532	0.00517	0.00502	0.00488
11	0.00475	0.00460	0.00446	0.00432	0.00419
12	0.00416	0.00402	0.00388	0.00375	0.00362
13	0.00366	0.00353	0.00340	0.00327	0.00315
14	0.00325	0.00312	0.00299	0.00287	0.00275
15	0.00289	0.00276	0.00264	0.00253	0.00241
16	0.00258	0.00246	0.00235	0.00223	0.00213
17	0.00232	0.00220	0.00209	0.00198	0.00188
18	0.00208	0.00197	0.00186	0.00176	0.00167
19	0.00188	0.00177	0.00167	0.00157	0.00148
20	0.00170	0.00159	0.00150	0.00140	0.00132
21	0.00154	0.00144	0.00135	0.00126	0.00117
22	0.00140	0.00130	0.00121	0.00113	0.00105
23	0.00127	0.00118	0.00109	0.00101	0.00094
24	0.00115	0.00107	0.00099	0.00091	0.00084
25	0.00105	0.00097	0.00089	0.00082	0.00075
26	0.00096	0.00088	0.00081	0.00074	0.00068
27	0.00088	0.00080	0.00073	0.00067	0.00061
28	0.00080	0.00073	0.00066	0.00060	0.00055
29	0.00073	0.00066	0.00060	0.00054	0.00049
30	0.00067	0.00061	0.00055	0.00049	0.00044
31	0.00061	0.00055	0.00050	0.00044	0.00040
32	0.00056	0.00050	0.00045	0.00040	0.00036
33	0.00052	0.00046	0.00041	0.00036	0.00032
34	0.00047	0.00042	0.00037	0.00033	0.00029
35	0.00044	0.00039	0.00034	0.00030	0.00026
36	0.00040	0.00035	0.00031	0.00027	0.00024
37	0.00037	0.00032	0.00028	0.00025	0.00021
38	0.00034	0.00030	0.00026	0.00022	0.00019
39	0.00031	0.00027	0.00023	0.00020	0.00018
40	0.00029	0.00025	0.00021	0.00018	0.00016

| TABLE 2: MONTHLY SAVINGS FACTORS | | | | | Time |
| Annual Rate of Return | | | | | Horizon |
10.5%	11%	11.5%	12%	12.5%	in Years
0.07940	0.07921	0.07903	0.07885	0.07867	1
0.03763	0.03744	0.03726	0.03707	0.03689	2
0.02375	0.02357	0.02339	0.02321	0.02304	3
0.01685	0.01668	0.01651	0.01633	0.01616	4
0.01274	0.01258	0.01241	0.01224	0.01208	5
0.01003	0.00987	0.00971	0.00955	0.00939	6
0.00811	0.00796	0.00780	0.00765	0.00750	7
0.00669	0.00654	0.00640	0.00625	0.00611	8
0.00560	0.00546	0.00532	0.00518	0.00505	9
0.00474	0.00461	0.00448	0.00435	0.00422	10
0.00405	0.00393	0.00380	0.00368	0.00356	11
0.00349	0.00337	0.00325	0.00313	0.00302	12
0.00303	0.00291	0.00280	0.00269	0.00258	13
0.00263	0.00252	0.00242	0.00231	0.00222	14
0.00230	0.00220	0.00210	0.00200	0.00191	15
0.00202	0.00192	0.00183	0.00174	0.00165	16
0.00178	0.00169	0.00160	0.00151	0.00143	17
0.00157	0.00148	0.00140	0.00132	0.00124	18
0.00139	0.00131	0.00123	0.00115	0.00108	19
0.00123	0.00116	0.00108	0.00101	0.00094	20
0.00110	0.00102	0.00095	0.00089	0.00083	21
0.00098	0.00091	0.00084	0.00078	0.00072	22
0.00087	0.00080	0.00074	0.00069	0.00063	23
0.00077	0.00071	0.00066	0.00060	0.00055	24
0.00069	0.00063	0.00058	0.00053	0.00049	25
0.00062	0.00056	0.00052	0.00047	0.00043	26
0.00055	0.00050	0.00046	0.00041	0.00038	27
0.00050	0.00045	0.00041	0.00037	0.00033	28
0.00044	0.00040	0.00036	0.00032	0.00029	29
0.00040	0.00036	0.00032	0.00029	0.00026	30
0.00036	0.00032	0.00028	0.00025	0.00023	31
0.00032	0.00028	0.00025	0.00022	0.00020	32
0.00029	0.00025	0.00022	0.00020	0.00017	33
0.00026	0.00023	0.00020	0.00018	0.00015	34
0.00023	0.00020	0.00018	0.00016	0.00014	35
0.00021	0.00018	0.00016	0.00014	0.00012	36
0.00019	0.00016	0.00014	0.00012	0.00011	37
0.00017	0.00015	0.00013	0.00011	0.00009	38
0.00015	0.00013	0.00011	0.00010	0.00008	39
0.00014	0.00012	0.00010	0.00008	0.00007	40

Loan Length in Years	TABLE 3: MONTHLY LOAN PAYMENT FACTORS Annual Rate of Return				
	3%	3.5%	4%	4.5%	5%
1	0.08469	0.08492	0.08515	0.08538	0.08561
2	0.04298	0.04320	0.04342	0.04365	0.04387
3	0.02908	0.02930	0.02952	0.02975	0.02997
4	0.02213	0.02236	0.02258	0.02280	0.02303
5	0.01797	0.01819	0.01842	0.01864	0.01887
6	0.01519	0.01542	0.01565	0.01587	0.01610
7	0.01321	0.01344	0.01367	0.01390	0.01413
8	0.01173	0.01196	0.01219	0.01242	0.01266
9	0.01058	0.01081	0.01104	0.01128	0.01152
10	0.00966	0.00989	0.01012	0.01036	0.01061
11	0.00890	0.00914	0.00938	0.00962	0.00986
12	0.00828	0.00851	0.00876	0.00900	0.00925
13	0.00775	0.00799	0.00823	0.00848	0.00873
14	0.00730	0.00754	0.00778	0.00803	0.00829
15	0.00691	0.00715	0.00740	0.00765	0.00791
16	0.00656	0.00681	0.00706	0.00732	0.00758
17	0.00626	0.00651	0.00676	0.00702	0.00729
18	0.00600	0.00625	0.00650	0.00676	0.00703
19	0.00576	0.00601	0.00627	0.00653	0.00680
20	0.00555	0.00580	0.00606	0.00633	0.00660
21	0.00535	0.00561	0.00587	0.00614	0.00642
22	0.00518	0.00544	0.00570	0.00597	0.00625
23	0.00502	0.00528	0.00555	0.00582	0.00610
24	0.00488	0.00514	0.00541	0.00568	0.00597
25	0.00474	0.00501	0.00528	0.00556	0.00585
26	0.00462	0.00489	0.00516	0.00544	0.00573
27	0.00451	0.00478	0.00505	0.00534	0.00563
28	0.00440	0.00467	0.00495	0.00524	0.00554
29	0.00431	0.00458	0.00486	0.00515	0.00545
30	0.00422	0.00449	0.00477	0.00507	0.00537
31	0.00413	0.00441	0.00469	0.00499	0.00529
32	0.00405	0.00433	0.00462	0.00492	0.00523
33	0.00398	0.00426	0.00455	0.00485	0.00516
34	0.00391	0.00420	0.00449	0.00479	0.00510
35	0.00385	0.00413	0.00443	0.00473	0.00505
36	0.00379	0.00407	0.00437	0.00468	0.00500
37	0.00373	0.00402	0.00432	0.00463	0.00495
38	0.00368	0.00397	0.00427	0.00458	0.00490
39	0.00363	0.00392	0.00422	0.00454	0.00486
40	0.00358	0.00387	0.00418	0.00450	0.00482

| TABLE 3: MONTHLY LOAN PAYMENT FACTORS | | | | | Loan |
| Annual Rate of Return | | | | | Length |
5.5%	6%	6.5%	7%	7.5%	in Years
0.08584	0.08607	0.08630	0.08653	0.08676	1
0.04410	0.04432	0.04455	0.04477	0.04500	2
0.03020	0.03042	0.03065	0.03088	0.03111	3
0.02326	0.02349	0.02371	0.02395	0.02418	4
0.01910	0.01933	0.01957	0.01980	0.02004	5
0.01634	0.01657	0.01681	0.01705	0.01729	6
0.01437	0.01461	0.01485	0.01509	0.01534	7
0.01290	0.01314	0.01339	0.01363	0.01388	8
0.01176	0.01201	0.01225	0.01251	0.01276	9
0.01085	0.01110	0.01135	0.01161	0.01187	10
0.01011	0.01037	0.01062	0.01088	0.01115	11
0.00950	0.00976	0.01002	0.01028	0.01055	12
0.00899	0.00925	0.00951	0.00978	0.01005	13
0.00855	0.00881	0.00908	0.00935	0.00963	14
0.00817	0.00844	0.00871	0.00899	0.00927	15
0.00784	0.00811	0.00839	0.00867	0.00896	16
0.00756	0.00783	0.00811	0.00840	0.00869	17
0.00730	0.00758	0.00787	0.00816	0.00845	18
0.00708	0.00736	0.00765	0.00794	0.00824	19
0.00688	0.00716	0.00746	0.00775	0.00806	20
0.00670	0.00699	0.00728	0.00758	0.00789	21
0.00654	0.00683	0.00713	0.00743	0.00775	22
0.00639	0.00669	0.00699	0.00730	0.00761	23
0.00626	0.00656	0.00687	0.00718	0.00750	24
0.00614	0.00644	0.00675	0.00707	0.00739	25
0.00603	0.00634	0.00665	0.00697	0.00729	26
0.00593	0.00624	0.00656	0.00688	0.00721	27
0.00584	0.00615	0.00647	0.00680	0.00713	28
0.00576	0.00607	0.00639	0.00672	0.00706	29
0.00568	0.00600	0.00632	0.00665	0.00699	30
0.00561	0.00593	0.00626	0.00659	0.00693	31
0.00554	0.00586	0.00619	0.00653	0.00688	32
0.00548	0.00581	0.00614	0.00648	0.00683	33
0.00542	0.00575	0.00609	0.00643	0.00678	34
0.00537	0.00570	0.00604	0.00639	0.00674	35
0.00532	0.00566	0.00600	0.00635	0.00670	36
0.00528	0.00561	0.00596	0.00631	0.00667	37
0.00523	0.00557	0.00592	0.00628	0.00664	38
0.00519	0.00554	0.00589	0.00624	0.00661	39
0.00516	0.00550	0.00585	0.00621	0.00658	40

Loan Length in Years	TABLE 3: MONTHLY LOAN PAYMENT FACTORS Annual Rate of Return				
	8%	8.5%	9%	9.5%	10%
1	0.08699	0.08722	0.08745	0.08768	0.08792
2	0.04523	0.04546	0.04568	0.04591	0.04614
3	0.03134	0.03157	0.03180	0.03203	0.03227
4	0.02441	0.02465	0.02489	0.02512	0.02536
5	0.02028	0.02052	0.02076	0.02100	0.02125
6	0.01753	0.01778	0.01803	0.01827	0.01853
7	0.01559	0.01584	0.01609	0.01634	0.01660
8	0.01414	0.01439	0.01465	0.01491	0.01517
9	0.01302	0.01328	0.01354	0.01381	0.01408
10	0.01213	0.01240	0.01267	0.01294	0.01322
11	0.01142	0.01169	0.01196	0.01224	0.01252
12	0.01082	0.01110	0.01138	0.01166	0.01195
13	0.01033	0.01061	0.01090	0.01119	0.01148
14	0.00991	0.01020	0.01049	0.01078	0.01108
15	0.00956	0.00985	0.01014	0.01044	0.01075
16	0.00925	0.00954	0.00985	0.01015	0.01046
17	0.00898	0.00928	0.00959	0.00990	0.01021
18	0.00875	0.00905	0.00936	0.00968	0.01000
19	0.00855	0.00885	0.00917	0.00949	0.00981
20	0.00836	0.00868	0.00900	0.00932	0.00965
21	0.00820	0.00852	0.00885	0.00917	0.00951
22	0.00806	0.00838	0.00871	0.00904	0.00938
23	0.00793	0.00826	0.00859	0.00893	0.00927
24	0.00782	0.00815	0.00849	0.00883	0.00917
25	0.00772	0.00805	0.00839	0.00874	0.00909
26	0.00763	0.00796	0.00831	0.00866	0.00901
27	0.00754	0.00788	0.00823	0.00858	0.00894
28	0.00747	0.00781	0.00816	0.00852	0.00888
29	0.00740	0.00775	0.00810	0.00846	0.00882
30	0.00734	0.00769	0.00805	0.00841	0.00878
31	0.00728	0.00764	0.00800	0.00836	0.00873
32	0.00723	0.00759	0.00795	0.00832	0.00869
33	0.00718	0.00754	0.00791	0.00828	0.00866
34	0.00714	0.00750	0.00787	0.00825	0.00863
35	0.00710	0.00747	0.00784	0.00822	0.00860
36	0.00707	0.00744	0.00781	0.00819	0.00857
37	0.00703	0.00741	0.00778	0.00816	0.00855
38	0.00701	0.00738	0.00776	0.00814	0.00853
39	0.00698	0.00735	0.00773	0.00812	0.00851
40	0.00695	0.00733	0.00771	0.00810	0.00849

| TABLE 3: MONTHLY LOAN PAYMENT FACTORS | | | | | Loan |
| Annual Rate of Return | | | | | Length |
10.5%	11%	11.5%	12%	12.5%	in Years
0.08815	0.08838	0.08862	0.08885	0.08908	1
0.04638	0.04661	0.04684	0.04707	0.04731	2
0.03250	0.03274	0.03298	0.03321	0.03345	3
0.02560	0.02585	0.02609	0.02633	0.02658	4
0.02149	0.02174	0.02199	0.02224	0.02250	5
0.01878	0.01903	0.01929	0.01955	0.01981	6
0.01686	0.01712	0.01739	0.01765	0.01792	7
0.01544	0.01571	0.01598	0.01625	0.01653	8
0.01435	0.01463	0.01490	0.01518	0.01547	9
0.01349	0.01378	0.01406	0.01435	0.01464	10
0.01280	0.01309	0.01338	0.01368	0.01398	11
0.01224	0.01254	0.01283	0.01313	0.01344	12
0.01178	0.01208	0.01238	0.01269	0.01300	13
0.01138	0.01169	0.01200	0.01231	0.01263	14
0.01105	0.01137	0.01168	0.01200	0.01233	15
0.01077	0.01109	0.01141	0.01174	0.01207	16
0.01053	0.01085	0.01118	0.01151	0.01185	17
0.01032	0.01065	0.01098	0.01132	0.01166	18
0.01014	0.01047	0.01081	0.01115	0.01150	19
0.00998	0.01032	0.01066	0.01101	0.01136	20
0.00985	0.01019	0.01054	0.01089	0.01124	21
0.00973	0.01007	0.01042	0.01078	0.01114	22
0.00962	0.00997	0.01033	0.01069	0.01105	23
0.00952	0.00988	0.01024	0.01060	0.01097	24
0.00944	0.00980	0.01016	0.01053	0.01090	25
0.00937	0.00973	0.01010	0.01047	0.01084	26
0.00930	0.00967	0.01004	0.01041	0.01079	27
0.00925	0.00961	0.00999	0.01037	0.01075	28
0.00919	0.00957	0.00994	0.01032	0.01071	29
0.00915	0.00952	0.00990	0.01029	0.01067	30
0.00911	0.00948	0.00987	0.01025	0.01064	31
0.00907	0.00945	0.00984	0.01022	0.01062	32
0.00904	0.00942	0.00981	0.01020	0.01059	33
0.00901	0.00939	0.00978	0.01018	0.01057	34
0.00898	0.00937	0.00976	0.01016	0.01055	35
0.00896	0.00935	0.00974	0.01014	0.01054	36
0.00894	0.00933	0.00972	0.01012	0.01052	37
0.00892	0.00931	0.00971	0.01011	0.01051	38
0.00890	0.00930	0.00970	0.01010	0.01050	39
0.00889	0.00928	0.00968	0.01008	0.01049	40

Years Income is Needed	TABLE 4: LUMP SUM FACTORS Annual Rate of Return				
	6%	6.5%	7%	7.5%	8%
10	8.6458	8.4436	8.2479	8.0586	7.8753
11	9.3609	9.1219	8.8913	8.6689	8.4543
12	10.0547	9.7767	9.5094	9.2523	9.0049
13	10.7278	10.4088	10.1031	9.8098	9.5286
14	11.3808	11.0191	10.6733	10.3428	10.0266
15	12.0143	11.6081	11.2211	10.8521	10.5003
16	12.6289	12.1768	11.7473	11.3390	10.9508
17	13.2252	12.7257	12.2527	11.8043	11.3793
18	13.8037	13.2557	12.7381	12.2491	11.7868
19	14.3649	13.7672	13.2045	12.6742	12.1743
20	14.9094	14.2611	13.6524	13.0805	12.5429
21	15.4376	14.7378	14.0827	13.4689	12.8935
22	15.9501	15.1980	14.4960	13.8401	13.2269
23	16.4472	15.6423	14.8930	14.1949	13.5439
24	16.9296	16.0712	15.2743	14.5340	13.8455
25	17.3975	16.4852	15.6406	14.8581	14.1323
26	17.8515	16.8848	15.9925	15.1679	14.4051
27	18.2920	17.2707	16.3305	15.4640	14.6645
28	18.7193	17.6431	16.6551	15.7470	14.9112
29	19.1338	18.0026	16.9670	16.0175	15.1459
30	19.5360	18.3497	17.2665	16.2761	15.3690
31	19.9262	18.6848	17.5543	16.5232	15.5813
32	20.3047	19.0082	17.8307	16.7594	15.7831
33	20.6719	19.3205	18.0962	16.9851	15.9751
34	21.0282	19.6219	18.3512	17.2009	16.1577
35	21.3739	19.9129	18.5961	17.4071	16.3313
36	21.7092	20.1937	18.8314	17.6042	16.4965
37	22.0346	20.4649	19.0574	17.7927	16.6536
38	22.3502	20.7267	19.2745	17.9727	16.8029
39	22.6556	20.9794	19.4831	18.1449	19.9450
40	22.9535	21.2233	19.6834	18.3094	17.0801
41	23.2403	21.4576	19.8749	18.4659	17.2080
42	23.5131	21.6794	20.0552	18.6125	17.3273
43	23.7844	21.8989	20.2328	18.7561	17.4435
44	24.0476	22.1107	20.4033	18.8934	17.5540
45	24.3029	22.3152	20.5671	19.0247	17.6592
46	24.5506	22.5126	20.7245	19.1501	17.7592
47	24.7909	22.7032	20.8756	19.2700	17.8543
48	25.0240	22.8872	21.0208	19.3846	17.9447
49	25.2502	23.0648	21.1603	19.4941	18.0307
50	25.4697	23.2362	21.2942	19.5988	18.1126
51	25.6826	23.4017	21.4229	19.6988	18.1904
52	25.8891	23.5615	21.5465	19.7945	18.2644
53	26.0895	23.7157	21.6652	19.8859	18.3347
54	26.2839	23.8646	21.7793	19.9732	18.4017
55	26.4725	24.0083	21.8888	20.0567	18.4653

| TABLE 4: LUMP SUM FACTORS | | | | | Years |
| Annual Rate of Return | | | | | Income is |
8.5%	9%	9.5%	10%	10.5%	Needed
7.6979	7.5261	7.3597	7.1986	7.0426	10
8.2471	8.0471	7.8540	7.6675	7.4874	11
8.7669	8.5377	8.3172	8.1048	7.9002	12
9.2587	8.9997	8.7511	8.5124	8.2831	13
9.7242	9.4348	9.1578	8.8925	8.6383	14
10.1647	9.8445	9.5388	9.2468	8.9679	15
10.5816	10.2303	9.8958	9.5772	9.2737	16
10.9761	10.5935	10.2303	9.8853	9.5574	17
11.3495	10.9356	10.5438	10.1725	9.8206	18
11.7028	11.2578	10.8375	10.4403	10.0648	19
12.0372	11.5611	11.1127	10.6900	10.2913	20
12.3536	11.8467	11.3705	10.9228	10.5015	21
12.6531	12.1157	11.6121	11.1398	10.6965	22
12.9364	12.3690	11.8385	11.3422	10.8774	23
13.2046	12.6075	12.0507	11.5309	11.0453	24
13.4584	12.8321	12.2495	11.7068	11.2010	25
13.6986	13.0436	12.4357	11.8709	11.3454	26
13.9259	13.2428	12.6102	12.0238	11.4795	27
14.1410	13.4303	12.7738	12.1664	11.6038	28
14.3446	13.6069	12.9270	12.2993	11.7192	29
14.5372	13.7732	13.0706	12.4233	11.8262	30
14.7195	13.9298	13.2051	12.5389	11.9255	31
14.8920	14.0773	13.3311	12.6466	12.0176	32
15.0553	14.2162	13.4492	12.7471	12.1031	33
15.2098	14.3469	13.5599	12.8408	12.1824	34
15.3560	14.4700	13.6636	12.9281	12.2559	35
15.4944	14.5860	13.7608	13.0095	12.3242	36
15.6254	14.6952	13.8518	13.0855	12.3875	37
15.7493	14.7980	13.9371	13.1562	12.4463	38
15.8666	14.8948	14.0171	13.2222	12.5008	39
15.9775	14.9860	14.0920	13.2838	12.5513	40
16.0821	15.0714	14.1618	13.3409	12.5980	41
16.1791	15.1503	14.2260	13.3931	12.6405	42
16.2731	15.2264	14.2876	13.4430	12.6809	43
16.3621	15.2981	14.3453	13.4895	12.7183	44
16.4464	15.3656	14.3994	13.5328	12.7531	45
16.5261	15.4292	14.4501	13.5733	12.7853	46
16.6015	15.4891	14.4976	13.6109	12.8152	47
16.6729	15.5454	14.5421	13.6461	12.8430	48
16.7405	15.5985	14.5838	13.6789	12.8687	49
16.8045	15.6485	14.6229	13.7094	12.8926	50
16.8650	15.6956	14.6595	13.7379	12.9148	51
16.9222	15.7399	14.6938	13.7645	12.9353	52
16.9764	15.7816	14.7260	13.7892	12.9544	53
17.0277	15.8209	14.7561	13.8123	12.9721	54
17.0762	15.8579	14.7843	13.8338	12.9885	55

Years Income is Needed	TABLE 4: LUMP SUM FACTORS Annual Rate of Return		
	11%	11.5%	12%
10	6.8914	6.7448	6.6028
11	7.3134	7.1453	6.9828
12	7.7031	7.5131	7.3301
13	8.0628	7.8511	7.6475
14	8.3949	8.1615	7.9377
15	8.7014	8.4466	8.2029
16	8.9844	8.7086	8.4454
17	9.2457	8.9492	8.6670
18	9.4869	9.1702	8.8696
19	9.7095	9.3733	9.0547
20	9.9151	9.5598	9.2240
21	10.1049	9.7311	9.3787
22	10.2800	9.8885	9.5201
23	10.4418	10.0331	9.6494
24	10.5911	10.1659	9.7675
25	10.7289	10.2879	9.8755
26	10.8561	10.4000	9.9743
27	10.9736	10.5029	10.0645
28	11.0820	10.5975	10.1470
29	11.1822	10.6844	10.2224
30	11.2746	10.7642	10.2913
31	11.3599	10.8375	13.3543
32	11.4387	10.9049	10.4119
33	11.5114	10.9667	10.4645
34	11.5785	11.0235	10.5126
35	11.6405	11.0758	10.5566
36	11.6977	11.1237	10.5968
37	11.7505	11.1678	10.6336
38	11.7992	11.2082	10.6672
39	11.8442	11.2454	10.6979
40	11.8858	11.2795	10.7259
41	11.9240	11.3108	10.7515
42	11.9585	11.3389	10.7743
43	11.9912	11.3653	10.7958
44	12.0214	11.3897	10.8154
45	12.0492	11.4120	10.8333
46	12.0750	11.4325	10.8496
47	12.0987	11.4514	10.8646
48	12.1206	11.4687	10.8783
49	12.1409	11.4846	10.8908
50	12.1595	11.4992	10.9022
51	12.1768	11.5126	10.9127
52	12.1927	11.5249	10.9222
53	12.2074	11.5363	10.9309
54	12.2210	11.5467	10.9389
55	12.2335	11.5562	10.9462

GLOSSARY

12b-1 Fee A fee, typically 0.25%–1.0% of a fund's net asset value, charged annually by some mutual funds to cover marketing expenses such as advertising and participation in mutual fund supermarkets. This fee is subtracted from the fund's earnings each year before they are distributed to the shareholders.

401(k) Plan The most common form of defined contribution pension plan in private industry.

Adjustable Rate Mortgage (ARM) A mortgage loan with interest rates that can vary during the life of the loan, usually tied to the interest rate of a benchmark bond.

Activities of Daily Living (ADL) Specified activities of normal independent life used by insurance companies to quantify the degree to which a person is unable to care for him or herself.

Amortization The reduction of debt by payments of principal and interest on a loan so that the debt is paid in full at the end of the term.

Asset Something of value owned by a person or company.

Asset Management Account See Cash Management Account

Average Annual Return The average return, gain or loss, an investment has earned each year over some number of years. Time periods frequently quoted are 3-year, 5-year, and 10-year. The return in any specific year may be above or below this average annual return.

Back Ratio A widely used measure in the mortgage loan industry. A person's total monthly loan payments are added to the proposed PITI and divided by that person's pretax monthly income.

Back-End Load A fee some mutual funds charge their shareholders when they sell shares in the fund. Typically, if a back-end load is charged it decreases and eventually disappears if the mutual fund is held for a specified period before being sold.

Beneficiary A person designated to receive some benefit from an insurance policy, pension, or will.

Benefit An insurance or pension payment made to a person in accordance with the terms of an insurance policy or pension.

Bond A security issued by a company or government organization that represents a loan from the bondholder to the bond issuer.

Capital Money initially placed in an investment. (See also capital gain and tax basis.)

Capital Gain Money made from selling something for more than its purchase price. When the difference between the selling price and the purchase price is negative it is called a capital loss.

Cash Balance Pension Plan A type of portable defined benefit pension plan in which pension accounts of employees grow at a rate guaranteed by the employer. Both the employee and employer usually make contributions to the employee's pension account, often based on a percentage of the employee's salary. Many companies are moving from traditional defined benefit to cash balance pension plans, resulting in reduced benefits for employees already close to retirement.

Cash Float Use of somebody else's money for a short period of time without having to pay interest. Traditionally, financial institutions were the only ones capable of benefiting from a cash float, but individuals can do so by purchasing items with a credit card and then paying the card balance in full when the bill comes due. In effect the credit card issuer loans the individual money for purchases made during the billing period interest free.

Cash Management Account A brokerage account with several premium features. One key feature is that all money in the account that is not in other investments is swept into a money market mutual fund, where it earns interest. Also called an asset management account and known by various brand names at various brokerage firms.

Cash Value 1. With reference to property and casualty insurance this is insurance that pays the insured person the depreciated cost (as opposed to replacement cost) of an insured item if that item is lost or destroyed. 2. With reference to life insurance this is the amount of money the insured person has accumulated in the savings account associated with a cash value life insurance policy.

Cash Value Life Insurance A life insurance policy that combines life insurance with an associated savings account that earns interest.

Certificate of Deposit (CD) A loan to a financial institution of a specified amount of money for a specified duration. The interest earned on such a CD is usually larger than for an account from which the depositor is free to withdraw all or part of the money at any time.

Closed-End Mutual Fund A mutual fund with a fixed number of shares, so that a share of the fund may sell for more or less than the net asset value of the fund.

COBRA Officially called the Consolidated Omnibus Budget Reconciliation Act of 1985; this law requires companies to offer the same health insurance to former employees that they offer to current employees for some period of time.

Co-Insurance A feature of some health insurance policies that obligates the insured person to pay some fixed percentage of any medical bills.

Collision Automobile insurance coverage that pays for damage to the insured vehicle if it is damaged in a collision.

Comprehensive Automobile insurance coverage that pays for damage or loss of the insured vehicle because of theft, vandalism or other covered causes.

Conforming Mortgage A mortgage loan that conforms to the standard for the industry so that it can be more easily securitized. Once securitized, these repackaged mortgages can be sold to investors. Conforming mortgages cannot exceed $252,700 in value. (See also security.)

Deferred Load See Back-end load.

Defined Benefit Pension Plan A pension plan in which the employer pays retired employees an annuity for the rest of their lives. The size of the annuity typically depends on the length of employment and the salary the person earned during the later years of their employment.

Defined Contribution Pension Plan A pension plan in which the employee can make tax sheltered contributions to a retirement account, where they grow free from income taxes. Many employers make some matching contributions to their employees' retirement accounts.

Disability Insurance, Any Occupation Disability insurance that replaces lost income if the insured person is disabled and unemployable in any occupation.

Disability Insurance, Own Occupation Disability insurance that replaces lost income if an insured person is disabled and unable to perform work in their profession, even if they are employable in some other line of work.

Distribution A payment of mutual fund earnings (dividends, interest, and capital gains) to the fund's shareholders.

Diversified Mutual Fund A mutual fund that must maintain a diversified portfolio of investments. A diversified stock mutual fund cannot have more than five percent of its net worth in any one company, and cannot own more than ten percent of any company's outstanding stock.

Dividend A payment a company makes to its stockholders to distribute some of the company's earnings rather than reinvesting those earnings in the company.

Equity 1. Referring to partial ownership of something, usually stock; an equity mutual fund is a fund that invests in stocks. 2. The amount of ownership a person has in something purchased using borrowed money, for example, equity in a house.

Expense Ratio The sum of all operating fees for a mutual fund as a percentage of that fund's net asset value. This is the most useful figure to use in comparing mutual funds' operating expenses.

FICO Score FICO stands for Fair, Isaac & Co., a company that produces a well-known credit worthiness score used widely in the mortgage loan industry. FICO scores range from a low of 450 to a high of 850.

First Dollar Insurance An insurance policy with no deductible. Such policies are almost never cost effective for the insured person.

Foreign Work Test A test applied by the U.S. Social Security Administration in determining whether a U.S. citizen living overseas is eligible to receive social security retirement benefits. The test has several stipulations, but the first states that a person can perform no more than 45 hours of foreign work per month and still be eligible to receive U.S. social security retirement benefits.

Front Ratio A widely used measure in the mortgage loan industry. The proposed PITI for a mortgage is divided by the person's pretax monthly income.

Front-End Load A sales fee charged by some mutual funds when they are purchased. The load is calculated as a percentage of the amount of money to be invested and this load is taken out first. Only the remaining money is actually invested in the mutual fund.

Fundamental Investing A style of investing. The emphasis is on finding good businesses. Once identified, fundamental investors estimate the firm's underlying value. This valuation is compared to the firm's current value on the stock market to determine if it is worth buying at its current price.

Guaranteed Renewable An insurance policy that is guaranteed to be renewable for some period of time without the customer having to again demonstrate insurability.

HMO Health Maintenance Organization, a common form of pre-paid medical care in which a customer receives any needed care at facilities of the organization for a fixed annual fee.

Individual Retirement Account (IRA) A special account with U.S. financial institutions in which the investment grows free of U.S. tax. There are limitations on deposits to and withdrawals from such accounts, as well as other tax benefits that depend on specifics of the account and the person who owns it.

Issue Age Rate Insurance See level premium insurance.

Large-Cap Stocks See Market Capitalization.

Level Premium Insurance Also called Issue Age Rate Insurance, this is insurance where the premium is fixed when the policy is first purchased and does not increase during the life of the policy. These policies are typically more expensive initially, since much insurance coverage becomes more expensive as one ages.

Liability 1. A debt owed by a person or company. 2. A person's legal obligation to pay penalties and expenses related to a lawsuit. A person can purchase liability insurance to cover the financial impact of a lawsuit.

Liquidity The degree to which an investment can be easily and quickly converted to cash.

Load A sales fee charged by some mutual funds.

Local Hire A person hired locally by an employer at an overseas location as compared to a person sent overseas on assignment.

Long-Term Care Insurance Insurance that pays the cost of long term care in a nursing home, extended care facility, or the insured person's home if the insured person becomes unable to live independently.

Loss of Use Provision A provision of some property and casualty insurance policies that pays the insured person if the insured property becomes unusable for some period of time.

Margin Account A brokerage account that allows the account holder to borrow money from the brokerage firm to make new investments. Such a loan uses investments in the account as collateral.

Market Capitalization The total market value of all outstanding stock in a company. (A company's stock price multiplied by the number of shares it has outstanding in the market.) Companies with large market capitalization are sometimes known as "large-caps", small companies as "small-caps", and medium sized companies as "mid-caps".

Market Timing A style of investing. Market timers try to judge when the stock market or an individual stock will make its next significant move up (or down) and try to buy (or sell) shares before the anticipated move.

Mid-Cap Stocks See Market Capitalization.

Money Market Account An account at a financial institution that pools funds from account holders and invests these in conservative investments that have high minimum investment requirements, but earn higher rates of return than are commonly available with smaller investments. At a bank these accounts are officially known as money market deposit accounts. At a brokerage firm they are called money market mutual funds.

Money Market Mutual Fund A money market account with a brokerage firm, as opposed to a money market deposit account, which is a similar account held at a bank.

Mutual Fund An investment company that invests its shareholders' money and distributes earnings (if any) from those investments annually to its shareholders.

Mutual Fund Supermarket Large collections of mutual funds offered by certain brokerage firms with or without a transaction fee. See also No Transaction Fee.

Net Asset Value The total value of investments held by a mutual fund at any time, divided by the number of shares of the fund outstanding at that time. It is the dollar value of one share of a mutual fund and is the price at which shares in open-end mutual funds are bought and sold.

Net Worth The sum of all assets owned by a person or company minus all liabilities owed by that person or company. Also called net financial worth.

No-Load Mutual funds that do not charge a front-end or back-end load. Some no-load funds may charge a 12b-1 fee.

No Transaction Fee Mutual funds that can be purchased from certain brokers without paying a front-end load or a brokerage commission. The costs incurred by the brokerage firm and mutual fund are passed to mutual fund shareholders in the form of higher 12b-1 fees.

Non-Cancelable An insurance policy that is guaranteed renewable for some period of time, and for which the premiums are fixed and cannot be raised by the insurance company after the policy is first purchased.

Open-End Mutual Fund A mutual fund without a fixed number of shares. As new money is invested in the fund, new shares are issued. The number of shares issued is equal to the amount of money invested divided by the fund's net asset value (NAV). The NAV does not change because new money is invested, but because the value of the fund's holdings changes.

Participation Another term for co-insurance. Co-insurance is often called participation by non-U.S. insurance companies.

Participating Insurance Policy An insurance policy from certain insurance companies in which the policyholders are part owners of the insurance company. Excess money earned by the company may be distributed to the policyholders.

PITI A common term in the mortgage industry. It is the sum of monthly payments for the principal on the mortgage loan, the interest on that loan, real estate taxes, and homeowners insurance.

Points A pre-payment of interest when a mortgage loan is originated. One point equals one percent of the mortgage loan amount. Paying points reduces the interest rate charged during the term of the loan.

PPO Preferred Provider Organization, a network of healthcare providers who have an agreement to provide healthcare at reduced cost to customers of particular health insurance companies. Care from these providers costs the policyholder less than care from a provider without an agreement with the insurance company. Often care provided by PPO participants is free or available at nominal cost to the policyholder.

Pre-Existing Condition A medical condition that a person has before purchasing a health insurance policy. Frequently, health insurance companies exclude such conditions from coverage.

Private Mortgage Insurance (PMI) Homebuyers who borrow more than 80% of the price of a house are required to pay private mortgage insurance premiums. This insurance pays the balance of the mortgage loan to the lender should the purchaser default on the mortgage.

Purchasing Power The quantity of goods and services some amount of money will buy at a specified time. As inflation drives prices higher more money is needed to maintain the same purchasing power.

Replacement Cost A provision of property and casualty insurance policies in which the insurance company agrees to pay a sum large enough to replace an insured item with a similar item purchased new. This is in contrast to cash value coverage, which pays the policyholder a smaller depreciated amount.

Sector Fund A mutual fund that invests only in companies in a particular industry or industry segment.

Security A financial instrument that can be traded on an exchange. When a loan is securitized it is turned into bonds that can be sold on a bond exchange.

Self-Insurance Fund Money kept available in savings to cover short periods of unemployment or disability, or unexpected emergency expenses. By keeping a self-insurance fund a person is not only better situated to deal with unexpected events, but can also save money on insurance by buying policies with higher deductibles.

Small-Cap Stocks See Market Capitalization.

Stock Usually refers to common stock, which is a security that represents partial ownership in a business and may entitle the stockholder to receive dividends if the company decides to distribute some of its earnings to its owners, the shareholders.

Street Name Investments that are bought and held in a brokerage account without the investor holding a physical share or bond certificate are said to be in street name. Investments held in street name can be more easily and quickly sold when liquidating investments.

Survivor Benefit 1. A feature of some pension funds that allows a surviving spouse to continue to receive pension benefits if the retired employee dies first. 2. A benefit paid by life insurance or social security to family members after the death of a person covered by insurance or social security.

Tax Basis The acquisition cost of an investment including any commissions and loads. When you reinvest mutual fund distributions (or stock dividends) that money is used to purchase additional shares. From a tax perspective that purchase represents your tax basis in a new investment. Mutual fund distributions (and stock dividends) are taxable in the year they occur whether or not they are reinvested. If reinvested distributions (or dividends) were not treated as the tax basis of a new investment then the reinvested distributions (or dividends) would be taxed both in the year in which they occurred and when the investment was sold for a capital gain.

Tax Bracket A range of income in which one is obligated to pay income tax on each additional dollar earned at some fixed percentage rate. Those in higher tax brackets pay more tax on each additional dollar they earn.

Tax Deferred An investment for which no income tax is owed until the investment is liquidated.

Term Life Insurance Life insurance sold for a fixed period of time that pays the beneficiary a fixed benefit if the insured person dies during the term of the policy.

Total Return The total amount earned on an investment; the combination of all interest, dividends and capital gains earned on that investment over a given holding period. (See also average annual return.)

Umbrella Liability Insurance Liability insurance that covers all possible liabilities unless expressly excluded. Such insurance typically has a high maximum benefit and supplements liability coverage provided by homeowners and automobile insurance policies.

Vested An employee is vested when he or she has worked for an employer long enough to be covered by that employer's pension or retirement plan.

INDEX

Symbols

12b-1 208–209
401(k) plan 78–80

A

Activities of daily living 153
Adjustable rate mortgage 116–117
ADL. *See* Activities of daily living
Asset management account. *See*
    Cash management ac-
    count
Automobile loan 118–119

B

Back ratio 110–112
Back-end load 208–209
Bill paying 95–96, 120–121
Bond 193. *See also* U. S. Treasur-
    ies
    callability of 200
    default risk 194
    inflation risk 196–197
    interest rate risk 200
    investment risk 194
Brokerage firm 101–105
    mutual fund supermarket 209

C

Capital 194–196
Capital gain. *See* Taxation: of
    investment
Cash float. *See* Credit card
Cash management account 103–
    104, 204

Cash value. *See* Insurance: auto
    and Insurance:
    homeowners. *See also*
    Insurance: life
CD. *See* Certificate of deposit
Certificate of deposit 100–101
College
    costs 57–58
    educational IRA 60
    state savings plans 61
Compounding 192
Credit card 37–38, 119–122
    avoiding late payment of 120–
    121
    cash float 120
Credit rating 122–124

D

Debt reduction 31–33
Debt service ratio 29, 31, 242
Defined benefit pension plan 70–
    71
Defined contribution pension plan
    78–80
Distribution. *See* Mutual fund:
    distributions
Dividend. *See* Stock. *See also*
    Taxation: of investment

E

Expense ratio 209

F

FDIC. *See* Federal Deposit Insur-
    ance Corporation

Federal Deposit Insurance Corporation 96–97
Financial statement
    net financial worth 21–22, 236–242
    net monthly income 25–29, 238–242
Foreign tax credit 221–222
Foreign work test 187–188
Front ratio 110–112
Front-end load 208
Fundamental investing 214–215

G

Government bond. *See* U. S. Treasuries

I

Individual Retirement Account 82–84
Insurance
    association 131
    auto 134–137. *See also* Insurance: umbrella liability
    cash value 133–134
    collision 135
    comprehensive 135
    discounts 136–137
    foreign country requirements 135–136
    international 135–136
    liability 134–135
    medical 135
    uninsured motorist 135
    of bank accounts 96–97
    of brokerage accounts 101
    of credit union accounts 96–97
    disability 155–160

adjustable rate. *See* Insurance: disability: level premium
any occupation 157
deductible. *See* Insurance: disability: waiting period
elimination. *See* Insurance: disability: waiting period
guaranteed insurable 159
how much is needed 156–157
inflation 159
level premium 158
own occupation 157. *See also* Insurance: disability: residual benefit provision
presumed disability clause 157–158
probationary period 158
residual benefit provision 157, 159
social security benefits 156
split occupation 157
taxation of benefits 157, 158
waiting period 157–158
waiver of premiums 159
workers' compensation 156
FDIC 96–97
foreign 132–133
group 130–131
health 144–151
    co-insurance 146–147
    COBRA 149–150
    deductible 145
    guaranteed renewable 144, 148
    medical evacuation 150–151
    medicare 150
    medivac 150–151
    non-cancelable 148
    participation. *See* Insurance: health: co-insurance

pre-existing condition 148–149
homeowners 137–141. *See also* Insurance: umbrella liability
  cash value 139
  discounts 141
  liability 141
  loss of use 140
  medical 141
  personal property 139–140
  replacement cost 138–139
  second home 139
  unoccupied provision 139
  vacation home. *See* Insurance: homeowners: second home
individual 131
liability. *See* Insurance: umbrella liability. *See also* Insurance: auto and Insurance: homeowners
life 160–173
  amount needed 168–173
  cash value 160, 162–163
  credit life 165
  declaring reduced and paid up 162–163
  decreasing term life 161–162
  extended term life 162–163
  fixed duration 161
  guaranteed rate structure 165
  guaranteed renewable 161
  incontestability clause 164–165
  level term life 161–162
  mortgage, insuring 161
  multiple indemnity clause 164
  policy dividend 165
  policy premium payment 165
  straight term life 161–162
  suicide clause 164
  term life 161–162
long-term care 151–155
  Activities of Daily Living 153
  assisted living care. *See* Insurance: long-term care: integrated policy
  custodial care. *See* Insurance: long-term care: level of care
  deductible. *See* Insurance: long-term care: waiting period
  duration 153–154
  guaranteed renewable 155
  home care. *See* Insurance: long-term care: integrated policy
  inflation 154–155
  integrated policy 153
  intermediate care. *See* Insurance: long-term care: level of care
  issue age rate premium. *See* Insurance: long-term care: level premium
  level of care 154
  level premium 155
  medicaid 152
  medicare 152
  mental disorders 154
  non-cancelable 155
  nursing home care. *See* Insurance: long-term care: integrated policy
  optional renewability 155
  skilled care. *See* Insurance: long-term care: level of care
  waiting period 154

medicaid. *See* Insurance: long-term care
medical. *See* Insurance: health
medicare. *See* Insurance: health and Insurance: long-term care
NCUA 96–97
non-cancelable. *See* Insurance: health and Insurance: long-term care
rating companies 129–130
replacement cost 133–134
SIPC 101
umbrella liability 142–143
IRA 82–84

L

Large-cap stock. *See* Market capitalization
Life expectancy 84
Liquidity 199
Load 208–209
Loan
auto. *See* Automobile loan
mortgage. *See* Mortgage loan
Local hire. *See* Taxation: as a local hire. *See also* Social security: totalization agreements
Long bond. *See* U. S. Treasuries: bonds
Long-term care insurance. *See* Insurance: long-term care

M

Market capitalization 210
Market timing 214
Medical insurance. *See* Insurance: health
Mid-cap stock. *See* Market capitalization

Money market account 100
money market deposit account 100
money market mutual fund 100. *See also* Cash management account
Mortgage loan 107–117
15-year fixed 54
30-year fixed 54, 109
adjustable rate 116–117
convertible 117
two-step 117
ARM. *See* Mortgage loan: adjustable rate
back ratio. *See* Mortgage loan: qualifying for
balloon 117
conforming 107–109
escrow account 115
FICO. *See* Mortgage loan: qualifying for
front ratio. *See* Mortgage loan: qualifying for
Loan To Value. *See* Mortgage loan: LTV
LTV 108–109, 112
origination fee 113
owner occupied. *See* Mortgage loan: qualifying for
PITI 110–112
PMI 112
points 113
pre-approval of 114
pre-qualifying for 113–114
principal, interest, taxes, and insurance. *See* Mortgage loan: PITI
Private Mortgage Insurance. *See* Mortgage loan: PMI
qualifying for 110–114
back ratio 110–112
FICO score 115

front ratio 110–112
owner occupied 108
tax deductibility of interest
109–110
Mutual fund 193–194, 205–212
categories of 209–212
based on capitalization 210
based on geography 211–
212
based on sector 211
based on style of investing
210–211
closed fund 206
closed-end 206
distributions 205–206
taxation of 205–206, 218–
219
expense ratio 209
load 208–209
12b-1 208–209
back-end 208–209
deferred. *See* Mutual fund:
load: back-end
front-end 208
money market. *See* Money
market account
net asset value 193–194, 205–
206
offshore 80–81, 207
open-end 205–206
overseas marketing of 206–
207
supermarket 209

N

National Credit Union Administra-
tion 96–97
NAV. *See* Net Asset Value
NCUA. *See* National Credit Union
Administration
Net Asset Value 193–194, 205–206

Net income 26, 239. *See also*
Financial statement: net
monthly income
Net worth 22, 23–24, 237. *See
also* Financial statement:
net financial worth
No Transaction Fee 209
No-load mutual fund 208

P

Participating insurance 165
Participation insurance 146–147
Pension plan. *See* Retirement:
pension plan
PITI 110–112
PMI 112
Private Mortgage Insurance. *See*
PMI
Purchasing power 196–197

R

Rating companies
of insurance companies 129–
130
of saving institutions 97–99
Replacement cost 138–139
Retirement
401(k) 78–80
Individual Retirement
Account. *See* Retirement:
IRA
IRA 82–84
pension plan 70–78
cash balance 73
defined benefit 70–71
defined contribution 78–80
vesting 70, 79
social security benefits 74–
78, 177–179. *See also*
Social security: receiving
benefits overseas

Risk 194–201
  liquidity 199
  of financial loss
    due to ill health. *See*
      Insurance: health and
      Insurance: long-term care
    due to injury. *See* Insur-
      ance: disability
    due to property
      damage. *See* Insurance:
      auto and Insurance:
      homeowners
  of investing
    loss of capital 194–196
    loss of purchasing power
      196–197
    lost opportunity 197–199
  reducing by matching invest-
    ments to time horizon
    195–196, 197, 198–
    199, 201–202
  volatility versus risk 199–200

S

Savings ratio 29, 30, 242
Sector fund 211
Securities Investors Protection
  Corporation 101
Self-insurance fund
  24, 30, 99, 126–127
SIPC. *See* Securities Investors
  Protection Corporation
Small-cap stock. *See* Market
  capitalization
Social security 175–190
  disability benefits 181–183
    average amount of benefit
    182
    beneficiaries 182
    eligibility for 181
    income exclusion 182
    waiting period 182
  electronic benefit transfer 189

medicare premiums while
  overseas 190
Personal Earnings and Benefit
  Estimate Statement. *See*
  Social security: Social
  Security Statement
receiving benefits overseas
  188–190
retirement benefits 177–179
  average amount of benefit
  76, 178, 179
  eligibility for 177. *See also*
  Social security: totalization agreements
  foreign work test 187–188
  how calulate 178
  reduction for early retirement 177
  reduction for earned income
  186–188
  spousal entitlement 178–
  179
Social Security Statement
  176–177
survivor benefits 179–181
  average amount of benefit
  180
  beneficiaries 180
  eligibility for 180
  how calculate 180–181
  primary insurance amount
  179
totalization agreements 183–
  186
  amount of benefit 185–186
  eligibility for benefits 184–
  185
  list of treaty countries 183–
  184
Windfall Elimination Provision 185–186
Speculator 212

Spending 35–41
   impact on future goals 36–38
   patterns
      changing 39–41
      indentifying 38–39
      tracking 36
Stock 193. *See also* Taxation: of
   investment
Stock picker 214–215
Street name 104–105. *See also*
   Brokerage firm
Survivor benefit. *See* Retirement:
   pension plan. *See also*
   Social security: survivor
   benefits

T

Tax treaties
   covering income taxes 225–
      228
     saving clause 226
   covering social security taxes
      228–230
Taxation
   alternative minimum tax 222
   as a local hire 223
   based on citizenship 220–221
   based on residency 220–221
   change of address filing 223
   deduction versus a tax credit
      222
   equalization package 223
   filing extensions 222
   foreign earned income exclu-
      sion 220–221
   foreign tax credit 221–222
   housing allowance 224
   of investment 217–220
     capital gains 218–219
     comparing taxable and tax-
       free investments 217
     dividend income 218
     effective tax rate 217–218

     interest income 218
     mutual fund distribution
       218–219
     stock award 219–220
     stock option 220
     tax basis 219
     withholding tax 220
   IRS form 1116 221–222
   IRS form 2555 221
   Section 911 220–221
   of social security benefits
      230–231
   statute of limitations 224
Term life insurance. *See* Insurance: life
Time horizon 43–44. *See also*
   Risk: reducing by matching investments to time
   horizon
Totalization agreements
   social security benefits. *See*
     Social security: totaliza-
     tion agreements
   social security taxes. *See* Tax
     treaties: covering social
     security taxes
Trader 212–213
   day trader 213

U

U. S. Treasuries
   bills 197–207, 204–205
   bonds 193, 197–207
   long bond. *See* U. S. Treasur-
     ies: bonds
   T-bills. *See* U. S. Treasuries:
     bills
Umbrella liability insurance. *See*
   Insurance: umbrella
   liability

V

Vesting 70, 79